UNIX by Experimentation

Timothy S. Ramteke

Prentice Hall
Upper Saddle River, New Jersey   *Columbus, Ohio*

Find ~ -name filename

Publisher: Charles E. Stewart, Jr.
Production Editor: Alexandrina Benedicto Wolf
Cover Photo: Photo Researchers, Inc.
Cover Designer and Coordinator: Karrie Converse-Jones
Production Manager: Deidra M. Schwartz
Marketing Manager: Ben Leonard

This book was set in Times Roman by Prentice Hall and was printed and bound by The Banta Company. The cover was printed by The Banta Company.

Printed in the United States of America

10 9 8 7 6 5 4 3 2

ISBN: 0-13-020944-9

Prentice-Hall International (UK) Limited, *London*
Prentice-Hall of Australia Pty. Limited, *Sydney*
Prentice-Hall of Canada, Inc., *Toronto*
Prentice-Hall Hispanoamericana, S. A., *Mexico*
Prentice-Hall of India Private Limited, *New Delhi*
Prentice-Hall of Japan, Inc., *Tokyo*
Editora Prentice Hall do Brasil, Ltda., *Rio de Janeiro*

Praise and glory to Christ the Lord,

who with love so infinite, and grace so amazing,

saved a worm such as me.

Contents

Unit 1
OPERATING SYSTEM CONCEPTS, 1

Unit 2
BASIC COMMANDS, 11

Unit 3
DIRECTORIES, 26

Unit 4
TEXT EDITING, 48

Unit 5
BASIC FILE MANIPULATION, 66

Unit 6
ADVANCED FILE MANIPULATION, 82

Unit 7
WORKING IN C SHELL AND tcsh, 102

Unit 8
UNIX NETWORKING, 130

Unit 9
PROGRAMMING IN BOURNE SHELL, 147

Appendix A
THE vi EDITOR, 168

INDEX, 179

Preface

Each unit is divided into the following sections: Concepts to Learn, Commands to Learn, Sample Session, Experiments, Homework, and Lab Assignments.

Concepts to Learn is a summary of concepts and terms discussed in the unit.

Commands to Learn is a summary of commands and options used in the unit. They can be studied before starting the unit to see what types of operations will be covered in the unit or they can be used as a reference to look back to the actual syntax of the commands.

The Sample Session section shows the actual output as commands are entered on the computer. Some commands are entered incorrectly on purpose to illustrate the error messages received. The commands are entered one by one, gradually advancing the reader to new skill levels without making the learning process difficult. The responses from the computer make the student feel as if he or she is sitting with the author next to the console. This experience is like that of bringing a computer into a classroom and projecting a session on the screen. An added advantage to this style is that the student doesn't have to take notes because a record of the session is right there in the text.

Parallel to the session, in a column on the right–hand side of the page, is a verbal explanation of all the action that is going on. This "by example" method allows the instructor to show the effects of UNIX commands as if they were a screen play being unfolded. This approach is much more effective than treating UNIX as a series of dry commands which don't fit together. Imagine trying to learn carpentry by only learning what each tool *can do* individually! It is far better to learn carpentry by learning how to *use* the tools to build a cabinet or whatever. Likewise, in the Concepts to Learn and the Commands to Learn sections you will learn what each individual command *can do* and in this and in the following section you will learn how to *use* those commands to accomplish certain tasks.

The section on Experiments allows the student to learn on his own by *seeing* what each command does without anyone else *telling* him. When this section is done first within each unit, it allows the student to draw conclusions by observing what happens. In this section students write in the output that they see from typing each command. Again, explanations on the right–hand side guide the learner.

A set of exhaustive homework exercises, at the end of each unit, allows professors to assign homework exercises which are simple as well as challenging.

Finally, a set of lab assignments is given at the end of each unit to see if the students can apply all the concepts which they have learned.

I welcome suggestions and comments at ramteke@pilot.njin.net.

Finally, I thank Bhupinder Sran for his insight into Unit 1, Bob O'Connell for his idea that this work should be turned into a text book, and Bill Yodlowsky for all his help and assistance. The readers will appreciate Bret Workman's superb editing which caused me much grief!

Unit 1

Operating System Concepts

TERMS TO LEARN

Batch Processing	Jobs are executed after a group of them are collected. Therefore the results of batch jobs are not available immediately.
CPU	Central Processing Unit. The Intel Pentium is an example of a CPU. This is where most arithmetic and logic operations are done.
Compiler	This is a program which converts a program written in a high–level language into machine code.
High–Level Language	C is an example of a high–level language. It is an easier language to program with than machine language.
Kernel	The UNIX operating system converted (or compiled) to machine language for the CPU which it is running on.
LAN	Local Area Network. A network of hosts, printers, and other devices within a facility (or a building).
Machine Language	The only kind of language a CPU understands. Everything which runs on a host must be converted sooner or later into machine language.
Modem	A device which allows you to send data over telephone lines. The receiving end of a communications link must also have a modem.
Multiprocessing	Many processes are run simultaneously.
NIC	Network Interface Card. An adapter in a host (or a PC) which connects it to a LAN.
NOS	Network Operating System. An operating system which is made to network computers over a LAN.
Operating System	Software which controls the operations of a computer. It handles all input/output, scheduling of jobs, and managing of memory. Windows 98 is an example of an operating system. An application, such as a word processor, communicates with the operating system in order to do its tasks.
Partition	A segment of RAM or a hard drive. One RAM partition is where one process can be loaded and run. One hard drive can contain many operating systems, but each one must have its own partition.
Process	A program which is currently running.
Spawning	This occurs when one process starts another one.

1

Telnet	This is a command which allows you to remotely log into a host. If you are not right at the console of a host, even if you are logging in from another host nearby, you are still logging in remotely. Remote login doesn't mean you are miles away from your host.
Timesharing	This allows many users to share CPU time simultaneously.
Virtual Memory	Part of the hard drive can be used to extend the range of RAM. This is called virtual memory.
WAN	Wide Area Network. A network which is more than 2 or 3 miles in diameter.

WHAT IS AN OPERATING SYSTEM

A computer has many resources. It has one or more CPUs (Central Processing Unit) where most of the processing is done. It also has RAM (Random Access Memory) where data and programs are stored as long as the power is on. A computer may also have floppy drives, hard drives, CD-ROM drives, printers, NICs (Network Interface Cards), and many other such devices and items. Each has its own purpose. Now imagine if all these devices started doing their "own thing" as they pleased. For example, a file that is supposed to be saved to the hard drive gets sent over the network instead or a program that is supposed to be read off the CD-ROM drive doesn't get read because it is doing something else at the time. Or suppose that when two users, who are logged on the same computer, send two different files over the network, these files get all mixed up instead of staying separated. What one user does would affect another. Just as it is clear that we need a captain to run a ship, it is obvious that we need a system program to run our computer. We need an operating system to be in charge and bring order to all the tasks that have to be performed on our computer.

An operating system is a system program which is in charge of the computer when it is turned on. Although a computer can run many processes simultaneously, it can work under only one operating system at a time. A PC can be booted up under UNIX or it can be booted up under DOS, for instance. But it cannot be booted up under both operating systems at any given time. Just as it is best for a ship to operate under one captain at any given time, so it is best that only one operating system should control a computer at any given time.

Besides bringing order to the operations of a computer, the operating system has other advantages. A primary one is that it makes it easy for programmers to write application programs such as word processors and spreadsheets. If it weren't for operating systems, programmers who want to write any program would need to write tedious commands in assembly language in order to communicate with the CPU and other hardware components. Many assembly language instructions would have to be written every time even when something as simple as writing a file to a diskette has to be done. This process would take a lot of time and the effort would have to be duplicated for each application. Also, different applications would perform operations differently. There would be no standard way of doing things. An operating system makes writing applications easier and provides consistency in how users interact with the computer.

The operating system hides the complexity of the hardware, that is, of the CPU and other components of the computer. Programmers find it easier to communicate with the hardware through the operating system. Hence, they can concentrate more on making programs friendlier for users and not have to be concerned about the hardware implementation of the details.

WHERE DOES THE OPERATING SYSTEM FIT

In Figure 1.1, we see that the heart of the operating system is called the *kernel*. The kernel takes care of all the hardware interfacing so that the software which sits on top of the operating system doesn't have to. Hence, when the software which interfaces with the operating system needs to do anything, it does it through the kernel. The interface which is provided to the kernel is defined by system calls which it provides.

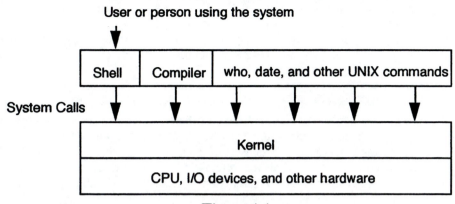

Figure 1.1

The software which accesses the kernel through system calls runs in what is called the *user mode*. Compilers, editors, and UNIX commands are examples of items which access the kernel. These run in the user mode since they are the objects which use the operating system. The operating system itself runs in what is called the *kernel mode*. It talks directly to the hardware and the low-level, physical components of a computer.

When a person logs onto a UNIX system, a command interpreter is provided for that user. This item of software is called the *shell*. When we enter commands to the operating system, we do it through the shell. If it detects a syntax error, an error message is displayed to us and the incorrect command doesn't go the kernel. Error messages from the kernel are displayed by the shell to the user in a manner which is understandable to us. If we enter a proper UNIX command, the shell will convert our command to a set of system calls and the kernel will go ahead and complete the task.

COMPONENTS OF AN OPERATING SYSTEM

Operating systems manage all the resources of a computer. These resources fall into four categories. They are processes, input/output devices, memory, and files. An operating system must be able to manage and streamline the operation of these four items.

Processes

A program which is currently being executed together with its working environment is called a *process*. It could be a command interpreter or a shell which is running, or it could be an editor, a mail program, or even a game which is running.

Multiprocessing: In the old days, when a mainframe was writing a file out to a disk or a printer, the CPU just waited and didn't do any processing until the file was written out to the physical device. When a record had to be read into RAM, again the CPU had to wait until all the data was read before it could start processing that data. Sometimes this waiting period was so long that the CPU had to be idle up to 80% of the time. The CPU works at the speed of electricity which is much faster than the speed at which physical I/O devices operate. Physical devices are slower because a magnetic tape may have to be forwarded to a certain place or the arm which contains the head to read a disk may have to come to a certain position before data transfer can occur. Such operations are much slower than the transfer of electric current in a CPU. And in an era when computers were very expensive, this was undesirable. Soon engineers developed a better method of utilizing the resources of the CPU called multiprocessing.

Multiprocessing or multiprogramming allows the CPU to save the work space of a job and put that job aside while waiting for its I/O to complete. Since RAM is divided into partitions, one partition contains the programs for the operating system itself, while each of the other partitions contains one job that was loaded into it. If there are four partitions of RAM available for extra programs, then the operating system can run four jobs at any given time. Then while the CPU is waiting for one job to complete its I/O operation, it can continue with a job which is in one of the other partitions.

Timesharing: Formerly, mainframes would run jobs only in a batch mode. This meant that once a group of jobs was obtained, then all those jobs would be executed together. This would require programmers to wait one or two hours before they could get the results of their programs.

Now timesharing allows users of the computer to share the CPU time. Since not all users require the services of the CPU all the time, the CPU can serve many users simultaneously, giving them the results of their work immediately. This creates what is called an interactive working environment. Workers obtain results immediately and their productivity goes up.

Process Table: When an operating system is running many processes concurrently using the timesharing concept, it must be able to store all the pertinent information about each process. This information is stored in what is called a *process table*. For each process that is still running, the process table contains what part of memory is allocated for its program and data. What files are opened and the location of the next records to be processed are also stored in the process table. All information that is needed to continue a process which has been suspended is stored in the process table. This way, a process which becomes active again is started in the same environment it was in when it was suspended. Basically, the process table contains all information needed to manage a process.

Signals can be sent to a process by the operating system to convey some piece of communication. For instance, when the operating system wants to suspend a process which has been using too much CPU time, it will send the CPU a specific signal to do this.

Spawning Processes: Every process is started by a particular user, someone who has an account on the computer system. Each user is identified by what is called the *user ID* or uid, for short.

One process can create another process, which can create others. This is called *spawning*. The uid of the parent process is associated with all the processes which it creates. Consider this example. When a person logs on, he or she is running a shell process. If that person executes an operating system command, then the shell spawns the process which is associated with that command. If a text editor is invoked, for example, then that process is created by the shell, and so forth.

I/O Devices

When a process needs to read a block of data from a device, such as a hard drive, the operating system must first send an I/O request on behalf of the process to the device–independent software. This software is written so that the operating system can send and receive data and signals regardless of what the actual device is. The device–independent software looks in the cache to see if the block of data is there; if not, then it will tell the device driver to fetch it. The software which is particular to the actual device is written in a device driver. Hence, each device needs its own device driver software. Now the process has to wait until the operation is complete. See Figure 1.2.

The hardware is signaled to perform the operation through the interrupt handler. When the hardware dumps the block of data into the cache, it will send a hardware interrupt to the interrupt handler. The interrupt handler will then signal the operating system through the device driver and the device–independent software that the I/O request is complete. Now the operating system can continue that process in the state it was in before it was suspended.

Memory Management

The Memory Hierarchy: Registers are part of the CPU. They are the fastest type of memory because they are right in the CPU where data is processed. However, there are only a handful of them. RAM is the next fastest type of memory, but there is more of it than CPU registers. Hard drives

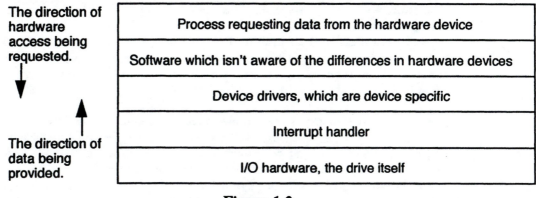

The direction of hardware access being requested.

The direction of data being provided.

| Process requesting data from the hardware device |
| Software which isn't aware of the differences in hardware devices |
| Device drivers, which are device specific |
| Interrupt handler |
| I/O hardware, the drive itself |

Figure 1.2

and floppies are also a type of memory, but they are slower to access than RAM or registers. However, hard drives can hold a lot more information than RAM or registers.

Memory Management Issues: With batch systems, memory is divided into fixed partitions. When a job needs to run, it is loaded from a hard drive into a free partition as soon as its turn comes up. Then the entire job stays in memory (or RAM) until the job is complete. There is no need to hold all the jobs in RAM at one time because the users are not running the jobs in an interactive mode. They don't need responses in real time. Jobs are loaded from the hard disk and executed as RAM becomes available. Users can expect to wait an hour or two to get their results.

With timesharing systems, however, responses to the tasks which the users require must be provided in real–time mode. In order to accomplish this, the operating system must run many jobs concurrently. As a result, however, there is typically not enough memory available to store them all.

Swapping: The simplest form of memory management for timesharing systems is called *swapping*. Here the partitions are not fixed. Entire jobs, not parts of them, are loaded into memory partitions of varying size. When a process has to wait for I/O, the entire job is swapped from RAM to the hard drive, then brought back into RAM when the I/O process is complete. Because partitions can change size as their requirements change, swapping provides a better use of memory than fixed–size partitions.

Virtual Memory: In this scheme of memory management, the size of the program or job that is running may be larger than the RAM that is allocated for that program. Hence, the rest of the job must reside on the hard disk until it is needed. Then it is swapped as needed. Because only parts of the programs which are running are stored in RAM, many more programs can reside in memory at any given time and many more programs can be executed at any given time.

In a typical job, execution of the code is usually confined to a group of programming lines at a given time. Hence, when a program is initially loaded for execution, only the first part of the program is loaded. Then as execution advances to the part of the code which resides on the hard drive, this part of the code is swapped with the part that is in memory and execution can continue. The operating system has to manage this process. Virtual memory, therefore, is the ability of an operating system to include the space available on the hard drive with the capacity of the real RAM. A technique called *paging* is used to achieve this.

Files

File Types: We work with two types of files: regular files and directory files. Regular files are files which can be written, overwritten, read, executed, etc. Directory files are folders where other files can be organized and stored. There are different kinds of regular files. Some files are text files, while others are application–specific files, such as WordPerfect files. Others are binary files; these files can be executed.

A text file is also called an ASCII file. We can see and understand ASCII files when displayed on the screen since they contain English characters. A nice thing about a text file is that it can be displayed on the screen by practically any operating system. Email, for example, that is sent in text format is understandable by any receiving host.

File Access: Basically, there are two ways to access files: sequential and random access. In sequential access records are stored in some kind of order, and they are usually processed in that order. Typically, they are all processed in one session. When all records need to be processed, sequential access proves to be the fastest method because a technique called buffering is used to read records in advance from I/O. A payroll program is an example of an application which uses sequential access

When records have to be accessed randomly, such as in a hotel reservation system, random access of records is more appropriate. Here, one record is processed at a time rather than the entire file.

File System: In UNIX, a hard disk partition is called a file system. A file system is divided into blocks of space called inodes (index nodes). Inodes are special kinds of blocks which contain information about the file, such as who is the owner of the file, when it was last modified, and its location on the disk. When a file needs to be accessed, it first looks at the root directory which is in a certain position on the hard drive. Here, it finds the inode for the first directory in the path. Using the inode number, the block number is calculated and the file may be found there. If there are more directories in the file's path, then additional inodes are referenced and additional block numbers are calculated. The format of a UNIX file system is completely different from that of a DOS partition.

THE UNIX OPERATING SYSTEM

Machine Language: Each type of CPU has its own set of instructions which it understands. An Intel CPU's instruction set, for example, is different from the instructions which Motorola's CPU understands. The set of instructions which each kind of CPU understands is called *machine language*. Assembly language is similar to machine language. Programmers find it easier to program in assembly language than in machine language. Once the program is written in assembly language, another program called an *assembler* will convert the assembly language into machine language so that the proper CPU can execute it. Programs written in machine or assembly languages run efficiently. However, they can be executed only on the CPU for which they were intended. (See Figure 1.3.)

High–Level Language: C, C++, COBOL, BASIC are examples of high–level languages. They are even easier to code than assembly language programs but require what is called a *compiler* to convert the code into machine language. Since each CPU type's instruction set is different, a different compiler is needed to compile the same program on different CPUs. (See Figure 1.4.)

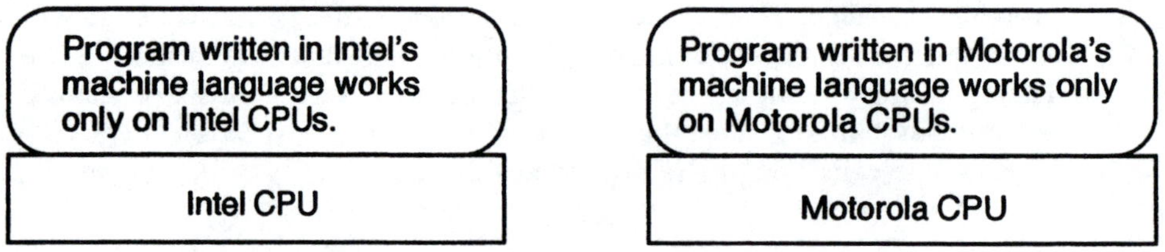

```
 _____          _____
| Program written in Intel's |        | Program written in Motorola's |
| machine language works      |       | machine language works only   |
| only on Intel CPUs.         |       | on Motorola CPUs.             |
|_____|        |_____|
|                            |        |                              |
|         Intel CPU          |        |         Motorola CPU          |
|_____|        |_____|
```

Figure 1.3 A machine–language program which needs to be executed on different CPUs must be rewritten for each CPU separately. All major operating systems, except UNIX, are written this way.

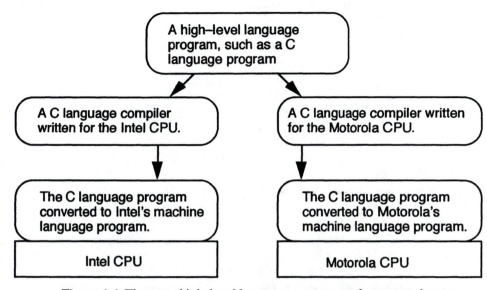

Figure 1.4 The same high–level language program can be executed on different CPUs without having to rewrite it, as long as you have the compilers for those CPUs. Unix is the only major operating system written in a high–level language, specifically, C.

However, the same high–level language program can execute on any computer regardless of its CPU type. This is because each compiler can convert the same program into the correct machine language code. Programs written in assembly language don't have this benefit. They are not portable. However, we can now run the same program on any CPU, as long as it is written in a high–level language. All we would need is a compiler for that type of CPU.

Different Operating Systems: Operating systems are usually written in assembly or machine language. This is done so that they can run more efficiently. I/O can be done faster because the operating system works more closely with the hardware.

There are several common operating systems. They only work on their specific platform or for the CPU for which they are intended. DOS works only on IBM–compatibles. MacOS works only on Macintoshes which use a Motorola chip rather than an Intel chip. MVS/XA is an operating system which runs only on IBM mainframes. Windows NT works only on PCs. Windows 3.1 is not an operating system at all, but only a GUI (Graphical User Interface) shell which makes working in an DOS environment more pleasant. Each of these operating systems is written in the assembly language of its particular CPU. You cannot run MacOS directly on a PC or Windows NT on a mainframe because they are written in assembly languages.

Where Does UNIX Work? UNIX is not written in assembly language like all other operating systems. Just as a high–level language can run on any computer as long as you have the compiler for it, so can you run UNIX on any computer as long as you have a C compiler for it. The C language was created for UNIX and UNIX is written in C. The C language was made to be more efficient than other high–level languages so UNIX enjoys the advantage of machine language coding and can be run on any CPU.

Software's ability to run on any computer is called *portability*. UNIX is portable. You can run UNIX on a PC, Mac, mainframe, a Sun server, or anything else. All you need for it is a C compiler since UNIX is written in C.

Open Systems: A major advantage obtained from portability is what is called *open systems*. Open systems means that you are not tied to one particular vendor. In the days of mainframe computers, you would have to pay a million dollars or more to buy one. It was just as expensive to develop applications for such hosts. However, if you didn't like your vendor, for whatever reason, you could not afford to just throw away the investment you had made in writing applications and rewrite them for a new kind of a mainframe. The vendors knew that, so you didn't get service.

With open systems, however, you can change your hardware equipment vendor a lot easier. Sure, you have to buy new equipment. But if your applications are written for UNIX, you can easily port those over to the new vendor's version of UNIX.

Because of a real need to be able to port (or transfer) your applications to different versions of UNIX, IEEE (Institute for Electronics and Electrical Engineers) has made and is continuing to develop a standard called POSIX which is used with UNIX.

Networking Comes Naturally to UNIX: When DOS was first written for the PC, other companies came along and had to write NOSs (Network Operating Systems). Novell's NetWare is a common NOS. However, in the mid–1980's NetWare wasn't sufficient if you wanted to do wide area networking. You had to resort to routers which ran other protocols and operating systems. If you needed email, you had to add other software.

UNIX was created in the late 1960's and networking was part of its original design. Hence, UNIX could always be run on stand–alone stations over LANs and WANs. Email and other network related functions come with UNIX. No wonder that when the TCP/IP protocols were first tested for the Internet, they were first tested on UNIX systems.

Other Advantages of UNIX: UNIX is an operating system that provides a simple user interface. It also provides a hierarchical file system as we now have it with DOS or folders in GUIs.

UNIX provides a simple consistent user interface to peripheral devices and networked hosts. In DOS, we have a directory tree for the A: drive, a different tree for the C: drive, and so on. In UNIX, however, there is only one root and one tree. The floppy drive can be mounted under one of the branches of the tree. Similarly, a host from a different country can be mounted on the same tree. A remote host may respond more slowly than the files that exist on your local computer, but it is seen as part of the same directory tree.

No other operating system runs faster on a PC than UNIX. It manages memory better and uses the resources of the computer more efficiently than all other operating systems.

UNIX allows piping. This is a feature that enables you to take the output of one command and make it the input of another command or utility. It also allows you to write complex programs using primitive commands.

Another nice thing about UNIX is that it is not the "new kid on the block." It has been around since 1969. It has been tested and tried by many scientists and practitioners. It is secure. It works on stand–alone hosts. It works over local area networks as well as enterprise–wide networks. UNIX has proven itself in all kinds of settings. Also, many high–quality UNIX applications can be obtained for free. For example, a free UNIX–based software called Apache is used on over 50% of the Web servers on the Internet.

Login name or user name
Separator   Host name   domain

ramteke@alankay.nj.devry.edu

Host address

User address or Email address

Figure 1.5

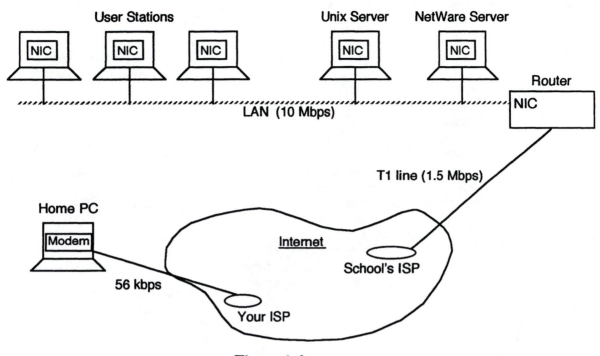

Figure 1.6

CONNECTING TO UNIX

In order to log into a UNIX server, you must first have a UNIX account. The account starts with your login name, then come the "@" sign and the host address. The host address includes the host name and the domain it is in. (See Figure 1.5.)

In Figure 1.6 we see a UNIX server. It has a host name and an Internet address. Here, we see that the UNIX server is part of a LAN. Because it is part of a LAN, it has a NIC (Network Interface Card). In fact, any device which is connected to the LAN must have a NIC. In this figure, if you were logged onto one of the user stations, you could telnet to the UNIX server. In Microsoft Windows, you would click on the Start button, select Run, type "telnet," and press Enter. Then you would have to use the Connect option to specify the address of the UNIX server to which you wish to be connected. When doing a telnet, you should provide only the host address and not the login name. The login name is entered when you see the login prompt as shown in the next unit. Then you can be connected over the Internet using a router.

If you have an Internet connection at home and if you are using a simple modem, you can connect to the Internet through an ISP (Internet Service Provider). You could connect to the same UNIX server from home using the same login procedure as outlined above. But you would first need to be connected to the Internet.

Sometimes you may want to save the log of your session to a file. You may want to save all your commands and their responses so that you can review or print your dialog at a later time. In the Windows 98 Telnet window, this is done by clicking on the Terminal pull–down window and selecting "Start Logging ...". Then you will get a dialog box prompting you to give the file name and where you want to save it on your PC. After that, your complete telnet session with the UNIX server will be saved in that file. After you are done working with your UNIX server, go to the Terminal pull–down menu of the Telnet program again and select "Stop Logging." Now you can view your session saved in the file or print it using Notepad or some other text editor.

HOMEWORK

1. What is the difference between batch processing and timesharing?
2. What is a program? A process? Where is information about a process stored?
3. What is the difference between machine language and a high–level language? Which is more portable?
4. What is the difference between an assembler and a compiler?
5. What are the advantages of UNIX?
6. What is the UNIX kernel? Does the kernel differ from CPU to CPU?
7. Explain the difference between kernel mode and user mode operation.
8. What are the four major parts of an operating system?
9. Explain the purpose of virtual memory.
10. When would a computer need a modem and when would it need a NIC?
11. What are the two ways to access files? How do they differ?
12. What is the purpose of an operating system?
13. Name other operating systems besides UNIX.
14. What is the difference between a regular file and a directory? What is the difference between an application–specific file and a text file?

Unit 2

Basic Commands

CONCEPTS TO LEARN

Logging Into the Server: You must have an account and a password provided by the UNIX server administrator in order for you to log on. You can log into a UNIX server more than once at any given time.

Logging Out: When your work is done, make sure you log out.

Shell: The shell is a command interpreter. Every UNIX account works with a shell. If you type in a non–UNIX command, the shell will not allow the command to be executed by the operating system; instead, it will display an error message. Depending on what the user prefers, there are different types of shells available. These are some examples:

sh	Bourne shell – the oldest shell.
csh	C shell – A popular shell
bash	Bourne–Again shell
tcsh	Pronounced "teesh" – A powerful shell

Standard Output: When the results of commands are displayed on the computer screen, it is called standard output.

Redirecting the Output: The output of a command can be redirected into a file by providing the file name after the > character.

Appending: The output of a command can be added to the end of a file (or appended) by using the >> characters.

Pattern Matching:

*	means 0 or more characters
?	means 1 and only one character
[0 – 9]	means only one digit
[!X]*	means all files which don't begin with X

COMMANDS TO LEARN

<arrows>	[DOS: doskey] Using the arrows on the arrow pad on most PC–based UNIX systems allows you to cycle through previously executed commands.
!!	Executes the last command again.
!n	Executes command whose number is n. Command numbers can be obtained by the history command.
!x	Executes the last command which started with the x character.
echo	[DOS: echo] Displays whatever follows it on the next line.

11

cal	Shows the calender for a given month or year.
cat	[DOS: type] Displays the contents of a file to the screen. More than one file can be typed out using one cat. "cat" stands for "concatenate" or "display all files listed one after the other."
clear	[DOS: cls] Clears the screen.
cp	Copies one file into another. No > is used.
date	[DOS: date] Shows the current date and time.
exit	Used to exit from the current shell.
history	Shows all the commands which were previously executed by the user.
history –n	Shows only the last n commands.
hostname	Shows the name of the server you are logged on.
logout	Allows you to logout.
ls	[DOS:dir] Shows which files exist in the current working directory. Only file names and directory names are listed.
ls –l	Shows filenames, directory names, sizes of the files, permissions, and other items. This is called a long listing.
ls –al	Shows all files, including hidden files. Hidden filenames begin with a dot.
man	Shows the manual page for the command that is listed here.
man –k	Finds all commands in the system which have to do with the keyword specified.
more	Similar to cat, but shows one screenful at a time. (Also, try the less command which is similar to more.)
b	This will go back one screen.
<Enter>	This key will go forward one line.
<Space>	The spacebar will go forward one screen.
h	Shows help for more.
q	Quits the more command.
mv	[DOS: rename or move] If a file is moved in the same directory, then this is a rename. If a file is moved into a different directory, then this is really a move.
passwd	Allows you to change your password. First, UNIX will verify that the proper user is trying to change the password and not just a professor who is angry because the user left the terminal unattended. This is done by asking for the old password. Then the new password is entered twice to make sure that the user can type the same password twice. Note whether the caps are on or off. UNIX is case sensitive, unlike DOS.
ps	Shows what processes are running. If you are stuck in a loop and can't get out of it, then telnet into the server from another window. Do this command to find out which process to kill and do "kill –9 <PID>" where PID is the process ID listed with ps.
sh	Allows you to go into the Bourne shell.
tcsh	Allows you to go into the tcsh shell.
telnet	Allows you to remotely login to a server.
touch	Creates the file if it doesn't exist. Otherwise, it updates the file time–date stamp.
rm	[DOS: del] Deletes a file or files. No questions are asked.
rm –i	Tells UNIX to ask if you really want to delete this file before deleting.
uptime	Shows how long the server has been up since it was last rebooted.
who	Shows who is currently logged on.
who am i	Shows your login name.
whoami	Also shows your login name.

```
OpenBSD/i386 (alankay) (ttyp0)                          Here I am logging into alankay.
login: tramteke                                         I enter my password, but it doesn't echo on
Password:                                               the screen.
Last login: May 20 02:17:41 from 204.142.105.4
Warning: no Kerberos tickets issued.
OpenBSD 2.2 (ALANKAY) #1: Mar 13 11:17:45 EST 1998


% {101} who                                             Who is currently logged on alankay?
tramteke ttyp0  May 20 02:18  (207.172.201.21)          Only I am logged on, from the IP address of
% {102} telnet alankay                                  207.172.201.21. This is the IP address of
Trying 204.142.105.4...                                 my PC.  Now telnet into alankay again
Connected to alankay.nj.devry.edu.                      (from alankay).
Escape character is '^]'.
OpenBSD/i386 (alankay) (ttyp2)
login: tramteke
Password:                                               Log on as before.
Last login: May 20 02:18:50 from 207.172.201.21
Warning: no Kerberos tickets issued.
OpenBSD 2.2 (ALANKAY) #1: Mar 13 11:17:45 EST 1998


% {101} who                                             I am logged in twice: once from the ".21" IP
tramteke ttyp0  May 20 02:18  (207.172.201.21)          address and once from the ".4" IP address,
tramteke ttyp2  May 20 02:19  (204.142.105.4)           which is alankay's address.

% {102} passwd
Changing local password for tramteke.                   First, change your password to something
Old password:                                           you can remember. I wasn't allowed to
passwd: Permission denied                               change it since I didn't enter my old pass-
passwd: /etc/master.passwd: unchanged                   word correctly.
% {103} passwd
Changing local password for tramteke.                   This time, I entered the old password cor-
Old password:                                           rectly, so I was able to change it. I must
New password:                                           enter the new password the same way twice.
Retype new password:
% {104} telnet alankay                                  To test the password change,  I telnet again
Trying 204.142.105.4...                                 from alankay to alankay.
Connected to alankay.nj.devry.edu.
Escape character is '^]'.

OpenBSD/i386 (alankay) (ttyp3)

login: tramteke                                         And the new password works.
Password:
Last login: May 20 02:19:51 from 204.142.105.4
Warning: no Kerberos tickets issued.
OpenBSD 2.2 (ALANKAY) #1: Mar 13 11:17:45 EST 1998

% {101} who                                             I see who is logged on.
tramteke May 20 02:18 (207.172.201.21)                  I am logged on three times now. At 2:18, I
tramteke May 20 02:19 (204.142.105.4)                   logged in from my own PC, and at 2:19 and
tramteke May 20 02:21 (204.142.105.4)                   2:21 I logged in from alankay.
```

```
% {102} logout
Connection closed by foreign host.
% {105} logout
Connection closed by foreign host.
% {103} who
tramteke May 20 02:18 (207.172.201.21)
% {104} cal feb 1915
cal: illegal month value: use 1-12
% {105} man cal
CAL(1)    OpenBSD Reference Manual
NAME
cal - displays a calendar
```

Now I am logging out of two of the sessions which I had started from alankay (IP of .4).

Notice that I only have one login now, the one I started from my own PC (IP of .21).
I want to find out what day of the week my mom was born on. However, I used the calender command incorrectly.
The man command will give me help on this command and many others. Only one line of this help is shown.

```
% {105} man man
% {106} cal 02 1915
February 1915
Su Mo Tu We Th Fr Sa
    1  2  3  4  5  6
 7  8  9 10 11 12 13
14 15 16 17 18 19 20
21 22 23 24 25 26 27
28
```

This helps me find out how to use the man command.
Here we go: this shows the calender for February of 1915.

```
% {109} clear
% {110} history
100  2:18     exit
101  2:19     who
102  2:19     telnet alankay
103  2:22     who
104  2:23     cal feb 1915
105  2:23     man cal
106  2:23     cal 02 1915
107  2:24     cal 04 1950
108  2:25     cal 04 2005
109  2:26     clear
110  2:26     history
```

Let's clear the screen.
Let's get a history of all the previous commands which were executed.

```
% {111} history 10
102  2:19     telnet alankay
103  2:22     who
104  2:23     cal feb 1915
105  2:23     man cal
106  2:23     cal 02 1915
107  2:24     cal 04 1950
108  2:25     cal 04 2005
109  2:26     clear
110  2:26     history
111  2:26     history 10
```

This command will show only the last 10 commands which were executed.

```
% {112} !c
clear
% {113} history 10
104  2:23     cal feb 1915
105  2:23     man cal
106  2:23     cal 02 1915
107  2:24     cal 04 1950
108  2:25     cal 04 2005
```

This command executes the last command I entered which began with the character "c". From the history output, we see it was the clear command. So this command is displayed and then executed. Now the screen is cleared again.

```
109   2:26     clear
110   2:26     history
111   2:26     history 10
112   2:26     clear
113   2:26     history 10
% {114} date
Wed May 20 02:27:22 EDT 1998
```

Let's see the current date and time.

```
% {115} uptime
2:27AM  up 14 days, 15:14, 1 user,
load averages: 0.19, 0.24, 0.41
% {116} whoami
tramteke
% {117} who am i
tramteke ttyp0    May 20 02:18
(207.172.201.21)
```

This command shows us how long alankay has been up since it was last rebooted. Other information is also provided about the server, such as the number of users logged on and its load. If you are having philosophical difficulties trying to figure out who you are, have no fear: UNIX will help you figure that out. Use either of these two methods to find your user name or login name.

```
% {118} !113
history 10
109   2:26     clear
110   2:26     history
111   2:26     history 10
112   2:26     clear
113   2:26     history 10
114   2:27     date
115   2:27     uptime
116   2:27     whoami
117   2:27     who am i
118   2:28     history 10
```

Redo command number 113. From the history output, we see that this executes the history 10 command again.

```
% {119} date
Wed May 20 02:28:45 EDT 1998
```

Notice that the time has changed.

```
% {120} !!
date
Wed May 20 02:28:48 EDT 1998
```

Redo the last command.

```
% {121} hostname
alankay
```

This command finds out which server you are logged on. If you have several sessions opened with several hosts, then you might need this command.

```
% {125} ls
```

The ls command lists the files (and directories) in the current directory. There are no files existing at the moment.

```
% {126} ps
PID   TT   STAT    TIME       COMMAND
16732 p0   Ss      0:00.51  -tcsh (tcsh)
20235 p0   R+      0:00.01  ps
```

The ps command finds out the processes which are running under your account. Right now there are PIDs (Process IDs) of 16732, which is the tcsh login shell that is running, and 20235, which is the ps command that was just executed. You will always have the ps entry.

```
% {127} tcsh
```

Go into another shell.

```
% {101} ps
PID   TT   STAT    TIME       COMMAND
2700  p0   R+      0:00.01  ps
8363  p0   S       0:00.12  -csh (tcsh)
16732 p0   Ss      0:00.51  -tcsh (tcsh)
```

Notice that you now have another process started.

```
% {102} csh
```

Go into C shell and you now have another process running.

```
% {101} ps
PID   TT   STAT    TIME       COMMAND
5368  p0   S       0:00.05  -sh (csh)
8363  p0   S       0:00.13  -csh (tcsh)
14003 p0   R+      0:00.00  ps
16732 p0   Is      0:00.51  -tcsh (tcsh)
```

Basic Commands

```
% {102} logout
Not a login shell.
% {103} exit
% {103} logout
Not a login shell.
% {104} exit
exit
% {128} ps
PID    TT   STAT     TIME       COMMAND
16732  p0   Ss       0:00.51    -tcsh
23925  p0   R+       0:00.01    ps
% {129} sh
$ ps
PID    TT   STAT     TIME       COMMAND
2439   p0   R+       0:00.00 ps
10923  p0   S        0:00.01 sh
16732  p0   Ss       0:00.52 -tcsh
$ ksh
$ ps
PID    TT   STAT     TIME       COMMANDD
4940   p0   R+       0:00.00    ps
10923  p0   S        0:00.02    sh
16732  p0   Ss       0:00.52    -tcsh
28560  p0   S        0:00.01    ksh
$ exit
$ exit
% {130} ps
PID    TT   STAT     TIME       COMMAND
16732  p0   Ss       0:00.52    -tcsh
17733  p0   R+       0:00.01    ps
```

UNIX doesn't allow me to log out using this shell since there are other shells running.

I must first exit out of the last shell.

However, since I am not in my login shell, I cannot log out.

After exiting the next to last shell, I may log out, but I don't.

Here is proof that I am in my login shell.

This is how we go into Bourne shell.

And this is how I would go into Korn shell.
This ps command shows that I have the Bourne shell (sh), Korn shell (ksh), and the tcsh shell (tcsh) running.

Exit from the Korn shell.
Exit from the Bourne shell.
Now, we are back in our original, or login, shell.

```
% {131} echo UNIX is fun
UNIX is fun
% {132} ls
% {133} echo UNIX is fun > fun1
% {134} ls
fun1
% {135} ls -l
total 2
-rw-r--r-- tramteke  prof 02:35 fun1
% {136} cat fun1
UNIX is fun
```

The echo command will place the characters you type after it on the next line, "echoing" the characters.
The ls command shows what files exist. None here.
The redirection will create the file called fun1. Instead of displaying the line on the screen, it is redirected to fun1.
The ls command verifies that this file exists.
The –l option shows permissions and other aspects of the file. The very first dash before the "rw" indicates that fun1 is a file. The other information shown will be explained later.
The cat command will display the contents of fun1, which was created in command 133.

```
% {137} cat fun1 > fun2
% {138} ls -l
total 4
-rw-r--r-- tramteke  prof 02:35 fun1
-rw-r--r-- tramteke  prof 02:36 fun2
% {139} echo gliding is fun > fun1
% {140} cat fun1
gliding is fun
% {141} cat fun2
UNIX is fun
% {142} cat fun1 fun2
gliding is fun
```

Adding a redirection here places the output in the file called fun2 instead of sending the output to the screen.
Here, we see that both files, fun1 and fun2, exist.

Redirecting the output "gliding is fun" to fun1 overwrites fun1. The old content of fun1 is lost.

In command 137, fun1 was copied into fun2. fun2 is still the same as before.
Doing a cat of more than one file shows each file, one after the other, without any separation.

Basic Commands

```
UNIX is fun
% {143} cat fun1 fun2 > fun3
% {144} cat fun3
gliding is fun
UNIX is fun
% {145} echo lazying is fun >> fun3
% {146} cat fun3
gliding is fun
UNIX is fun
lazying is fun
% {147} cat fun1 >> fun3
% {148} cat fun3
gliding is fun
UNIX is fun
lazying is fun
gliding is fun
% {149} ls
fun1 fun2 fun3
% {150} ls > fun1
% {151} cat fun1
fun1
fun2
fun3
% {152} echo echo
echo
% {153} echo cat
cat
% {154} cat echo
cat: echo: No such file or directory
% {155} cat cat
cat: cat: No such file or directory
% {156} uptime >> fun1
% {157} cat fun1
fun1
fun2
fun3
2:41AM  up 14 days, 15:28, 1 user
% {158} ls -l
total 6
-rw-r--r-- tramteke  prof  02:41 fun1
-rw-r--r-- tramteke  prof  02:36 fun2
-rw-r--r-- tramteke  prof  02:39 fun3
% {159} history > fun1
% {161} more fun1
   .  .  .
    .  .  .
69  15:54   logout
% {162} man more



h or H Help: display a summary of
these commands.
```

Here, the output of fun1 and fun2 is redirected from the screen to file3. Now the content of file3 is the content of both file1 and file2.

Using >> appends "lazying is fun" to the end of fun3. Notice, the first two lines show the previous contents of fun3 and the third line, "lazying is fun," is shown to be added by the append sign.

Here, the content of fun1, "gliding is fun," is added to the end of fun3 and command 148 confirms that.

The ls command shows that we now have three files.

The output of ls is redirected to fun1. The old content of this file is lost and now fun1 contains the names of the files in the current directory.

echo displays "echo."

echo, here, displays "cat."

We cannot print the file called "echo." This file doesn't exist.

Neither does the file called "cat".

The output of how long the host has been up is appended to fun1. Notice that when fun1 is typed, it is shown at the end of the file.

We still have three files in our current directory.

The output of any command can be redirected in a file. Here, the output of history is redirected into fun1. The content of fun1 is now my entire history of commands. The more command allows me to view one screen at a time. (The fun1 file is now too long to be shown here.)
In order to find out how to use a command, or what it does, use the man command. This example shows how to get information about the more command.
While in man, typing . . .

h	will give you help
<enter>	will scroll one line
<space bar>	will scroll one page forward
b	will scroll one page back

```
/pattern              *  Search forward
```

```
% {163} less fun1
...skipping...
48  9:56    passwd
69  15:54   logout
```

```
% {164} man -k move
colrm (1) - remove columns from a file
flock (2) - apply or remove an advi-
sory lock on an open file
insque, remque (3) - insert/remove
element from a queue
```

```
% {165} !! | more
man -k move | more
```

```
% {166} ls -l
total 3
-rw-r--r--  1 tramteke  prof  116 fun1
-rw-r--r--  1 tramteke  prof   12 fun2
-rw-r--r--  1 tramteke  prof   57 fun3
```

```
% {167} cp fun2 fun1
```

```
% {168} ls -l
total 3
-rw-r--r--  1 tramteke  prof   12 fun1
-rw-r--r--  1 tramteke  prof   12 fun2
-rw-r--r--  1 tramteke  prof   57 fun3
```

```
% {169} cat fun1
UNIX is fun
```

```
% {170} cat *
UNIX is fun
UNIX is fun
gliding is fun
UNIX is fun
lazying is fun
gliding is fun
```

```
% {171} mv fun2 fun1
```

```
% {172} ls -l
total 4
-rw-r--r--  1 tramteke  prof  12   fun1
-rw-r--r--  1 tramteke  prof  57   fun3
```

```
% {173} rm -i *
remove fun1? y
remove fun3? n
```

```
% {174} rm fun3
```

```
% {175} ls -l
```

```
% {176} touch funXL1 funL1 funXL2 fun1
% {176} touch XfunXL Xtime3
% {177} touch MfunX XL7 XL79 XM798 X3
```

q   will quit you out of man.

/   will look for the characters in the file which follow the slash. The line which contains that pattern is then placed toward the top of the screen.

The less command is similar to the more command, and on some systems it has more features than the more command.

If you don't know the name of a UNIX command, use the –k option for keyword. Here, we are looking at all the commands on the system which have to do with the keyword "move."

The list was so long that all the output went off the screen. Adding "| more" to a command will show the output of that command one screenful at a time. However "!!", pronounced "bang bang", will repeat the previous command, reducing the typing required.

We have three files called fun1, fun2, and fun3.

fun1 is 116 bytes long,

fun2 is 12 bytes long,

and fun3 is 57 bytes long.

After copying fun2 to fun1, the old content of fun1 is lost and the content of fun2 replaces that of fun1.

fun1 has the contents of fun2.

* means all files in the current directory.
Here, we are displaying the contents of . . .
first, fun1; then, fun2;
and last, fun3.

Moving fun2 to fun1 is different than copying.

Move is like doing a rename, if done in the same directory. Since fun2 is moved to fun1, the old content of fun1 is lost, (notice, no warning is given) and the content of fun2 replaces the content of fun1. fun2 no longer exists.

This command removes all files. The –i option asks the user if each file shown is really to be deleted or not. Here, we are deleting fun1 but not fun3.

Here, we are deleting fun3 directly without using the –i option. Now there are no files left.

The touch command will quickly create file(s) if they don't exist. If they do exist, it will update the time–date stamp.

```
% {178} ls
MfunX  X3     XL7    XL79   XM798
XfunXL Xtime3 fun1   funL1  funXL1
funXL2
% {179} ls -l
total 0
-rw-r--r--   tramteke   prof   0 MfunX
-rw-r--r--   tramteke   prof   0 X3
-rw-r--r--   tramteke   prof   0 XL7
-rw-r--r--   tramteke   prof   0 XL79
-rw-r--r--   tramteke   prof   0 XM798
-rw-r--r--   tramteke   prof   0 XfunXL
-rw-r--r--   tramteke   prof   0 Xtime3
-rw-r--r--   tramteke   prof   0 fun1
-rw-r--r--   tramteke   prof   0 funL1
-rw-r--r--   tramteke   prof   0 funXL1
-rw-r--r--   tramteke   prof   0 funXL2
% {180} echo *
MfunX X3 XL7 XL79 XM798 XfunXL Xtime3
fun1 funL1 funXL1 funXL2
% {181} cat X3
% {182} cat x3
cat: x3: No such file or directory
% {183} echo X*
X3 XL7 XL79 XM798 XfunXL Xtime3
% {184} echo *1
fun1 funL1 funXL1
% {185} echo *X*
MfunX X3 XL7 XL79 XM798 XfunXL Xtime3
funXL1 funXL2
% {186} echo ???
XL7
% {187} echo ?????
MfunX XM798 funL1
% {188} echo ????[0-9]
XM798 funL1
% {189} echo X????
XM798
% {192} echo *[0-9]
X3 XL7 XL79 XM798 Xtime3 fun1 funL1
funXL1 funXL2
% {193} echo *[A-z]
MfunX XfunXL
% {194} echo *[a-Z]
echo: No match.
% {195} echo [!X]*
X]: Event not found.
% {196} sh
$ echo [!X]*
MfunX fun1 funL1 funXL1 funXL2
$ exit
% {197} logout
```

We now have 11 files with which we can experiment.

Doing a long listing, we see that all these files have 0 bytes in them.

From command 170, remember that * means all filenames. Echoing * will echo all filenames.

Notice that X3 has nothing in it.
Although X3 exists, x3 doesn't. UNIX is case sensitive.

* also means 0 or more characters. Here, all filenames which begin with an X are displayed.
All filenames which end with a 1 are displayed.

All filenames which have X anywhere in their names are displayed. Remember that * means 0 or more characters.

? means one and only one character. This shows all filenames which have only three characters in their names.
All filenames which have exactly five characters are shown.

Here, we have all filenames which have five characters and end with a number. [0–9] means one digit.
All filenames which begin with an X and have four characters following them are shown.
All filenames which end with a digit are shown.

All filenames which end with an alphabetic character are shown. Upper-case characters come first, then lower-case. Hence, "[a–Z]" doesn't make sense.

We are looking for filenames which don't begin with X.
However, our shell (tcsh) doesn't use this syntax.
We go to the Bourne shell by typing "sh."
Here that syntax works.
Notice that the prompt changes in Bourne shell to $.
Now, we exit the Bourne shell
and log out.

EXPERIMENTS

Fill in all of the items in the experiments which either you enter or the operating system provides you. Underline or highlight the items which you enter and leave the system responses as they are.

Logging In and Logging Out

`login:`
`password:`

2.1 Before you start, get your user login name and the password for your account from your system administrator. Only then can you start working in UNIX.
Enter your login name here.
Enter your password. It will not appear on the screen. (Don't write down your real password.)

`%passwd`

2.2 First change your password. Don't type the "%"; it is just the prompt. Only type passwd.
Write down the dialogue, that is, everything the system asks you and your responses.
THROUGHOUT THIS BOOK, WRITE DOWN WHAT YOU SEE ON THE SCREEN IN THE LEFT COLUMN AND ALL THE EXPLANATIONS IN THE RIGHT COLUMN. You may simplify the system responses.

`%date`

2.3 What does this command do? (Write down the computer's response to your left.)

`%daye`

2.4 Type in "date" incorrectly and identify which of the following keys allows you to backspace and correct your typo:
[del]
^h or <Ctrl>h
[backspace]

`%who am i`

2.5 What does this command give you?

`%who`

2.6 Write in only your user name and two others if this list is long. What does this command do?

`%history 6`

2.7 What does this history command show you?

`%!3`

2.8 This one is a little tricky. What does a number placed after a bang, "!", do?

`%!5`

`%!!`

2.9 What does "!!" do?

`%date`

`%!!`

```
%uptime
```

2.10 Can you tell what these two commands do?

```
%clear
```

```
%cat
```

2.11 Suppose that some time in the future you lose your prompt. Which of these keystrokes will bring your prompt back?
^d or Ctrl–d
^c or Ctrl–c
<return>
<esc>

```
%logout
```

2.12 Never turn off the computer without logging out. Which of the following ways will also log you out?
exit
^d

echo, cat, and Redirection

```
%echo what
```

2.13 Now log back in and try this.

```
%echo What a day!
```

2.14 What does "echo" do?

```
%echo echo
```

2.15

```
%echo What > file1
```

2.16 Was anything displayed on the screen?

```
%ls
```

2.17 This shows a directory listing. Does it show only the names of the existing files or does it also show the contents of the files?

```
%cat file1
```

2.18 What does "cat" do? (It is short for the word "concat-enation.")

```
%echo Why > file1
```

2.19 What does the *output redirection operator* ">" do?

```
%cat file1
```

Does it allow anything to get displayed on the screen? (The screen is called *standard output*.)

What does ">" do with the items that were supposed to go on the screen?

```
%date > file1
%cat file1
```

2.20 Did this experiment erase the old contents of file1?

Why weren't the date and the time displayed on the screen?

```
%who am i > file1
%cat file1
```

2.21 Can whatever goes on the screen be redirected to a file?

```
%echo echo >> file1
```

2.22 The ">>" is called the *append redirection operator.*

```
%cat file1
```

2.23 What did Experiment 2.22 do to file1?

```
%who am i >> file1
```

2.24

```
%cat file1
```

2.25 Was file1 overwritten or was something added to its end?

```
%cat file1 > file2
```

2.26 Before running the next experiment, can you tell what the content of file2 should be?

```
%cat file2
```

Does the cat command send items to standard output? In other words, does it display something on the screen? What does the redirection ">" do with those items?

```
%echo file1 > file2
```

2.27 Does this experiment or Experiment 2.26 copy a file? Why?

```
%cat file2
```

```
%echo cat
```

2.28

```
%cat echo
```

2.29 Why does this experiment give an error while the previous one did not?

```
%cat file1 file2
```

2.30 Can you type out the contents of more than one file at a time?

```
%more file1
```

2.31 If this command doesn't work, try "pg file1". These commands allow you to view one screen at a time. Our files are small, so you can't appreciate the benefits of this command now.

```
%ls
```

2.32 This shows a *listing*. Does the listing show the contents of files or only their names?

```
%ls —l
```

2.33 The "–l" is an option to the command. Options are used to make commands do certain special things. Each command has its own set of options. Write down only the lines for file1 and file2. This is called a "long listing."

```
%ls —a
```

2.34 You don't have to write down the output. This option shows a listing for "all" files.

```
%
```

2.35 By trial and error show how both of these options can be used simultaneously.

```
%man ls
```

2.36 How many possible options are there for the `ls` command?

"man" stands for manual page. It gives information about the command. Pressing the following keys while in "man" will do what?
[Enter] key
[Space] bar
b
q

```
%
```

2.37 How would you find out what options exist for the `cat` command?

```
%man −k list

%!! | more
```

2.38 If the screen fills up with too many lines at one time, do !! | more. This will redo the last command so that the output is more readable. This command will be explained in Unit 4 when we go over piping.

Sometimes you don't know what command to use let alone how it is used, but do you know that it has something to do with "listing" or just "list." The man −k option will help you find names of commands that are related to some keyword.

```
%cp file1 file2
```

2.39 What does this command do? Is ">" used?

```
%mv file1 file3
```

2.40

```
%ls −l
```

2.41 Does file1 still exist? What happened to it?

```
%rm −i file*
```

2.42 Enter "y" for each file you created in these experiments. What does the "rm" command do? What about the "−i" option?

Pattern Matching

2.43 Now erase all other files you may have in your directory and create the following files using `echo` or `touch`. For this experiment, their content is not important, only their names:
file1, test1, file23, f, abf, af23, af5, af8, af99s, ax7, bf2, bf21.x
DO NOT ERASE ANY FILES WHICH BEGIN WITH A DOT. THEY ARE NEEDED FOR YOUR ACCOUNT.
For each of the following commands, name the files it lists:

```
%ls *

%ls f*

%ls *1

%ls *f*

%ls af[0−9]

%ls af[0−9]*

%ls ??[0−9]
```

```
%ls   ???

%ls   af?

%ls   a?[0-9]

%ls   [ab]*

%ls   *.x
```

2.44. Instead of `ls`, use the `echo` command a few times. For example, what difference do you see with `echo *`?

2.45. Instead of `ls`, use the `cat` command. What difference do you see?

```
%sh
$ls   [!a]*


$ls   [!a-b]*


$exit
%ls   *[0-9]
```

2.46. We have been working in C shell so far. In Bourne shell, you can negate patterns. To go into Bourne shell, simply type `sh` and use `exit` to come out of it .

HOMEWORK

1. Using only echo, cat, >, and >>, give the command which will accomplish the following:
   a. Display "BoomBoom" on the screen.
   b. Create a file called bb which contains the line "BoomBoom".
   c. Create a file called aa which contains the line "Just kidding".
   d. Add the contents of file bb to the end of file aa.
   e. Create a file called cc which has the contents of file bb.
   f. Add "nuf kidding" to the end of file aa.
2. Give the command to do the following:
   a. Copy file1 to file2.
   b. Rename file1 to file2.
   c. Clear the screen.
   d. Quickly create files called f1, f2, f5, and f7 with nothing in them.
   e. Change the password.
   f. Find out your user name.
   g. Find out who is logged on the system currently.
   h. Find out all the information about the date command.
   i. Find out all the commands which have to do with the word "date."

3. Explain what each of the following commands does:
   a. ls
   b. ls −a
   c. ls −al
   d. ls −la
   e. echo *
   f. cat *
   g. rm −i *

Basic Commands

4. Give the command to do the following:
   a. Redo the previous command.
   b. Find out all the previous commands executed.
   c. Redo command number 12.
   d. Redo the last command which started with the characters, "cat".
   e. Redo the last command which started with the character, "l".
   f. Redo the last command but be able to see its output one screen at a time.
5. How would you display the names of the files which meet the following conditions:
   a. Filenames which don't begin with a number?
   b. Files which have two "x"s anywhere in their names?
   c. Filenames that are only 5 characters long,
      that begin with an "x", and end with an "x"?
6. How would you display the contents of all the files which meet the following conditions:
   a. Filenames which begin with the letter "a"?
   b. Filenames which are 4 characters long and end with a "1"?
   c. Filenames which end with a number?
7. How would you safely delete the files which meet these conditions:
   a. All files in the current directory?
   b. Files which have "q" anywhere in their name?
8. How do you find the current time and how long your computer has been up?

LAB ASSIGNMENTS

1. Create a file called lab1. The lab should contain the output of the following commands in the order given. Separating the output of each command should be a blank line and another line which contains 20 dashes and the command itself. Hence, the lab1 file will start with a blank line, the dashes following the command, and the output of that command. This cycle is repeated for each command. Do not use a text editor. Before you start make sure you have at least three files in the current directory including a file called "memo." Have this file contain the text "Onward we go with UNIX!" Here are the commands:
   a. Show the current time.
   b. The names of the users who are currently logged on. *who*
   c. The name of the UNIX host you are logged on to. *Hostname*
   d. The amount of time that the UNIX host has been up since the last time it was rebooted. *uptime*
   e. The list of commands which have to do with the keyword, "copy." *man -k copy*
   f. All the filenames in your current directory. *ls -l*   *ls*
   g. A long listing of all the file names in your current directory.
   h. The contents of the file called "memo." *cat memo*
   i. The last 8 commands which you have executed up to this point. *History 8*

2. Using only the commands learned in this unit, create a file called fileA with the following content:

   ```
   as I wander
   under the sky
   ```

   Then add this line to the top of fileA. You will need more than one command and maybe another file.

   ```
   I wonder
   ```

   Save the long listing in a file called fileB.
   Create fileC that contains the contents of fileA and fileB and your user name.
   Hand in the history of the commands needed to do this assignment.

Directories

CONCEPTS TO LEARN

Files: Files are items which can generally be displayed using the cat command. Directories are special types of files. However, we won't be referring to them as files.

Directories: These are called folders in window environments. If you have to search through 200 files in your login directory, for example, it would be difficult to find the particular file which you are looking for. But if all these files were organized inside directories with descriptive names, then searching for a specific file would not be as tedious, assuming that your organization of the directories and files is well structured.

Root Directory: There is only one root directory on a UNIX host. All users on the host share the same root. Floppy drives and printers and other networked hosts can all be mounted on your host. However, they are all under the same root directory. In DOS, that is not the case. Drive A has a different root than drive C, and so on.

Login Directory: This is the directory where a user is placed when she or he first logs on. This is also called the home directory.

Path: The list of directories specifying where a file is located.

Full Pathname: The path starting with the root or starting with /. Changing a directory using a full pathname works the same way no matter from which directory you are making the change.

Relative Pathname: The path starting from your current working directory. This path never starts with a /. It may start with a single dot, double dots, or a directory name which exists in the current working directory. Changing a directory using a relative pathname starts from where you are currently in the directory tree.

UNIX File Structure: Under the common root directory which everyone on a UNIX system shares, there are certain directories where certain files are stored. Typically, the following directories would be used to place the files shown.

/bin	Binary executable files, such as cat and other executables.
/etc	System files, such as the passwd files, giving all the users on the system or /etc/group where the groups are listed.
/tmp	Files, such as garbage files, which need to be deleted automatically every so often.
/dev	Printers, disk drives, and other devices are mounted here.
/var	Various files, such as mail files, can be stored here.

COMMANDS TO LEARN

cd (or cd ~)   [DOS: cd] Changes the current directory to the login directory.

cd <dirname>	Changes the directory to the directory specified. This directory current directory.
cd ..	Changes the directory to the parent directory.
cd /	Changes the directory to the root directory.
chmod	Changes the permissions for a file or a directory. The first digit ___ permission for the owner (or the creator) of the file; the second digit s ___ ...es the permission for the group members; and the third digit specifies the permission for anyone who is not in the group. (See Figures 3.3 and 3.4 on page 43.) 0 means no permissions. Add 4 if you want read, add 2 if you want write or overwrite, and add 1 if you want executable permissions.
cp	Copies a file or a directory.
cp –r	[DOS: xcopy /s] Copies a directory (recursively) to another directory. Recursive means that all subdirectories and files will be copied.
find ~	[DOS: dir filename /s] Looks for a file starting at your login directory. You should always use ~ when using the find command. Otherwise, the entire directory tree is searched and that may easily take ten minutes. find ~ –name "file1" –print will look for the file whose name is "file1" and then print the path where that file(s) is found on the screen.
mkdir	Creates a new directory.
mv	Moves a file or directory. If the file is in the same directory, then it is renamed. Both what is to be moved and where it is to be moved must be specified.
pwd	Prints the working or current directory to the screen.
rm	Deletes a file.
rm –r	[DOS: deltree] Deletes a directory tree. Recursively deletes all directories and subdirectories and their files.
rmdir	Removes a directory.
umask	Sets the default permissions to files which will be created in the future.

SAMPLE SESSION

```
:ramteke {109} pwd
/home/ramteke
:ramteke {110} ls
file1       unit5
lab1        unit1
```

pwd shows us where we are in the current directory tree. Starting at root, we come down to a directory named home and then down to my login directory called ramteke. I have four files in my login directory.

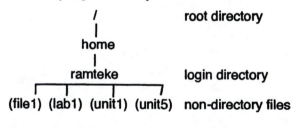

```
:ramteke {111} cd ..
:home {112} pwd
/home
:home {113} cd ..
: {114} pwd
/
: {114.1} cd ..
(error)
```

cd .. brings us up to the parent directory of where we were. We were in ramteke and so now we come up one level to home. A pwd done here confirms that.

Now we go up another level.

And we are at root.

If we try to go up another level, we find out that the root directory has no parent.

Here are all the files and directories in the root directory:

```
: {115} ls
altroot  bsd        dev    mnt         sbin    tmp      web
bin      bsd.dist   etc    quota.user  stand   usr
boot     bsd.old    home   root        sys     var
```

```
{116} cd home
:home {117} pwd
/home
:home {118} ls -l ramteke
file1
lab1
unit1
unit5
```

To go down a directory tree, you must provide the directory name. To go up, use cd .. Here we have come down to home from root.

Do not do the ls command here. There might be thousands of login directories here, one for each user. ls -l ramteke gives the directory listing of ramteke only.

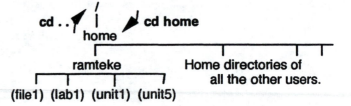

We will study the grep command and piping in a later unit. For now, take my word for it that the grep command will find my directory entry under home.

```
:home {119} ls -l | grep ramteke
drwx------ 6 ramteke  prof 512 May 25 ramteke
```

```
:home {120} cd ramteke
:ramteke {121} cd ../..
: {122} pwd
/
```

If we want to go down from /home to my directory, we must do a cd ramteke.
Doing a cd ../.. will make us go up two directory levels, all the way to the root directory. A pwd confirms this.

```
: {123} cd
:ramteke {124} pwd
/home/ramteke
:ramteke {124.1} cd home
(error)
:ramteke {125} cd /home
:home {126} pwd
/home
:home {127} cd ..
: {128} cd bin
:bin {129} cd
:ramteke {130} cd /bin
:bin {131} cd /ramteke
/ramteke: No such directory.
:bin {132} cd /home/ramteke
:ramteke {133} cd bin
bin: No such file or directory.

:ramteke {134} cd /bin
:bin {135} pwd
/bin
:bin {136} cd ~
:ramteke {137} pwd
/home/ramteke
:ramteke {138} mkdir lab2
:ramteke {139} ls -l
total 11476
-rw-r--r--    ramteke   file1
-rw-r--r--    ramteke   lab1
```

Doing a cd by itself will place us in our login directory. Again, doing a pwd confirms that.

If we want to go up to home, this command will not work because home is not under ramteke. You could do a cd .. or you could do a cd /home. That is, starting from the root directory (/), come down to home. home is under root. A pwd confirms that this worked.
A cd .. brings us up to root again.
We can come down to bin, this is another directory which is under root. Doing a simple cd would bring us back to our login directory. Here, we go back to bin.
We try to come back to the login directory, but the ramteke directory is not under root so we get an error.
To get to ramteke, we use the full path, that is, the path starting with the root (/). A full path must begin with a slash and must specify all the directories leading to the directory to access.
We go back to bin using a full pathname.

Doing a cd ~ is like doing a simple cd. It takes us to our login directory. In UNIX, many call a tilde (~) a squiggle, an exclamation mark (!) a bang, and a backslash (\) a backwhack.
Now let us create a directory called lab2 under ramteke.
Notice that the current directory is still ramteke. Directories are made under the current working directory, whatever it is.

```
drwxr-xr-x   2 ramteke   lab2
drwxr-xr-x   2 ramteke   unit1
drwxr-xr-x   2 ramteke   unit5
:ramteke {140} cd lab2
:lab2 {141} pwd
/home/ramteke/lab2
:lab2 {142} ls
:lab2 {143} mkdir eng
:lab2 {144} ls -l
total 2
drwxr-xr-x   2 ramteke eng
:lab2 {145} mkdir comp sci
:lab2 {146} echo tasting > test
:lab2 {147} ls -l
total 8
drwxr-xr-x   2 ramteke   comp
drwxr-xr-x   2 ramteke   eng
drwxr-xr-x   2 ramteke   sci
-rw-r--r--   1 ramteke   test
```

Doing an ls –l shows the files and directories. Files are shown with a dash at the beginning of the entry. Directory entries begin with the letter "d."

Now we go down to lab2 which we just created.
A pwd confirms that.

This brand new directory doesn't have files in it yet.
Let us make a directory here called eng.
Notice its existence.

Make another two directories under lab2 and create a file called test. Now this is what we have:

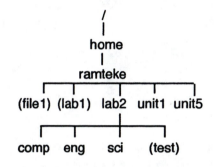

```
:lab2 {148} cat comp
:lab2 {149} cat test
tasting
:lab2 {150} cd test
test: Not a directory.
:lab2 {151} pwd
/home/ramteke/lab2
:lab2 {152} cd comp
:comp {153} pwd
/home/ramteke/lab2/comp
:comp {154} mkdir prgms projs
:comp {155} ls -l
total 4
drwxr-xr-x   2 ramteke   prgms
drwxr-xr-x   2 ramteke   projs
:comp {156} cd projs
:projs {157} pwd
/home/ramteke/lab2/comp/projs
:projs {158} ls
:projs {159} mkdir best good
:projs {160} cd ..
:comp {161} pwd
/home/ramteke/lab2/comp
:comp {162} cd ..
:lab2 {163} cd eng
:eng {164} mkdir resrch hws qzs
:eng {165} ls -l
drwxr-xr-x   2 ramteke   hws
drwxr-xr-x   2 ramteke   qzs
drwxr-xr-x   2 ramteke   resrch
```

We are still in lab2. From here we cannot type out comp because it is a directory. However, we can type out test since it is a regular file.
Neither can we change the current directory to test.

We are still in lab2.

comp is a directory, so we can change the directory to it.
Here is the proof.

While we are in comp, we create two more directories.
They are listed here.

Let us now change the working directory to projs under comp.

Notice that the directory is empty since it was just created.
Create two additional directories under projs.
Go up one level to comp.

Go up another level to lab2.
Now go down to eng.
While in eng, create these three directories.
List them.

```
:eng  {166}  cd  hws
:hws  {167}  mkdir  may  june
:hws  {168}  ls  -l
total 4
drwxr-xr-x   2  ramteke    june
drwxr-xr-x   2  ramteke    may
:hws  {169}  pwd
/home/ramteke/lab2/eng/hws
```

In hws, create may and june. The following directory tree shows what we have now under ramteke, our login directory. I haven't shown the upper part of the directory. We still need to add the subdirectories under sci.

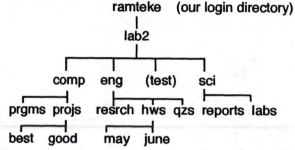

```
:hws  {170}  cd  ~/sci
 (Error)
:hws  {171}  cd  ~/lab2/sci

:sci  {172}  cd
:ramteke  {174}  cd  lab2
:lab2  {175}  ls  -l
total 8
drwxr-xr-x   4  ramteke  comp
drwxr-xr-x   5  ramteke  eng
drwxr-xr-x   2  ramteke  sci
-rw-r--r--   1  ramteke  test
:lab2  {176}  cd  sci
:sci  {177}  mkdir  reports  labs
:sci  {178}  cd  labs
:labs  {179}  pwd
/home/ramteke/lab2/sci/labs
:labs  {180}  cd  reports
reports: No such file or directory.
:labs  {181}  cd  ..
:sci  {182}  cd  reports
:reports  {183}  cd  /labs
/labs: No such file or directory.
:reports  {184}  cd  ../labs
:labs  {185}  pwd
/home/ramteke/lab2/sci/labs
:labs  {186}  cd  ../..
:lab2  {187}  pwd
/home/ramteke/lab2
:lab2  {188}  cd  sci/labs
:labs  {189}  pwd
/home/ramteke/lab2/sci/labs
:labs  {190}  cd
:ramteke  {191}  cd  /eng
/eng: No such file or directory.
:ramteke  {193}  cd  eng
eng: No such file or directory.
:ramteke  {195}  cd  lab2
:lab2  {196}  cd  eng
```

Starting from a tilde, which means from the login directory, we go down to sci. We get an error.
We need to specify the lab2 directory, which is between sci and ramteke, our login directory. Now we are in sci.
Let us go to our login directory.
And then let us go down to lab2.
Doing an ls -l shows the three directories and one file under lab2.

In order to add the subdirectories for sci, let us come down here and then create them.
Let us go down the labs branch.
Doing a pwd shows us that we are there.

We cannot go down to reports from labs.

We must go up to the parent directory, that is, sci.
From there, we can come down to reports.
Starting from the root, or using a full pathname, we cannot come down to labs. It is not directly under root.
However, first going up one level from reports using .., we can come down to labs. We must go up to sci and then come down.
From labs, if we go up two levels in the directory tree, we get to lab2.

To go down two levels, we must give the directory names.

This brings us back to our login directory.
The eng directory isn't under root.

Neither is it under ramteke.

We must first come down to lab2.
Then eng is available.

```
:eng {198} cd hws/june
:june {199} pwd
/home/ramteke/lab2/eng/hws/june
:june {200} cd ~/lab2/comp
:comp {201} pwd
/home/ramteke/lab2/comp
:comp {202} cd projs/good
:good {203} pwd
/home/ramteke/lab2/comp/projs/good
:good {204} cd ../../eng
../../eng: No such directory.
:good {205} cd ../../../eng
:eng {206} pwd
/home/ramteke/lab2/eng
:eng {207} cd /qzs
/qzs: No such file or directory.
```

From eng, we change our directory to june. However, we must specify hws, the directory through which we must pass.

Starting from the login directory (~), we can come down to comp, via lab2.

We can come down to good via projs.

If we go up two sets of (..) or two directories from good, that brings us to comp. eng is not under comp so we get an error. We need to go up three levels to the lab2 directory before we can come down to eng.

The qzs directory is not under root. This gives us an error. If we use a full pathname, starting from root (/), we can come down to qzs.

```
:eng {208} cd /home/ramteke/lab2/eng/qzs
:qzs {209} pwd
/home/ramteke/lab2/eng/qzs
:qzs {210} cd ../resrch
:resrch {211} pwd
/home/ramteke/lab2/eng/resrch
:resrch {212} cd ../../comp
:comp {213} cd ~/lab2/sci
:sci {214} pwd
/home/ramteke/lab2/sci
:sci {215} cd ..
```

The .. brings us up to eng and the /resrch brings us down there.

Going up two levels from resrch takes us to eng and then to lab2. From there comp is accessible.
Starting from the login directory (~), we come down to sci via lab2.
A cd .. brings us up to lab2.

Working in other directories without changing directories:
The test file is in lab2. See the figure for command 169.
Its content is "tasting." This file was created in command 146.
If we do an ls from sci, we get the items that are in sci: labs and reports.
An ls .. will show the directory listing for the parent directory, that is, for lab2.
To do a listing for eng without changing the working directory, we go up one level from sci and then specify eng.
Similarly, if we give the path, the relative path in this case, for projs, we get the two items that are in that directory.
Notice, our current working directory isn't changed.
It is still sci.
Coming up to the lab2 directory, if we do an ls, it gives us what is in lab2.

```
:lab2 {217} cat test
tasting
:lab2 {218} cd sci
:sci {219} ls
labs      reports
:sci {220} ls ..
comp eng  sci  test
:sci {221} ls ../eng
hws      qzs       resrch
:sci {222} ls ../comp/projs
best good
:sci {223} pwd
/home/ramteke/lab2/sci
:sci {224} cd ..
:lab2 {225} ls
comp eng  sci  test
:lab2 {226} ls sci
labs      reports
:lab2 {227} ls comp
prgms projs
:lab2 {228} ls comp/projs
best good
```

If we do an ls by specifying the directory name with it, we get to see what is in that directory. This is what is in sci.
This is what is in comp.

This is what is in projs.

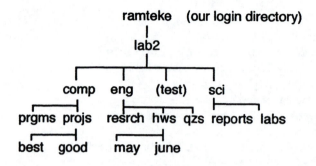

The directory tree is shown again above for reference.

```
:lab2 {229} ls .
comp eng   sci    test
```
Doing an ls with a single dot shows the current directory. Here we now have three directories and one file.

```
:lab2 {230} cat test
tasting
```

```
:lab2 {231} cd comp/projs
:projs {231.1} cat  test
(error)
```
Coming down to projs,
we try to display the contents of test. However, this file is not under projs. It's under lab2.

```
:projs {232} cat ../../test
tasting
```
This time we try to display the contents of test by providing the path to it since test is not under projs.

```
:projs {233} cd ..
:comp {234} cat ../test
tasting
```
From comp, when we do a cat on test to display its contents, we only need to specify that the test file is one level above comp.

```
:comp {235} cd
:ramteke {236} cat lab2/test
tasting
```
To print test from the login directory, we need to provide lab2 as the path to test. Notice, the current directory is unchanged. Only a cd changes the working directory.

```
:ramteke {237} cd lab2
:lab2 {238} cat test
tasting
```

Here we display the test file using a full path.

```
:lab2 {239} cat /home/ramteke/lab2/test
tasting
:lab2 {240} cd
```
The find command searches files starting at the current directory that is given by the single dot. It finds files, using the –name option, whose name is test. All such files can then be deleted, printed, or whatever. Here, we display them using the –print option.

```
:ramteke {241} find . -name "test" -print
./lab2/test
```
The file is found under lab2 only.

Here, we are moving the test file to lab2/eng/hws.

```
:ramteke {242} mv lab2/test lab2/eng/hws
:ramteke {243} find . -name "test" -print
./lab2/eng/hws/test
```
When that is done, test doesn't exist in lab2 anymore. The find command finds the file under hws, just where we moved it.

```
:ramteke {244} cp lab2/test lab2/eng/hws
cp: lab2/test: No such file or directory
```
This copy command confirms that test is indeed not under lab2.

```
:ramteke {245} cp lab2/eng/hws/test lab2
```
Copy test from hws to lab2.

```
:ramteke {246} find . -name "test" -print
./lab2/eng/hws/test
./lab2/test
```
This find command shows that the file whose name is test is in two places: hws and lab2.

```
:ramteke {247} rm -i lab2/test
remove lab2/test? y
```
Here we delete test from lab2.
To confirm the delete, we enter y.

```
:ramteke {248} cd lab2/eng/hws
```

```
:hws {249} cd test                          From hws, we try to change to test.
test: Not a directory.                       But test is not a directory.
:hws {251} ls -l                             In command 242, we moved test under hws.
total 6                                      Here it is with the june and may directories.
drwxr-xr-x   2 ramteke  june
drwxr-xr-x   2 ramteke  may
-rw-r--r--   1 ramteke  test
:hws {252} pwd
/home/ramteke/lab2/eng/hws
:hws {253} mv test ..                        Here, we are moving test up one level to eng.
:hws {254} ls                                Doing an ls confirms that test was moved.
june may                                     Doing a find from the login directory (~) shows the file test
:hws {255} find ~ -name "test" -print
/home/ramteke/lab2/eng/test                  under eng.
:hws {256} mv ../test .                       Here, we move test from eng back to hws, the current
:hws {257} ls                                directory. The single dot is necessary, since it specifies
june may   test                              where the file is to be moved.
                                             In command 256, the path had to be given to access test,
                                             because it wasn't under the current directory.
:hws {258} mv test ../../comp                Here, we don't give the path for test. It is in the current
                                             directory of hws. This file is moved to comp which is two
                                             "dot–dot"s above hws.
:hws {259} mv ../../comp/test .              Here, we bring that file from comp back to hws, the current
:hws {260} ls                                directory.
june may   test
:hws {261} mv test ../../comp/projs/good         test is moved to good.
:hws {262} find ~ -name "test" -print            Yes, test is found under good.
/home/ramteke/lab2/comp/projs/good/test
:hws {263} mv ../../comp/projs/good/test ../..   Now move test to lab2.
:hws {264} find ~ -name "test" -print            Yes, test is found under lab2
/home/ramteke/lab2/test
:hws {265} mv ~/lab2/test ~/lab2/sci/labs        Move test to labs.
:hws {266} find ~ -name "test" -print            Yes, test is found in labs.
/home/ramteke/lab2/sci/labs/test
:hws {267} mv ../../sci/labs/test .              Move test from labs back to hws.
:hws {268} ls                                    Yes, test is in hws.
june may   test
:hws {269} mv test june                          Move test to the june directory.
:hws {270} ls                                    Yes, test is not in hws.
june may
:hws {271} ls june                               It is under june.
test
:hws {272} mv june/test may                      Move test from june to may.
:hws {273} ls may                                Yes, test is under may.
test
:hws {274} mv may/test /                         Move test to root.
Permission denied                                I have no permission to add files there.
:hws {275} mv may/test /home                     Can I place test in home?
Permission denied                                No. I am not allowed.
:hws {276} mv may/test /ramteke                  ramteke is not under root.
Permission denied
:hws {277} mv may/test /home/ramteke             I can place test in my login directory or
:hws {278} ls /home/ramteke                      any directory under it.
file1      test       unit5
lab1       unit1
```

```
:hws  {279}  cd                          This brings us back to the login directory.
:ramteke  {280}  pwd
/home/ramteke
:ramteke  {281}  cp -r lab2 lab2.bak      In our login directory, let us duplicate the entire directory
                                          tree. The -r option will do the recursive copy.
                                          Doing a find on hws confirms that now we have two
:ramteke  {283}  find ~ -name "hws" -print
/home/ramteke/lab2/eng/hws               occurrences of it, once under each of the trees.
/home/ramteke/lab2.bak/eng/hws           Now let us proceed to remove the lab2.bak tree.
:ramteke  {284}  rmdir lab2.bak           We cannot delete this directory using rmdir, since there are
Directory not empty                       other files and directories under it.
:ramteke  {286}  cd lab2.bak              We go to lab2.bak.
:lab2.bak  {287}  rmdir eng               We still cannot delete the eng directory for the same reason
rmdir: eng: Directory not empty           as earlier.
:lab2.bak  {288}  cd eng                  Hence, we come down to eng.
:eng  {289}  ls                           We do a listing.
hws       qzs       resrch
:eng  {290}  rmdir hws                    We cannot remove the hws directory. It has may and june
rmdir: hws: Directory not empty           directories in it.
:eng  {291}  cd hws                       We go to hws.
:hws  {292}  ls
june may
:hws  {293}  rmdir june                   We remove june and may.
:hws  {294}  rmdir may
:hws  {295}  pwd                          We check our working directory.
/home/ramteke/lab2.bak/eng/hws
:hws  {296}  cd ..                        Now, we can move up one level to eng.
:eng  {297}  rmdir hws                    We remove the hws directory successfully.
:eng  {298}   ls                          Then we see that the qzs and resrch directories are left.
qzs       resrch
:eng  {300}  rm qzs                       We cannot use the rm command to remove a directory.
rm: qzs: is a directory                   It is used to remove regular files.
:eng  {301}  rmdir qzs                    We remember that rmdir will remove directories and we do
:eng  {302}  rmdir resrch                 that successfully.
:eng  {303}  pwd
/home/ramteke/lab2.bak/eng
:eng  {304}  cd ..                        We move up to lab2.bak.
:lab2.bak  {305}  rmdir eng               From there we can remove the eng directory.
:lab2.bak  {306}  ls                      Now we have only the comp and sci directories left.
comp sci
:lab2.bak  {307}  cd ..                   We come back to the login directory.
```

```
:ramteke {308} rmdir lab2.bak
lab2.bak: Directory not empty
:ramteke {309} rm -r lab2.bak
:ramteke {310} ls
file1        lab2       unit5
lab1         unit1      test
```

We try to remove the lab2.bak directory using the rmdir command while there are other items in it, but we can't. However, with the –r option and the rm command commonly used with regular files, we can. We delete lab2.bak in one swoop, both it and its entire directory tree.
lab2.bak is gone. (Be careful with the rm –r command!)

```
:ramteke {311} mv test lab2/comp
:ramteke {312} cd lab2/comp
:comp {313} ls
prgms projs test
:comp {314} ls -l
total 6
drwxr-xr-x   2 ramteke prgms
drwxr-xr-x   4 ramteke projs
-rw-r--r--   1 ramteke test
```

We move the test file to comp.
We change the working directory there.
And see that test is there.

In a long listing, we see that the directories, prgms and projs, are there as directories. test is the file which we just moved here from the login directory.

```
:comp {315} cat test
tasting
:comp {316} chmod 000 test
:comp {317} ls -l
total 6
drwxr-xr-x   2 ramteke prof prgms
drwxr-xr-x   4 ramteke prof projs
----------   1 ramteke prof test
```

We see the contents of test. For the following commands, refer to Figures 3.3 and 3.4 on page 43.
We set the permissions for test so that the owner, ramteke, cannot read, write, or execute. That is the first 0. The second zero gives the same permission to members of the same group — prof. Finally, the third 0 in this chmod command gives the same permissions, or rather lack of permissions, to users who are not members of the group.

```
:comp {318} cat test
cat: test: Permission denied
:comp {319} chmod 400 test
:comp {320} ls -l
total 6
drwxr-xr-x   2 ramteke prof prgms
drwxr-xr-x   4 ramteke prof projs
-r--------   1 ramteke prof test
```

Sure enough, I cannot even read the file.

Changing the permission so that I can read the file, we see that now the first r is in the long listing. This means that I can read the file now. Basically, only the owner of the file may change the permissions of a file.

The r in this entry means that I can read the file.

```
:comp {321} cat test
tasting
:comp {322} echo 1111 > test
test: Permission denied.
:comp {323} chmod 600 test
:comp {324} ls -l
total 6
drwxr-xr-x   2 ramteke prof prgms
drwxr-xr-x   4 ramteke prof projs
-rw-------   1 ramteke prof test
```

Now, we can read the file.

However, we cannot overwrite it since we have only the read permission set.
Here, we add 2 to the 4 to give both write and read access.
We verify that.

Now the read and write permissions are set.
We can read the file.

```
:comp {325} cat test
tasting
:comp {326} echo testing 1 2 3 > test
:comp {327} cat test
testing 1 2 3
:comp {328} echo new testing > new
:comp {329} ls -l
total 8
-rw-r--r--   1 ramteke prof new
drwxr-xr-x   2 ramteke prof prgms
drwxr-xr-x   4 ramteke prof projs
-rw-------   1 ramteke prof test
```

And we can overwrite it.

However, when we create a new file (here we call the file new) the permissions are set so that anyone can read the file. Notice the three r's for the permissions for new. Do we need to do a chmod 700 every time we create a new file? Is there a way to set default file permissions for files which will be created in the future?

```
:comp {330} umask 077
```

The answer is yes. The umask command allows us to set default file permissions. Notice, no filename is given here because the command refers to files which are yet to be created. 0 for the first digit gives the owner all rights, and 7 for the group members and 7 for the public give them no rights. The numbering for umask is just the opposite of that for chmod. See Figure 3.5 on page 44.

```
:comp {332} echo brand new > b.new
:comp {333} ls -l
total 10
-rw-------     1 ramteke prof b.new
-rw-r--r--   1 ramteke prof new
drwxr-xr-x   2 ramteke prof prgms
drwxr-xr-x   4 ramteke prof projs
-rw-------   1 ramteke prof test
:comp {334} rm *
rm: prgms: is a directory
rm: projs: is a directory

:comp {335} ls -l
total 4
drwxr-xr-x   2 ramteke prof prgms
drwxr-xr-x   4 ramteke prof projs
:comp {336} echo 111111 > again
:comp {337} ls -l
total 6
drwxr-xr-x   2 ramteke prof prgms
drwxr-xr-x   4 ramteke prof projs
-rw-------   1 ramteke prof again
:comp {338} logout
```

Does the umask command work? Almost. Here, we created a new file called b.new and checked its permissions. But instead of giving the owner read, write, and executable privileges, it gave us only read and write. There must be something about how the operating system is set up that keeps us from giving executable privileges by default. However, the read and write privileges for the owner and no privileges for others worked properly.

Delete all files. The –i option would be a safe way of doing this. This doesn't delete the directories. The –r option would.

Be careful with the rm command, especially when (or if) you start doing system administrative commands.
All the files are deleted, but not the directories.

Let us test again to see if the umask command is still in effect. Here we create a file called again.
We check its permissions.

Sure enough, we have the default permissions set as expected. Bye.

EXPERIMENTS

To make the organizing of files easy, files are stored in directories in UNIX. This is like when similar documents are stored in the same manila folder in an office desk. UNIX, however, considers directories themselves (our manila folders) as a special kind of file.

What is it Like on Your Computer System?

3.1 Now let's see how your system is set up. Log in as usual and see in which directory the operating system places you. This is called the *home* directory. To see what directory you are in, use the pwd command. The top–most directory is called the *root* directory and it is "/". The name that appears after the first slash is the first directory under the root. This way, all the directories are listed, separated by slashes, until your home directory is listed at the end. (Usually, the home directory's name is similar to your login name.) In the space below, write all the directories *under* each other starting with the root (already given) and ending with your home directory, similar to how I did it for my account. You will need to refer to this diagram in future experiments.

%pwd

Directories

```
%cd ..
%pwd

%ls -l | more
```

3.2 pwd stands for print working directory on the screen. In the last experiment, your home directory was printed. What did cd .. do?

What is your current directory now?

If there are many accounts on your server, this will be a long list. In that case, just enter q to exit more.

Do you see your home directory listed here? Don't be concerned if you don't.

```
%cd ..
%pwd

%ls -l | more
```

3.3 Continue doing cd .., pwd, and ls –l until your working directory becomes the root.

Starting from your home directory, how many cd ..'s were needed in order to reach the root?

With more, enter q to exit.

```
%cd
%pwd
```

3.4 What does cd do?

```
%cd /
%pwd
```

3.5 What does cd / do?

```
%
%pwd

%ls -l | more
```

3.6 Look at the directory tree that you came up with in Experiment 3.1. Using the first directory under root, change the directory to that one. Write in your actual commands on the left.

3.7 Now change all the directories using the directory path from Experiment 3.1 until you get to your home directory. Write in your commands.

For example, using the figure for command 110 on page 27, if I were to go to my home directory from the root, I would use the following sequence of commands:
cd home, pwd, ls –l,
cd ramteke, pwd, and ls –l.
The pwd and ls –ls are not necessary, but they allow you to see where you are and where you are going. Now show how you would go down your directory tree.

```
%cd
%rm -i *
```

3.8 Before you continue you may want to remove all unwanted files. No files from Unit1 are needed. First, get to your home or login directory.

```
%mkdir exp2
%pwd
```

3.9 Now let us create a new directory in your home directory. Does your working directory change because of it?

```
%ls -l
```

Is exp2 listed as a file or a directory.

```
%cd exp2
%pwd

%ls -l
```

3.10 What command changes your directory?
(You may need to delete a directory that you created by mistake. In that case use the rmdir directory name.) Why isn't there anything in the exp2 directory?

Creating a Directory Tree

3.11 Under the exp2 directory, we want to build the directory tree shown in Figure 3.1 so that all our files would have appropriate places to be stored. I will lead you in creating one part of this directory tree. If you can follow how it is being created, you should be able to create the rest of it. First, fill in all the missing directories using your tree from Experiment 3.1 in the following figure:

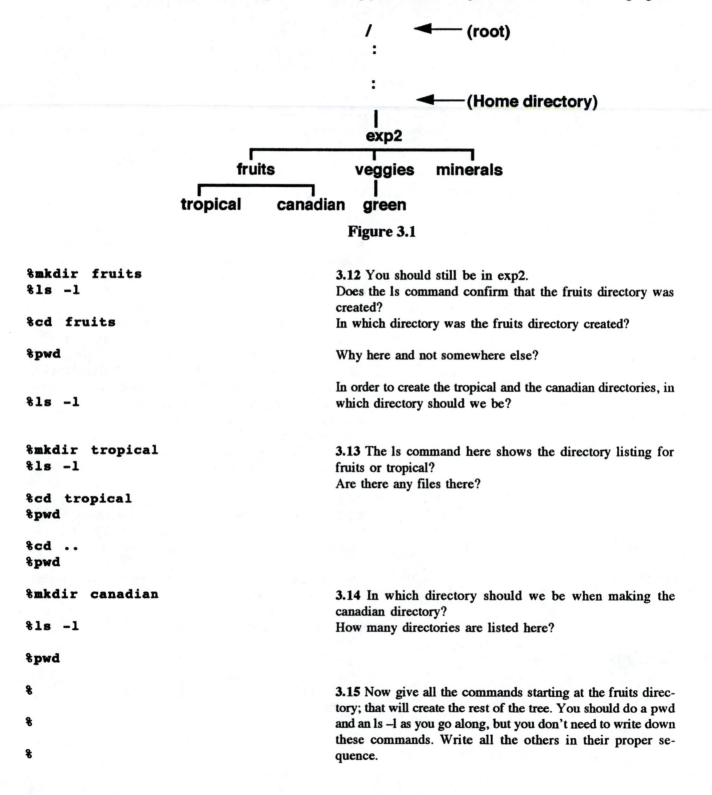

Figure 3.1

```
%mkdir fruits
%ls -l

%cd fruits

%pwd


%ls -l



%mkdir tropical
%ls -l

%cd tropical
%pwd

%cd ..
%pwd

%mkdir canadian

%ls -l

%pwd

%

%

%
```

3.12 You should still be in exp2.
Does the ls command confirm that the fruits directory was created?
In which directory was the fruits directory created?

Why here and not somewhere else?

In order to create the tropical and the canadian directories, in which directory should we be?

3.13 The ls command here shows the directory listing for fruits or tropical?
Are there any files there?

3.14 In which directory should we be when making the canadian directory?
How many directories are listed here?

3.15 Now give all the commands starting at the fruits directory; that will create the rest of the tree. You should do a pwd and an ls –l as you go along, but you don't need to write down these commands. Write all the others in their proper sequence.

```
%

%
```

Changing Directories

```
%cd
```
3.16 Go to your home directory.

```
%
```
3.17 How do you go to exp2?

```
%
```
3.18 How do you go to fruits?

```
%
```
3.19 Now go up to exp2.

```
%
```
3.20 Now go to green directly from exp2. You have to give the directory path to green, that is, via veggies, separated by a slash.

```
%
```
3.21 Go to exp2 directly. You will need two ..s separated by a slash.

```
%
```
3.22 Go to minerals.

```
%
```
3.23 Show the steps to go from minerals to tropical.

```
%
```
3.24 There are two ways to represent directory paths. One is called a *full pathname* and the other one is called the *relative pathname*. A full path is given starting with the root "/", but a relative path doesn't start with the root. For example, cd / usr/homeDirectory/exp2 is an example of a full pathname, while cd exp2 or cd ../.. are examples of relative pathnames since they don't begin with root "/". Using your directory tree, go to exp2 using a full pathname.

```
%
```
3.25 From exp2, go to minerals using a relative pathname. Then from there go to tropical using a full pathname.

```
%
```

Moving and ßFiles

```
%
%pwd
```
3.26 Go to fruits using a full pathname. Confirm that by using pwd.

```
%echo One more > memo1
```
3.27 Create a file in that directory.

For the following experiments do not use the cd command — do not change directories.

```
%ls -l
%mv memo1 file1
```
3.28 The mv command moves the file. Where did memo1 go?

```
%ls -l
```
Was it renamed?
If so, to what name?

```
%cat file1
```

```
%mv  file1  memo1
%mv  memo1  tropical
%ls  -1

%cd  tropical
%ls  -1

%cat  memo1

%cd  ..

%ls  -1  tropical

%cat  tropical/memo1


%cat  memo1




%mv  tropical/memo1  .
 (don't  miss  that  dot!)




%mv  memo1  ../veggies
%ls

%ls  ../veggies

%cat  ../veggies/memo1


%mv  ../veggies/memo1  .
%ls

%
%
%
%

%
%
%
%

%
%
%
%
```

3.29 Rename file1 back to memo1.
Does memo1 get renamed?
What is the difference between this mv command and the one in Experiment 3.28?

In Experiment 3.28, was file1 an existing directory?

In this experiment is tropical an existing directory?

So why is memo1 now moved, although before it was renamed?

3.30 We can do a directory listing of tropical without changing directories. The same is true about typing out the file, memo1. However, you must remember to specify the path, in this case, tropical/.

What happens if you don't specify the path?

3.31 In Figure 3.2, the original tree is shown on top. Next to (a) and (b), write the commands that will change the tree as shown. Can you do it without looking back?

3.32 This time, we want to bring memo1 back into fruits. The mv command must first specify what is being moved—memo1. Since it is not in the current working directory, we must specify its path—tropical. The single dot means to move it to the current directory, fruits, in this case.

3.33 Move memo1 to the veggies directory. See Figure 3.2(c). Is memo1 in fruits anymore?

Is memo1 in veggies?

Can we type out memo1 from fruits, without actually changing the directory to veggies?

3.34 Let's bring memo1 back. Don't forget that dot at the end of the command. What does it stand for?

3.35 Now move memo1 to the green directory, do a listing of that directory, do a cat of it, and move memo1 back to fruits.

3.36 Similarly, move the file to exp2, confirm the move, do a cat of it, and bring it back.

3.37 Now move memo1 to tropical, do tropical's listing, do a cat of memo, and move memo back to fruits.

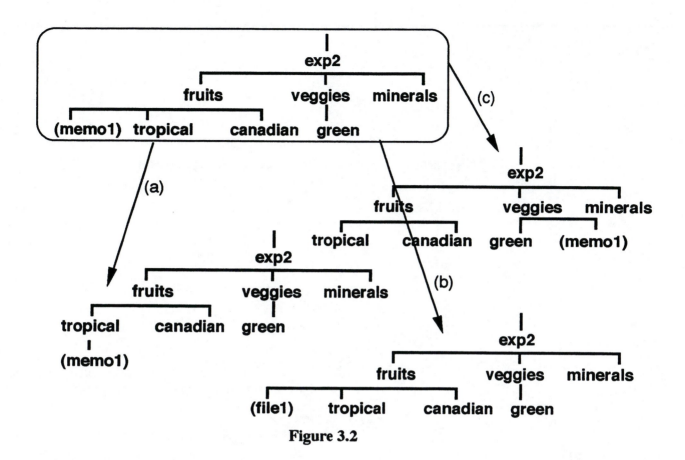

Figure 3.2

```
%
%
%


%
%


%cd
%pwd

%cp  -r  exp2  exp2Copy
%cp  -r  exp2  exp2Bkup
%cd  exp2/fruits

%pwd

%ls

%rm  -i  memo1
%rmdir  tropical
%rmdir  canadian
%ls
```

3.38 The cp command is similar to the mv command, except that it makes a copy of the file. Copy memo1 to the veggies directory and do a listing of both the fruits and the veggies directories to confirm the copy.

3.39 Now do a cat of the copy of memo1 that is in fruits and of the copy that is in veggies.

3.40 Now go to the home directory, and make a copy of the entire tree structure starting with exp2. Explore exp2Copy to make sure that the entire structure is copied. Also copy exp2 to exp2Bkup. We will need that tree segment later on. The "r" stands for recursive. Caution: do not copy a file on itself.

Removing Directories

3.41 Now follow these steps as we remove the fruits branch of the tree. Notice that, before a directory is removed, any existing files should be removed. Also, do an ls and a pwd before doing a rmdir to make sure you know what you are removing.

```
%cd ..
%pwd


%ls



%rmdir fruits


%

%

%

%

%

%cd
%pwd


%rm -ir exp2Copy




%cd exp2Bkup
%cd fruits
%ls -l
%
```

3.42 Now list all the steps to remove all the rest of the directories under (and including) exp2.

3.43 You should still be in your home directory. What did this command do? How could it be dangerous?

Long Listings and File Permissions

3.44 You should still have the exp2Bkup directory. Go to the fruits directory and do a long listing. Unlike the last unit, copy all information that is displayed there. You should have memo1 and two directories there.

Figure 3.3 shows a listing that I did on my account. The very first dash in the first line means that Exam1 is a regular file. The "d" under it in the next line means that myScripts is a directory file. "tim" is the owner of these files and "academic" is the group to which he belongs. The number just before "tim" indicates the number of links or copies that exist of this listing entry. There are 2 entries for myScripts. Exam1 is 45 bytes long. The names and information about the files in myScripts takes 85 bytes of space.

For Exam1, "rwx" means that "tim" can read, write, and execute that file; "r-x" means that the users in the group "academic" cannot write or update that file; and "r--" means that all other users may only read that file. Executable privilege for a directory means the that directory can be searched. Refer to Figure 3.4.

Using your output from Experiment 3.44, answer these questions:

What directories are listed under fruits?

How many bytes is memo1?

Explain the privileges for memo1.

Directories

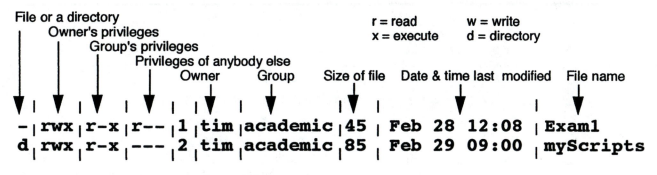

Figure 3.3

Explain the privileges for canadian.

How many files exist in fruits?

Who is the owner and the group for memo1?

Changing Permissions: How can we change the permissions? For example, in Figure 3.3 we see that Exam1 is readable by anyone in the academic group. I could live with that, since only other teachers are included in that group. However, students who are not part of the academic group also have read privileges. We want to give full privileges to the owner and, just to be safe, no privileges to anyone else.

Referring to Figure 3.4, we see that the permission code for the owner should be a 7 and it should be a 0 for both the group and anyone else that is not in the group. The way I would do that is:

```
%chmod 700 Exam1
```

This command stands for "change the file mode." As another example, to make myScripts have the full permission set for the owner, read and execute permissions for the group, and only read permission for anyone else, would require this command:

```
%chmod 754 myScripts
%ls -l
```

3.45 Can you change the permissions for memo1 so that you can only write to it, group members can only read it, and everyone else can only execute it? Do an ls -l to verify it.

```
%
%ls -l
```

3.46 Change all members of your home directory so that you have full permissions, but group members and anyone else have no permissions. Verify your file mode changes.

```
%echo last one > memo2
%ls -l memo2
```

3.47 Now create a file called memo2.
Is its permission set equal to 700?
Notice that new files are created with a default permission set.

```
%rm
```

---	0	no privileges	--x	1	execute only	
-w-	2	write only	-wx	3	write and execute	
r--	4	read only	r-x	5	read and execute	
rw-	6	read and write	rwx	7	read, write, and execute	

Figure 3.4 Permission sets and their codes for chmod.

---	7	no privileges	--x	6	execute only
-w-	5	write only	-wx	4	write and execute
r--	3	read only	r-x	2	read and execute
rw-	1	read and write	rwx	0	read, write, and execute

Figure 3.5 Permission sets and their codes for umask.

```
memo2
%umask 077
%echo last one > memo2
%ls -l memo2
```

3.48 Let us delete memo2 and try again. First let us change the default permission set using the umask command, then re-create the file. Have we changed the default permission set? The umask command uses the chmod codes in reverse order. (See Figure 3.5.) That is, with umask, the code for all permissions is 0, while for chmod it is 7.

The UNIX File Structure

3.49 Now let us explore the file structure of your UNIX system. Figure 3.1 (on page 38) is an example of a directory tree. Starting with the root, find these directories in your system, if you have them, and draw the directory tree that contains them:

/ (or root), bin, dev, etc, tmp, usr

Starting with bin, in order, these names stand for: binary or executable files, devices, miscellaneous, temporary files, and user.

Are there any files that are not directories in the root directory?

Who are the major owners of the files in root?

What aspect of the permissions allows anyone to do a cd to any of the directories in root?

In which directory do you find these executable files: cat, echo, date, and others?

Do the permissions of most of the files in bin allow anyone to execute them?

Do they allow anyone to change or overwrite them?

In which of these directories do the passwd and the group files exist?

Is there another bin directory under the usr directory? If so, which of these files do you find familiar?

HOMEWORK

1. Give the correct command to change to the specified directory in each case.
   a. the parent directory (or one level higher)
   b. the root directory
   c. the login directory
   d. the directory called local, which is under the login directory
2. Give the command to perform each of the following operations:
   a. Find out what is the current working directory.
   b. Find out what files and directories exist in the current working directory.
   c. Find out in which directory the file named lab2 exists.
   d. Rename the file lab2 to lab2a.
   e. Copy the file lab2 to lab2a.
   f. Create a directory called DirA.
   g. Make a copy of the directory DirA and all its files and subdirectories to another directory called DirA.cpy.
   h. Delete the directory DirA without using an option. Assume that it is empty.
   i. Delete the directory DirA and all files and subdirectories under it.

File Permissions:
3. Change the permissions for a file called lab2 as specified in each of the following instances:
   a. Owner is to write and execute only; group members are to read only; and all others are to read and execute only.
   b. Owner is to read, write, and execute; group members are to read and write only; and all others are to write and execute only.
   c. Owner is not to do anything; group members are to write only; and all others are to read and execute only.
4. In Question 3 above, what would you have to do if these permissions were to be set for all files in the current directory? What if these permissions were to be set for all files whose names begin with the characters "lab"?
5. For Question 3 above, give the umask command for each. Remember, no filename should be specified.

Making Directories:
6. Draw the directory tree for each part of (a) and (b) as it would appear if I had started from my login directory. Assume that there are no other directories or files in my home directory. Remember, when a directory is created, it is created in the current working directory. Keep track of your working directories as you draw the tree.
   a. cd, mkdir A, mkdir F, cd A, mkdir E, cd E, mkdir B D, cd .., mkdir C, cd ../F, cd ../A, mkdir G, cd
   b. cd, mkdir A, mkdir C, cd C, mkdir N, cd .., cd A, mkdir G L, cd G, cd ../.., mkdir F, cd F, mkdir J D H, cd ~, cd C/N, mkdir I K, cd K, mkdir M E, cd .., mkdir B, cd
7. Give all the commands needed to create the directory tree shown in Figure 3.6 in sequential order:

Changing Directories:
8. Using Figure 3.6, give the command needed to change the directories as specified in each case. Use relative pathnames.
   a. From old go to rock.   b. From old go to easy.
   c. From old go to country.   d. From old go to mysongs.
   e. From country go to classical. f. From country go to mysongs.
   g. From country go to easy.   h. From country go to indian.
   i. From mysongs go to current.   j. From mysongs go to roll.

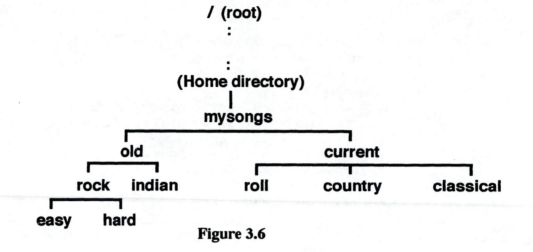

Figure 3.6

9. Assuming that the path to mysongs is /home/student/mysongs, give the command needed to change the directories as specified in each case in Question 8 above, using full pathnames.
10. When working near the top of a directory tree or in the bottom of a directory tree, are full pathnames used more often? What about relative pathnames?

Working in Directories:
11. Suppose there is a file called fileA in the old directory in Figure 3.6. Using relative pathnames, perform the following tasks. Do not change your current working directories.
   a. From old show the contents of fileA.
   b. From indian show the contents of fileA.
   c. From roll show the contents of fileA.
   d. From mysongs show the contents of fileA
   e. From old show the directory listing of old.
   f. From mysongs show the directory listing of current.
   g. From hard show the directory listing of old.

Moving Files in Directories:
12. Suppose there is a file called fileA in the old directory at the beginning of each of the following questions. Using relative pathnames, move fileA to the directory specified in each case. The "from" specifies the current working directory; fileA starts in the old directory in each case. Do not change your current working directories. Each question requires two commands. Refer to Figure 3.6.
   a. From old to mysongs and then back to old again.
   b. From mysongs to mysongs and then back to old again.
   c. From hard to indian and back to old again.
   d. From hard to easy and back to old again.
   e. From roll to roll and back to old again.
   f. From roll to mysongs and back to old again.
   g. From current to country and back to old again.
13. For Question 12 above, what would need to change if copying were to be done instead of moving?

LAB ASSIGNMENTS

For each of the following lab assignments, submit a history of the commands needed to perform the specified tasks. The history should not contain errors of any kind.

1. To begin this lab, type:

   ```
   script  session1
   ```

   Now go to your login directory. Do a directory listing of your login directory to verify that no file named BugFile exists. Then go to the directory which is the parent of your login directory. (In this unit, it was assumed to be /home. In your case, it may be different.) From the parent directory of your login directory, change the permissions of your login directory so that others can go there and create a file. Now have one of your friends go into your login directory and create a file called BugFile. Then do a directory listing again of your login directory without changing your directory to verify that they created such a file. Tell your friend to get out of your directory and then set permissions to your login directory so that only you have all the permissions and others have none. Then verify that this has been correctly done using command 119 on page 28 (with your login directory name). Then do a <Ctrl>D to terminate the script command. Now type out the file named session1.

2. Create a directory tree in your login directory that is called Cars. Cars has two directories called Family and Power. Family has two directories called Sedans and Wagon. Power has two directories called Nigerian and European. In Nigerian create a file called TestCar that has the contents, "Testing Pure Power!".

   Draw the directory tree.

   From your login directory, create a copy of the Cars directory tree called CarsCopy.

   Using one command, verify that there are two versions of TestCar. *find ~*

   Without using the rm –r command, delete the CarsCopy tree. *Rmdir*

   Go to the directory called Family. From there do all these tasks:
   cat ../Power/Nigerian/TestCar
   See the contents of TestCar, *& cat ../Power*
   do a directory listing of Power, *✓*
   move TestCar to Family, *mv ../Power/Nigerian/TestCar TestCar*
   and then copy Testcar into Cars.
   cp TestCar ../

Unit 4

Text Editing

CONCEPTS TO LEARN

Reading and Sending Email

The University of Washington has created two very simple UNIX programs which are widely used. Pine is the program to read and send email and Pico is the program for text editing. To enter the email program, type pine in lower–case letters. First, it will ask you if you want to get a copy of the documents. Just answer no. You really don't need them; pine is very easy to use. Then you will get the menu shown in Figure 4.1. Don't try using the mouse. It is a text–based application, so the arrow keys should work.

As the menu shows, to get help, press the "?" key or highlight the help option, then press <Enter>. To add or edit an entry in the address book, select the "A" option. When sending email, address book entries will allow you to use nicknames instead of the full email addresses which require the "@" sign and periods.

Suppose that someone asked me if I received their mail. First, I would highlight the "Folder List" option and that would bring me to a new screen as shown in Figure 4.1. Here I would select the "Inbox" to see if I have any incoming mail. This would bring me to the screen shown on the lower left. Here, I see a message for me. If I want to go back to the main menu, I press "M". If I want to delete it, I press "D". To view the message, I press "V". These commands and their meanings are all shown on the bottom of each screen. There are other options which are not shown in the figure. These allow you to reply to the person who sent you the message or forward the message to other recipients.

To send mail, I would select the "Compose Message" option from the main menu. That would take me to the screen shown on the bottom right. Here, I give the address to which the mail is supposed to go. If I want someone else to get a "carbon" copy of the mail, I would enter their address. If there is file in my login directory which I want to attach with the mail, that file name would be entered next to the "Attachment" label. Finally, I should give the subject of the message. The "Cc" and the "Attachment" sections are optional.

Then I am ready to type the message. If I change my mind, I can cancel the sending altogether. To send the mail, I press the "X" key while holding down the <Ctrl> key. The mail will be sent once I quit pine. You should never send mail when you are upset with a person. It is better to communicate touchy subjects in person.

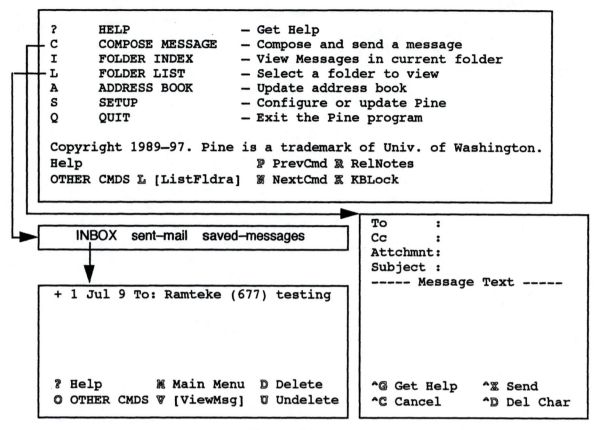

```
    ?      HELP           — Get Help
  ┌ C      COMPOSE MESSAGE — Compose and send a message
  │ I      FOLDER INDEX    — View Messages in current folder
  ┌ L      FOLDER LIST     — Select a folder to view
  │ A      ADDRESS BOOK    — Update address book
  │ S      SETUP           — Configure or update Pine
  │ Q      QUIT            — Exit the Pine program
  │
  │ Copyright 1989—97. Pine is a trademark of Univ. of Washington.
  │ Help                        P PrevCmd  R RelNotes
  │ OTHER CMDS L [ListFldra]    N NextCmd  K KBLock
```

```
       INBOX  sent—mail  saved—messages
```

```
 + 1 Jul 9 To: Ramteke (677) testing
```

```
 ? Help        M Main Menu  D Delete
 O OTHER CMDS  V [ViewMsg]   U Undelete
```

```
 To        :
 Cc        :
 Attchmnt:
 Subject :
 ----- Message Text -----
```

```
 ^G Get Help    ^X Send
 ^C Cancel      ^D Del Char
```

Figure 4.1

The pico Text Editor

Figure 4.2 shows the screen which one sees when running the pico text editor. The text entered on the first five lines of the screen is what I typed in when creating a file. It is a simple C program. To enter the editor, type pico in lower case letters. You may also specify the file name as an argument when entering pico. This program uses the same interface as the pine email program. All the command procedures are shown on the lower portion of the screen. The most important one is how to get help. <Ctrl>G allows you to do that.

The arrow keys allow you to move the cursor. To save the file, do a <Ctrl>O. To copy a line or several lines, first do <Ctrl>K for every line which needs to be copied. Then do a <Ctrl>U to restore those lines where they were and then, after moving the cursor where you want the text to be copied, do another <Ctrl>U. This copies the text that was in the buffer into that place in the file.

When saving a file, you are prompted to save the file under a different name, if you wish. When this is done, you end up with two versions of the file. The old version is saved with the name that you previously specified and the new version is saved under the new name.

Running a C or C++ Program

The Free Software Foundation has a great C/C++ compiler called gcc. All programs written for it must have an extension of .cc to make it run.

To run a C or a C++ program, type the source code as shown in Figure 4.2. Then save it as a text file with the file name "test.cc", and then exit pico. Now enter the following:

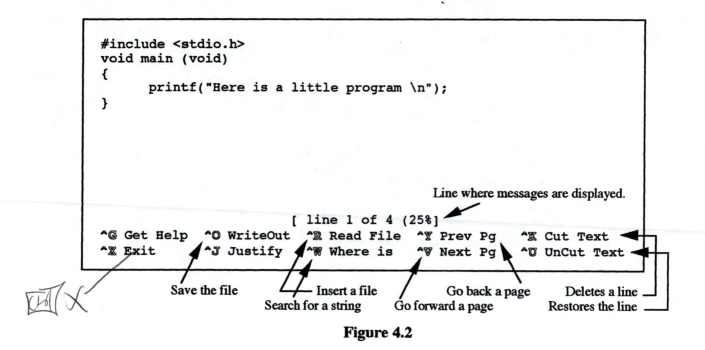

```
#include <stdio.h>
void main (void)
{
        printf("Here is a little program \n");
}
```

Line where messages are displayed.

[line 1 of 4 (25%]

^G Get Help   ^O WriteOut   ^R Read File   ^Y Prev Pg   ^K Cut Text
^X Exit   ^J Justify   ^W Where is   ^V Next Pg   ^U UnCut Text

Save the file   Insert a file   Go back a page   Deletes a line
              Search for a string   Go forward a page   Restores the line

Figure 4.2

```
%gcc_test.cc
%a.out
```

If the program works, you will see the output. If it doesn't, error messages will be displayed showing the line numbers where the syntax is incorrect. In that case, go back into the pico editor, correct the program, and rerun it.

The vi Editor

The vi editor is important for UNIX systems administrators to learn. If you are serious about learning UNIX, then you should learn vi. Appendix A goes into the vi editor in detail. Here, we will use a minimum set of vi commands.

The vi editor has basically two modes in which it operates. The command mode is where keys which are pressed on the keyboard are not entered as text in the file. Instead, they are interpreted as commands to the editor. To get into the command mode, press the <Esc> key once. The other mode is the text–insertion mode. One way to get into this mode is to press the character "i". This command is given while in the command mode.

Here are some important commands for the vi editor:

:w	Writes (or saves) the file.
:q	Quits (or exits) vi.
:q!	Allows you to quit vi without saving the file.
dd	Deletes one line.
h	Moves the cursor to the left. (Left arrow key may also work).
k	Moves the cursor up. (Up arrow key may also work).
j	Moves the cursor down. (Down arrow key may also work).
l	Moves the cursor to the right. (Right arrow key may also work).
i	Allows you to go in the text–insertion mode.
x	Deletes one character.

The emacs Editor

The Free Software Foundation has a great text editor which is free and popular with UNIX users. It is called "emacs". Emacs was created by the same person who started Java many years earlier. To enter emacs, type emacs in lower–case letters. You may also enter a file name after it.

One of the nice things about emacs is its ability to edit two d
simultaneously by opening two windows. Can your Windows edit

Here are some important emacs commands:

Help

<Ctrl>h	Starts help.
<Ctrl>ht	Starts the emacs tutorial.
<Ctrl>h<Ctrl>h	Lists the emacs help subcommands.

Moving the Cursor

<Ctrl>v	Goes to the next screen.
<Esc>v	Goes back one screen.
<Ctrl>b	Goes back one character (or use the left arrow key).
<Ctrl>f	Goes forward one character (or use the right arrow key).
<Ctrl>p	Goes back one line (or use the up arrow key).
<Ctrl>n	Goes forward one line (or use the down arrow key).
<Ctrl>a	Goes to the beginning of the current line.
<Ctrl>e	Goes to the end of the current line.
<Ctrl><	Goes to the beginning of the file.
<Ctrl>>	Goes to the end of the file.

File Control

<Ctrl>x<Ctrl>c	Exit emacs.
<Ctrl>x<Ctrl>f	Inserts a file from your directory.
<Ctrl>x<Ctrl>s	Saves the file using the old name.
<Ctrl>x<Ctrl>w	Saves the file using a new name.

Text Blocks

<Ctrl>k	Deletes the rest of the line starting at the cursor.
<Ctrl>@	Marks the block of text starting at the current position.
<Ctrl>w	Deletes the block of text from the mark (the posittition of the last <Ctrl>@) to the current position of the cursor.
<Ctrl>y	Yanks or restores the block of text that was deleted.

Windows

<Ctrl>x 2	Creates two windows on the screen.
<Ctrl>x o	(That's the letter "o.") Moves the cursor to the other window.
<Ctrl>x 1 (Number 1)	Deletes the window which doesn't have the cursor.
<Ctrl>x 4f	Finds and inserts a new file into the window.

String Replacements

<Esc>x replace–string <Enter>	All strings are replaced throughout the file. Emacs will ask for the old string and the new string.
<Esc>%	Starts the query replace sequence after which one of the following choices should be made:
	<Space> or y Changes the strings and finds the next match.
	<del> or n Doesn't change the string and finds the next match.
	<Ctrl>g Terminates the replace command.

Other Commands

<Ctrl>l (letter L)	Refreshes the screen. Whenever the screen is not in sync, this is useful.
<Ctrl>u 5	The command given after this one will be done 5 times. Other numbers can also be used.
<Ctrl>g	A very useful command. Terminates the command you are currently in. If you are stuck in a place where you cannot get out, use this command.
<Del>	Deletes a command. (<Backspace> doesn't usually work. If you use <Backspace> by mistake, you may need <Ctrl>g to get out.)

Job Control

%	This symbol is used in front of a job number whenever a command needs to know what job you are referring to.
&	This symbol placed at the end of a command will run the command in the background. Running a process in the background means that, although the process is taking a while to complete, you get your prompt back to enter new UNIX commands and do other tasks.
^Z	Suspends a process which is running and returns the prompt to enter a new command.
bg	This will background the job specified. See the instructions for & above. Job numbers should be specified using the % symbol.
fg	If a job is in the background and you want to attend to it, then foreground the job. For example, if you suspend an emacs session by doing a <Ctrl>Z, you will get your UNIX prompt back. You can then do other UNIX jobs. When you want to continue with your emacs session, you foreground it. If only one job is running, you need not provide the job number.
jobs –l	Shows the jobs which are running. Job numbers are assigned for the processes under each account. Hence, jobs for multiple users could have the same job number active under the users' accounts but all of those jobs would have separate process IDs.
kill –9	Allows you to kill a job (or process). The option of –9 is not necessary all the time.
ps	Shows all processes which are active under your account. This is given in the process table. The PID (Process ID) is the identification which is unique for the whole system.
sleep	Not a useful command unless you are experimenting with job control or running shell scripts. It makes you wait for a specified amount of seconds before you can continue with your work or session.
stop	Suspends a job which is running in the process table.
stty all	Gives you the key sequence to suspend a job among other terminal settings. Usually it is ^Z.

SAMPLE SESSION

It is a little difficult to illustrate a session when working with menus. Therefore, to keep the illustrations simple, the entire windows are not shown here. Figures 4.1 and 4.2 (pages 49 and 50) give a better idea of how these windows look. Keeping the illustrations simple also shows only the important parts of each window, thereby not cluttering them with too many items.

pine

```
{101} pine

┌─────────────────────────┐
│ ? HELP                  │
│ C COMPOSE MESSAGE       │
│ L FOLDER LIST           │
│                         │
│ Q QUIT                  │
└─────────────────────────┘

c
```

First, let us send ourselves some email. Simply type pine and this will give you a menu which is more completely shown in Figure 4.1.

We want to compose and send a message, so we choose "C".

```
To        :ramteke@pilot.njin.net
Cc        :
Attchmnt:
Subject :Just having fun
----- Message Text -----
Dear Myself,

Just testing this Email
program.

tiM
```

Since I am sending myself a message, I enter my own address. I can enter any valid address here.

I don't want to send copies to anyone, so the "Cc" entry is blank. I also have no files to attach to this email so "Attchmnt:" is also blank. The subject is entered as shown.

In the message area, I type the letter and sign it. Other folks create elaborate signatures. I simply capitalize the last letter of my first name.

^x
Send message? **Y**

```
? HELP
C COMPOSE MESSAGE
L FOLDER LIST

Q QUIT
```

As seen earlier in Figure 4.1, to send the message I press <Ctrl> x. Then pine asks me if I really want to send it. I respond with a "Y" for yes.
This brings me back to the main menu.

Q
Really Quit Pine? **Y**

Then I simply quit. I must quit for the mail to be sent.

{102} pine

Now let's see if I received the mail. We go back into pine.

```
? HELP
C COMPOSE MESSAGE
L FOLDER LIST

Q QUIT
```

L

```
INBOX   sent-mail  saved-messages
```

Choose "L" for folder list.
Here we select "INBOX".

INBOX

```
+ 1 Ramteke Just having fun
```

The Inbox shows one message waiting to be read.

V

```
Dear Myself,

Just testing this Email
program.

tiM
```

We press "V" to view it.

And here is the message which I sent to myself.

M

We press "M" to go back to the main menu.

```
? HELP
C COMPOSE MESSGAGE
L FOLDER LIST

Q QUIT
```

Q
`Really Quit Pine? Y`

Finally, we quit.

pico

Now let us use pico to learn how to edit files in UNIX. Simply type "pico" and then the file name. Here the file we are going to create is called list1. If it had already existed, then you would see that file on the pico screen. However, this is a new file and we type the three items which you see on the screen.

{103} pico list1

```
Stove
Sleeping bag
Tent
```

`<Ctrl>X`
`Save modified buffer? Y`
`File name: list1 <Enter>`

Pressing the X key while holding down the <Ctrl> key will make us exit pico. When we try to exit pico without saving the file, it asks us if we want to save the file, so we enter Y. Then pico will allow us to change the file name. We don't want to do that so we simply press <Enter>.

Now let us create another file called list2.

{104} pico list2

```
Towels
Fishing gear
```

`<Ctrl>O`
`File name: list2 <Enter>`

Here is its content.

We write the file or, in other words, we save it but don't exit pico. We see list2 on the screen and it is also in RAM. Here are the files on the hard drive of the UNIX server as they are saved:

list1

```
Stove
Sleeping bag
Tent
```

list2

```
Towels
Fishing gear
```

```
Towels
Fishing gear
_
```

`<Ctrl>R`
`File to insert: list1`

```
Towels
Fishing gear
Stove
Sleeping bag
Tent

_
```

Here is our file called list2 again on the screen. Let us add the list1 file to the end of list2. First, we place the cursor where we want to insert the file list1, at the bottom of the file list2. We place the cursor at the end of the list2 file. That is shown with a dash at the end of the file.

Then we do a <Ctrl>R to retrieve the file.

We are prompted for the name of the file to insert and we enter list1.

Now our screen will have 5 lines, 2 from list2 and 3 from list1. Notice that the file which was retrieved was inserted at the location where the cursor was located.

```
    Towels
    Fishing gear
    Stove
    Sleeping bag
    Tent
```

<Ctrl>K
<Ctrl>K

```
    Towels
    Fishing gear
    Stove
```

<Ctrl>U

```
    Sleeping bag
    Tent
    Towels
    Fishing gear
    Stove
```

<Ctrl>X
Save modified buffer? **Y**
File name: **list3**

{104.1} **cat list1**
{104.2} **cat list2**
{104.3} **cat list3**

{105}**vi list2**

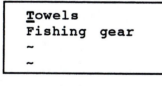

```
    Towels
    Fishing gear
    ~
    ~
```

i
i

```
    iTowels
    Fishing gear
```

<Esc>
dd

Now let us delete the last two lines and then move them to the top of the file. To do that, we move the cursor up two lines. We place the cursor under the "S" in "Sleeping."

Then we kill the last two lines by entering <Ctrl>K twice. And since we want to move those deleted lines to the top of the file, we move the cursor there.

Then, by pressing <Ctrl>U, we undelete those two lines at the top of the file. At this time, we could undelete those same two lines one or more times. If we were now to undelete at the bottom of the file, we would in effect be making a copy of those lines rather than doing a move. The two lines stay in the buffer to be undeleted wherever and as often as you wish until you delete other lines. Then the new deleted lines can be undeleted in the same fashion.

Now we exit pico. As we exit pico, we are allowed to change the name of the file which is to be saved. We change it to list3. These are the three files which now exist in our account and which we can print:

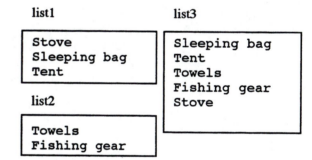

list1
```
Stove
Sleeping bag
Tent
```
list2
```
Towels
Fishing gear
```
list3
```
Sleeping bag
Tent
Towels
Fishing gear
Stove
```

The vi Editor

When calling the vi editor, we give it the filename list2. This brings up list2 on the screen. There are tildes at the end of the file to show us where the file ends. The cursor is under the "T" of Towels.

When vi starts up, it starts in the command mode and waits for a command. If we press i, that will place the editor in the text–insert mode and nothing will be shown on the screen. The second time we press i, it will be treated as text and vi will insert it on the screen and not interpret it as a command.

Now let us go back into command mode. This is done by pressing <Esc>. Then we press the letter d twice. The input is not displayed on the screen because we are in the command mode. The double d is interpreted as a command and it means to delete the entire line.

```
┌─────────────────────────┐
│                         │
│   F̲ishing   gear        │
│                         │
└─────────────────────────┘
```

`:q`
`:q!`

`{106}emacs list4`

```
┌─────────────────────────────┐
│   abcd    abcd    abbc       │
│   dcde    abcd    bcde       │
│   abcd    dcde    abb̲c       │
└─────────────────────────────┘
```

`<Ctrl>a`
`<UpArrow>`

```
┌─────────────────────────────┐
│   abcd    abcd    abbc       │
│   d̲cde    abcd    bcde       │
│   abcd    dcde    abbc       │
└─────────────────────────────┘
```

`<Ctrl>x<Ctrl>s`

`<Ctrl><Shift>@`
`<DownArrow>`
`<Ctrl>e`
`<Enter>`

```
┌─────────────────────────────┐
│   abcd    abcd    abbc       │
│   dcde    abcd    bcde       │
│   abcd    dcde    abb̲c       │
└─────────────────────────────┘
```

`<Ctrl>w`

```
┌─────────────────────────────┐
│   abcd    abcd    abbc       │
└─────────────────────────────┘
```

`<Ctrl>y`

```
┌─────────────────────────────┐
│   abcd    abcd    abbc       │
│   dcde    abcd    bcde       │
│   abcd    dcde    abb̲c       │
└─────────────────────────────┘
```

`<Ctrl>u 2 <Ctrl>p`
`<Ctrl>a`

```
┌─────────────────────────────┐
│   a̲bcd    abcd    abbc       │
│   dcde    abcd    bcde       │
│   abcd    dcde    abbc       │
└─────────────────────────────┘
```

`<Ctrl>y`

We are still in the command mode. If we had typed the colon (:) and w, we would have saved the file. Let us just quit vi without saving it. If we type :q, vi will not quit since the file wasn't saved. Hence, we do a :q! which means to quit the editor without saving the file.

The emacs Editor

I have found that Windows 95's telnet client will not support vi very well. That is also true of emacs. Make sure you have a good telnet client before you start using emacs. Emacs doesn't use two modes. If a command is to be given, then either the <Ctrl> or the <Esc> key is first pressed. When using the <Ctrl> key, keep the key down while pressing the next character. When using the <Esc> key, let go of it and then press the next character.
Here, I have entered text for a file called list4. The cursor is on the last character of the last line.
<Ctrl>a will place the cursor at the beginning of the line.
The up arrow will bring the cursor to the middle line.

This double <Ctrl> key sequence will save the file using the same name we started out with. In other words, list4 is now resaved.
Let us now copy the last two lines of the file to the top of the file. First we mark a block of text. The <Ctrl><Shift>@ command will mark the current position in the file. The down arrow and <Ctrl>e will bring the cursor to the end of the last line.

Now the bottom two lines are marked as a block.

<Ctrl>w deletes that block and we now have only the first line left on the screen.
Since we want to do a copy, let us restore the block at the bottom of the screen, the same place where we deleted it. This is done with a "yank" or <Ctrl>y.

Now let us go up by doing <Ctrl>p (previous line) two times. (<Ctrl>u *n* does the command following it *n* times.) Then doing a <Ctrl>a will bring us to the beginning of the line. <Ctrl>< would have brought the cursor to the same position easily.

Here we yank the buffer again and the same block of text which was deleted before is placed at the beginning of the file.

```
dcde    abcd    bcde
abcd    dcde    abbc
abcd    abcd    abbc
dcde    abcd    bcde
abcd    dcde    abbc
```

`<Ctrl><`
`<Esc>%`
`Query replace: dcde <Enter>`
`Replace dcde with: xxxx <Enter>`

```
dcde_   abcd    bcde
abcd    dcde    abbc
abcd    abcd    abbc
dcde    abcd    bcde
abcd    dcde    abbc
```

`Query replace dcde with xxxx`
`(? for help) y`

```
xxxx    abcd    bcde
abcd    dcde_   abbc
abcd    abcd    abbc
dcde    abcd    bcde
abcd    dcde    abbc
```

`Query replace dcde with xxxx`
`(? for help) n`
`<Ctrl>g`
`<Ctrl>x<Ctrl>s`
`<Ctrl>x<Ctrl>c`

Now let us get ready to replace some of the dcde strings with xxxx. Since only some of them are going to be replaced, we need to do a query replace.

First, place the cursor at the top of the file.

Now invoke the query replace command.

Provide the string which we want to change, dcde.

Then provide the string which we want to replace it with, xxxx.

First, the cursor falls after the top left occurrence of dcde. We press y to make the change.

Then the cursor falls on the dcde word of the second line.

Here we press n to not make the change.

We decide not to make any more changes, so we terminate this command by pressing <Ctrl>g.

Now we save the file.

Then we exit emacs.

Job Control

Nowadays everyone works with window interfaces, and if a job takes a while to complete, one can simply open another window while it is being completed. Nonetheless, learning job control gives a student a better feeling for how processes are handled by the operating system.

`{107} sleep 7`

Here is a simple command which asks the operating system to wait for 7 seconds. After 7 seconds, we get our prompt back.

`{108} sleep 15`

Here we have to wait 15 seconds to get our prompt back. Many jobs like sorting files or downloading a file can take a while. We want to be able to continue with our session without having to wait for the job to complete so we can get our prompt back. Putting a job in the background means just that; a job can run while we go about running other commands. The ps command shows that we are in our tcsh shell and the jobs command shows us that there are no jobs running right now under our account.

```
{109} ps
PID    TT    STAT    TIME      COMMAND
23379  p2    R+      0:00.01   ps
24319  p2    Ss      0:00.40   -tcsh
{110} jobs -l
{111} sleep 100 &
[1] 24435
```

By placing & at the end of the command, the process can keep running while we execute other commands. We now don't have to wait for the prompt to come back.

```
{112} sleep 200
^Z
Suspended
{113} ps
PID    TT   STAT   TIME      COMMAND
18569  p2   R+     0:00.01   ps
19241  p2   T      0:00.01   sleep 200
24319  p2   Ss     0:00.42   -tcsh
24435  p2   S      0:00.01   sleep 100
{114} jobs -l
[1]    - 24435 Running        sleep 100
[2]    + 19241 Suspended      sleep 200


{115} stop %1
[1]    + Suspended signal sleep 100
{116} jobs -l
[1]    + 24435 Suspended     sleep 100
[2]    - 19241 Suspended     sleep 200
{117} bg %1
[1]         sleep 100 &
{118} bg %2
[2]         sleep 200 &
{119} jobs -l
[1]    + 24435 Running        sleep 100
[2]      19241 Running        sleep 200
{120} fg %2
sleep 200
^Z
Suspended
{121} jobs -l
[1]    - 24435 Running        sleep 100
[2]    + 19241 Suspended      sleep 200
{122} kill %1
[1]      Terminated           sleep 100
{123} jobs -l
[2]    + 19241 Suspended      sleep 200
{124} emacs test1
```

```
+---------------------------------+
|   We are in emacs!              |
+---------------------------------+
```

```
^Z
Suspended
{125} ls
col4  mine  testA
{126} vi test4
```

```
+---------------------------------+
| now                             |
| we are in vi                    |
+---------------------------------+
```

```
^Z
Suspended
```

Here, we start a job and afterwards realize that this job will take some time, so we suspend it with the <Ctrl>Z character sequence.

In the process table we see that both of these jobs are listed. PID, the process ID, is a system–wide identification number for the process.

The job number is specific only under the account which it is running. Notice that sleep 100 & from command 111 keeps the job running in the background. However, sleep 200 which was suspended in command 112 is listed as suspended.

To stop job number one, use this command. Use the % sign to identify the job number. Now it is suspended.

In fact, both jobs are now suspended.

Backgrounding a job allows us not only to start a job but also to do other things.

We have started both jobs in the background.

And this command confirms that. Both jobs are running.

To run a job in the foreground means that the terminal on which we are entering commands is now associated with that job; so if we foreground job 2, our terminal becomes locked while we wait for the prompt to come back.

We decide to suspend it using <Ctrl>Z.

Job number 2 is suspended.

To kill a job means to terminate it.

Now only job number 2 is in the process table and it is suspended.

We could start another process such as the emacs editor. Sometimes we type something in the file, then wish we could find out a name of a file in the current directory before we continue. The way to do that is to suspend the emacs session by using <Ctrl>Z.

Then we can find the name of the file we are looking for. Incidentally, we could also go into another process like vi.

Then we can suspend that job also. In vi, you must be in the command mode to suspend a job.

```
{127} jobs -l
[2]   19241 Suspended sleep   200
[3] - 26880 Suspended emacs   test1
[4] + 8508  Suspended vi      test4
{128} fg %3
emacs test1
```

Now we find out that there are three jobs in the process table.

If we bring job number 3 to the foreground, we find ourselves back in the emacs session.

```
┌─────────────────────────┐
│  We are in emacs!       │
└─────────────────────────┘
```

```
^Z
Suspended
{129} jobs -l
[2]    19241 Suspended sleep 200
[3]  + 26880 Suspended emacs test1
[4]  - 8508  Suspended vi    test4
{130} fg %4
vi test4
```

Here, we get out of job number 3.

If we bring the vi session to the foreground, we go back into vi.

```
┌─────────────────────────┐
│  now                    │
│  we are in vi           │
└─────────────────────────┘
```

```
^Z
Suspended
{131} jobs -l
[2]    19241 Suspended sleep 200
[3]  - 26880 Suspended emacs test1
[4]  + 8508  Suspended vi test4
{132} logout
There are suspended        jobs.
{133} kill -9 %2
[2]       Terminated        sleep 200

{134} kill %3
{135} logout
There are suspended jobs.
[3]       Terminated   emacs  test1
{136} jobs -l
[4]  + 8508  Suspended   vi   test4
{137} kill %4
{138} logout
[4]       Terminated         vi test4
```

Here, we suspend job number 4.

We still have the other three jobs on hold.

We are not allowed to log out if we have jobs that are suspended.

So we kill one job. Sometimes you may need to use the –9 option to make sure the job is dead. (Some jobs are like cats. They have 9 lives.)

Of course, we still can't log out. One more job is still pending.

There is still one job which needs to be killed.

After we do that,

we can log out. It is better to kill all jobs instead of just closing the telnet window.

EXPERIMENTS

```
%pico lab4.1
```

```
┌─────────────────────────┐
│  I went                 │
│  to check out           │
│  how tall I was!        │
└─────────────────────────┘
```

4.1 Go into the pico editor and enter this file with its three lines.

4.2 Do you have to press any key to start typing text on the screen?

Do the arrow keys allow you move the cursor around?

4.3 Which of the following keys or key sequences allow you to delete a character?

      \<Del\>

      \<Backspace\>

      \<Ctrl\>h

4.4 Place the cursor on the first character of the top line. Press \<Ctrl\>K. What does it do? Give your answers in the left–hand column.

4.5 Now press \<Ctrl\>U three times. What does \<Ctrl\>U do?

4.6 Restore the screen as shown in Experiment 4.1. Using the \<Ctrl\> commands, copy the first two lines to the bottom of the file. Starting with the cursor on the top left corner, give the commands in the order which enabled you to accomplish that task.

```
%pine
A
```

4.7 Go into this email program and type "A". What does A allow you to do?

```
A
```

4.8 Now type A again. Find out the email address of a person next to you in lab. Fill his or her first name in the Nickname box and enter the entire email address. Complete the addition of this email address in your email address book.

```
C
```

4.9 Go back to the main menu. Type "C". What does this option provide?

4.10 Enter the nickname of the person you put in the address book in Experiment 4.8. Which keys allow you to complete sending the message?

4.11 Have your friend send you email. Then both of you quit the email program. How do you quit?

4.12 Now that you have used pine to create an entry in the address book and to send a message, you should be able to figure out how to read your email. Can you do that? Start at the main menu. Give the commands to view the mail which your partner sent you.

```
R
```

4.13 While viewing the message, type "R". What does this command allow you to do?

```
D
```

4.14 Complete replying to the message, then type "D". What does this command allow you to do?

```
%vi song1
```

```
I went
to check out
how tall I was!
```

4.15 Quit pine and get into the vi editor. Give the name of the file as song1. Type "i" (lower case) as soon as you enter vi. Then type in the file. If the file is not correct or gets messed up, don't worry about it. You should be able to get it right by the time we are done with these experiments.

```
<Esc>
q
```

4.16 Now press the <Esc> key. Then press q. The <Esc> key brings you into command mode. Did the q get entered as text on the screen? What do you think the <Esc> key does? What does it mean to go into command mode?

4.17 While in the command mode, that is after pressing the <Esc> key, try the following keys out. What is the function of each one?

h	j
k	l

4.18 Can you move the cursor by using the arrow keys?

4.19 While in the command mode, what do the following keys do?

x	u
dd	u

4.20 See if you can fix up the file so that it is as shown in Experiment 4.15. To insert text, try either a or i. To get out of the text–insertion mode, press <Esc>. The i command will allow you to insert text before the position of the cursor and the a will allow you to insert text after it.

4.21 Even if you can't correct the file, try these commands. Notice, they begin with a colon. What do they do?

```
:w
:q
```
If the :q doesn't work, try:
```
:q!
```

```
%cat song1

%echo Sha La La > song2

%emacs song3
```

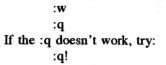
```
I went
to check out
how tall I was!
Unfortunately,
I found out how
small I was.
```

4.22 Type out the file and copy its contents.

4.23 Create a file called song2. We will use it here.

4.24 We are going into emacs now. You should remember a few things about emacs before going into it.

> Make sure you have a good telnet client that handles the terminal settings correctly.
> If the screen goes fluky, do a <Ctrl>l (letter L).
> If you get stuck in a command, do <Ctrl>g.
> Don't use the <Backspace> key, but rather the <Del> key.

Go into emacs and enter the file as shown. Don't bother to correct any mistakes you might make. It is not important that the file be exactly as shown.
Do your arrow keys allow you to move the cursor in all four directions?

4.25 What do the following commands do?
```
<Ctrl>a
<Ctrl>e
<Ctrl>h
```

4.26 What is the difference between the following two commands?

> <Ctrl>x<Ctrl>s
> <Ctrl>x<Ctrl>w

4.27 Do a <Ctrl>x<Ctrl>f and give song2 as a file name when asked to do so. What did this command do?

4.28 Bring the cursor to the top line. Do these commands in order and give their purpose:

> <Ctrl>k
> <Ctrl>u3<Ctrl>k

Now bring the cursor down past the last line and do:

> <Ctrl>u

4.29 Now do a <Ctrl>y again twice. Explain what <Ctrl>y does in your own words.

Can you paste the lines at any position in the file?

4.30 Now delete all duplicate lines so that the file looks something like it was shown earlier. Do these commands in order and explain what each one does.

> <Ctrl>x2
> <Ctrl>xo   (That's not a zero.)
> <Ctrl>xo
> <Ctrl>x4f   (Give song2 as the file name.)

4.31 What is the key sequence to copy a line from one window into the other? Try it.

4.32 What do the following commands do?

> <Ctrl>x1
> <Ctrl>x<Ctrl>s
> <Ctrl>x<Ctrl>c

Job Control

`%stty all`

4.33 If this command doesn't work, try stty a. If that doesn't work, find out from the man page which option will display the stty settings. Here, the output may be long. From the output, give the keystrokes for suspending a job. I will assume it is <Ctrl>z.

`%sleep 5`

4.34 How many seconds does this job take to complete?
Do you lose your cursor and prompt during this time?
Does UNIX allow you to enter any new commands or start any new processes during this time?

`%sleep 10`

4.35 How many seconds does this job take?

`%jobs -l`

4.36 Are there any jobs running right now? I am assuming there aren't any.

`%sleep 500`
`^z`

4.37 Start this long job and then suspend it by using the <Ctrl>z sequence.

```
%jobs -l
```
4.38 Are there any jobs listed here?
If so, what is their status?

```
%ps
```
4.39 Does this command show the new job which was suspended?
Which number is common between the output of this command and that of Experiment 4.38?

```
%bg %1
%jobs -l
```
4.40 Is the job, sleep 500, still suspended? Or is it now running?
Do you get your prompt back or is it waiting for the sleep command to complete?
The command bg stands for background. When you background a job, do you continue running the job? Are you allowed to start other UNIX processes or jobs?

```
%stop %1
%jobs -l
```
4.41 What does the stop command do?

```
%bg %1
```
4.42 Can you start the job in the background again?

```
%fg %1
```
4.43 Here, we are bringing the job to the foreground.
Do you get your prompt back or is UNIX waiting for the sleep command to complete?
The command fg stands for foreground. When you foreground a job, do you continue running the job? Are you allowed to start other UNIX processes or jobs?

4.44 Now suspend the job again and then kill it.
Does the kill command take the job out of the process table?

```
^z
%kill -9 %1
%jobs -l

%ps
```

HOMEWORK

pine:
1. In Figure 4.1 on page 49, there is a screen with sent mail and saved messages options. Using the help command, explain the purpose of these options and how to use them.
2. Starting with the main menu, give the keystrokes needed to change the email address of a person you have stored in the address book. Use the help command.
3. What does the <Space> key do when you are reading mail?

pico:
4. In pico, go to the help screen and find out two new commands which weren't mentioned in this unit. Explain what they do and how to execute them.
5. How do you find specific character strings in pico?
6. In pico, can you replace a specific character string with another one for all occurrences of that string in the document?
7. In pico, what does <Ctrl>C do?
8. Does <Ctrl>Z allow you to suspend a pico session?

The vi Editor:

9. What are the two modes of operation in vi?
10. What are two ways to quit vi? What is the purpose of each quit.
11. What key allows you to give commands to the vi editor?
12. What key allows you to enter text on the vi screen?
13. What do all the squiggles (~) mean on a vi screen?
14. How do you save a file in vi?

The emacs Editor:

15. How many modes of operations does emacs have?
16. All commands given to emacs begin with which keys? What is the difference in how these keys are used?
17. There are some stray characters on the screen that don't belong there. How do I get rid of them?
18. How do I get help? How do I run the emacs tutorial?
19. How do I move the cursor up 7 lines?
20. How do I move the cursor at the end of the line?
21. I have only five lines on the screen. The cursor is on the top–left most character. Give the keystrokes to copy the first two lines to the bottom of the screen. Give two ways to do that.
22. What command allows you to quit a command?

Job Control:

23. What are the different statuses a job can have and what do they mean?
24. Which item in the jobs –l listing is the same as that of the ps output?
25. How can you start a job which is going to take a long time to complete so that you can start another job?
26. If an emacs session is suspended and is assigned a job number of 3, how can you get back into that emacs session?
27. How can you suspend a job which is currently running in the foreground?
28. What are the two ways to terminate a job?

LAB ASSIGNMENTS

pine:

1. Create a file in your login directory that has the first two lines of a song. Call this file mysong. Then send email to your instructor telling something you like about her or him. Attach the file you created. Send a copy of that mail to your lab partner.
2. Reply to a message your lab partner sends you and attach your version of mysong to your reply. Also send a copy of your reply to your instructor.

pico and gcc:

3. Create the following program using pico. Enter it exactly as shown. Save it as program1.cc. You don't need to know what it means. Compile and execute it, correcting all syntax errors. Then save the output to the end of the same program.

```
#include <stdio.h>
void main (void)
{  int i;
   for(i = 1; i <= 3; ++i)
      printf("Line: %d\n", i);
}
```

Text Editing

The vi Editor:

4. Using vi, create a file called pg1 and re–enter the first three lines of the program in the above question. Then quit vi and go back into it again. Now add the last three lines of the file. Quit and print out the file.

The emacs Editor:

5. Do the given steps below. For each step give the commands needed to accomplish the task except for the operations done manually. You will create a file called Emacs1:

```
Line  1:  12345678901234567890123456789012345678901234567890
Line  2:  12345678901234567890123456789012345678901234567890
Line  3:  12345678901234567890123456789012345678901234567890
Line  4:  12345678901234567890123456789012345678901234567890
Line  5:  12345678901234567890123456789012345678901234567890
Line  6:  12345678901234567890123456789012345678901234567890
```

Step 1. Type only 1234567890 at the top left of your emacs screen.

Step 2. Copy 1234567890 four more times on the same line.

Step 3. Add "Line 1: " to the beginning of the line.

Step 4. Copy the first line two more times and change the line numbers manually to "Line 2:" and "Line 3: ".

Step 5. Split the screen, delete a line and undelete it.

Step 6. Go to the other screen and undelete that same line three times. Adjust the line numbers manually to "Line 4:", "Line 5:", and "Line 6".

Step 7. Now move these three lines after the end of the three lines in the original window.

Step 8. Reduce the two screens to one screen and move the cursor to the top left position.

Step 9. Change all occurrences of 345 to ===.

Step 10. Change all occurrences of 89 to ++ except for the second instance on the third line and the first instance on the fifth and sixth lines.

Step 11. Now save the file.

Job Control:

6. For this lab save the history of your commands and hand in a list of the commands for each of the following steps:

Step 1. Show that there are no jobs currently running.

Step 2. Go into vi to start editing the file called lab2.6. Then suspend it. Start another vi session to edit a file called lab4.6. Then suspend that also. Start a sleep 300 command in the background.

Step 3. Show the jobs which are currently running.

Step 4. Suspend the sleep 300 job, terminate the vi lab2.6 job, and show the status of your jobs.

Step 5. Try to log out.

Step 6. Go back to the vi session, exit it without suspending it, and show the status of your jobs.

Step 7. Start the sleep 300 job again so that you get your prompt back. Then suspend it again.

Step 8. Now start the sleep 300 job so that you don't get your prompt back right away.

Step 9. Suspend it. Show your job status, and then terminate that last job.

Unit 5

Basic File Manipulation

CONCEPTS TO LEARN

Creating a Flat File: When creating a file where you may need to manipulate fields in each line, it is best to separate each field with colons rather than just spaces. This is how it is done in the system file /etc/passwd.

The Password File: The file called passwd, under the /etc directory, is the location of a list of all users who have accounts on the UNIX server. There is one line for every user on the system. Each line has several fields which are separated by colons. Here is a line from the /etc/passwd file:

```
tramteke:*:1003:90:Timothy  Ramteke:/home/tramteke:/bin/tcsh
```

The first field is the user name (tramteke). The second field is a place for the encrypted password for this user. Here, only an asterisk is shown. The encrypted passwords are apparently stored in some other file for security's sake. 1003 is the uid. A user–ID (uid) is given to each user. The next field is the gid or the group–ID. This person is in group 90. In a file called /etc/group, you will find what each group is called. Then comes the user's full name. Other information about the user's phone number, room number, and other personal items can also be given here. Next, comes the login directory: /home/tramteke. Last is the login shell: /bin/tcsh.

Standard Output: The output of many commands is standard output or the console, as in "echo Matthew". The output can be redirected to a file using the right arrow (>), as in "echo Matthew > fileA".

Standard Input: The default input file for many commands is the console. However, if a filename is given, then that file is used as the input to the command. For example, cat fileA will use fileA as the input for the cat command. fileA is used as an argument to the cat command. Alternatively, cat < fileA will do the same thing. This, however, is a two–step process. First the cat command is executed and then fileA is redirected as the input for this cat command. This subtle difference between cat fileA and cat < fileA is not important to understand, but it helps to appreciate the flexibility of the UNIX operating system.

COMMANDS TO LEARN

cut		Cuts the characters specified in each line. The file stays unchanged.
	cut –c3,5	This will show only the 3rd and 5th characters of each line.
	cut –d: –f2	This will use the colon as the field delimiter and show only the second field in each line.
grep		Looks for the lines which the expression has specified.
	–i	Ignores the case (very useful).
	–l	Gives only filenames not the lines.
	–c	Counts the lines which match the expression.
head		Shows the first 10 lines of the specified file.
	head –5	Shows the first 5 lines of the specified file.
paste		This will paste two or more files next to each other side by side. A tab is used between the two columns.
sed		A sophisticated stream–editor.
	–l	Shows nonprintable characters, such as tabs and carriage returns.
	–d	Deletes the line that matches the expression given.
sort		This sorts out all the lines of the file specified.
	–r	Sorts in reverse order
	–o	Sorts a file and stores the sorted file back into itself. sort fileA > fileA will wipe out the contents of fileA because, in order to do the redirection, fileA is first deleted. Then UNIX does the sort. By this time, there is nothing to sort. However, sort –o fileA fileA will work properly.
	–t:	Uses the colon as the field separator. Other characters can be used in place of the colon.
	+3	Skips 3 fields before starting the sorting. If no –t option is used, the tab character is used to delimit (or separate) the fields.
	sort –t: +3	This will sort the file specified by using the fourth field as the sorting field. Contrast this with the options in cut.
tail		Shows the last 10 lines of the specified file.
	tail –5	Shows the last 5 lines of the specified file.
tr		Substitutes or deletes characters. Filename is not an argument.
		tr '[A–Z]' '[a–z]' < fileA Changes fileA's upper–case characters to all lower–case characters.
		tr '[a–z]' '[A–Z]' < fileA Changes fileA's lower–case characters to all upper–case characters.
		tr –d . < fileA Displays fileA without any periods.
wc		Does a word count, giving the number of characters, words, and lines.
	–l	Gives only the number of lines.
	–w	Counts only the number of words.

SAMPLE SESSION

{101} **echo Matthew Henson**   Let us begin with something familiar. This echo command
Matthew Henson   will merely echo whatever is on the line.
{102} **echo Matthew Henson > fileA** This will redirect it to fileA.
{103} **cat fileA**   Here it is: the name redirected to the file is Matthew Henson.
Matthew Henson
{104} **cat fileA > fileB**   Here the output is redirected to fileB.
{105} **cat fileB**   Sure enough, fileB has what was redirected from fileA.
Matthew Henson

```
{107} cat > testA
Matthew     :Henson         :NPole      :1909
Vilhjalmur  :Stefansson     :Arctic     :1910
Roald       :Amundsen       :SPole      :1911
Sherpa      :Tenzing        :Everest    :1953
^d
{110} cat < testA
Matthew     :Henson         :NPole      :1909
Vilhjalmur  :Stefansson     :Arctic     :1910
Roald       :Amundsen       :SPole      :1911
Sherpa      :Tenzing        :Everest    :1953
{111} sort testA
Matthew     :Henson         :NPole      :1909
Roald       :Amundsen       :SPole      :1911
Sherpa      :Tenzing        :Everest    :1953
Vilhjalmur  :Stefansson     :Arctic     :1910
{112} sort < testA
Matthew     :Henson         :NPole      :1909
Roald       :Amundsen       :SPole      :1911
Sherpa      :Tenzing        :Everest    :1953
Vilhjalmur  :Stefansson     :Arctic     :1910
{113} cat testA
Matthew     :Henson         :NPole      :1909
Vilhjalmur  :Stefansson     :Arctic     :1910
Roald       :Amundsen       :SPole      :1911
Sherpa      :Tenzing        :Everest    :1953
{114} sort testA > testB
{115} cat testB
Matthew     :Henson         :NPole      :1909
Roald       :Amundsen       :SPole      :1911
Sherpa      :Tenzing        :Everest    :1953
Vilhjalmur  :Stefansson     :Arctic     :1910
{116} sort < testA > testB
{117} cat testB
Matthew     :Henson         :NPole      :1909
Roald       :Amundsen       :SPole      :1911
Sherpa      :Tenzing        :Everest    :1953
Vilhjalmur  :Stefansson     :Arctic     :1910
{118} sort > testB < testA
{119} cat testB
Matthew     :Henson         :NPole      :1909
Roald       :Amundsen       :SPole      :1911
Sherpa      :Tenzing        :Everest    :1953
Vilhjalmur  :Stefansson     :Arctic     :1910
{120} cat
a
a
b
b
c
c
^D
```

Here, no input filename is given so the input file is taken from the keyboard or the console. The keyboard is standard input. The file is terminated by pressing <Ctrl>D. The output of this command is redirected to testA. Hence, this file is read from the keyboard and placed in testA.

Now the testA file is redirected as input to the cat command. However, this time the output isn't redirected so it is displayed on the screen. This is the same as doing cat testA.

Here, the output isn't redirected to a file. Default output is the screen so the screen is called standard output. The file testA doesn't change, and only the sorted version of testA is displayed on the screen. Each line is sorted.

Similar to command 110, the sort command is executed. The input for this command is taken from the file, testA. This has the same effect as command 111.

Notice, testA hasn't changed. Only the output was sorted.

This command will sort testA and instead of displaying the output on the screen, UNIX redirects it to testB. The file testB is now the sorted version of testA.

We can redirect the input to the sort command and redirect the output to testB.

We can switch the order of the input and output redirection. It has the same effect. The file testB is still the sorted version of testA.

Here is an interesting command. Remember, command 107 did not provide an input filename so the input came from the keyboard. Here also no input filename is given, so the input comes from the keyboard. As command 115 did not redirect the output and caused the output to go to the screen, so here, the output goes to the screen. Hence, whatever we type is displayed by the cat command.

```
{121} sort
b
c
a
^D
a
b
c
```

The same is true with this sort command. Whatever we type before <Ctrl>D is taken as the input file. The entire file must be entered before it can be sorted.

Next comes the head command. It is like the cat command. However, only the first 5 lines of the file are printed in command 122 and only the first two lines are printed in command 123.

```
{122} head -5 /etc/passwd
root:*:0:0:The System Administator,,,:/root:/bin/
uucp:*:66:1:UNIX-to-UNIX Copy:/var/spool/uucppublic:/usr/libexec/uucp/
uuciconobody:*:32767:32767:Unprivileged user:/nonexistent:/sbin/
aloiacon:*:1000:20:Anthony Loiacono:/home/aloiacon:/bin/tcsh
wyodlows:*:1001:20:William Yodlowsky,,,:/home/wyodlows:/bin/
{123} head -2 /etc/passwd
root:*:0:0:The System Administator,,,:/root:/bin/
uucp:*:66:1:UNIX-to-UNIX Copy:/var/spool/uucppublic:/usr/libexec/uucp/
```

```
{124}head -20 /etc/passwd > passy
{125} wc passy
       20        55      1281 passy
{126} wc -l passy
20 passy
```

Here we take the first 20 lines of the passwd file and store it in our own file called passy. The wc command gives the number of lines, words, and characters, including carriage returns. The -l option gives only the number of lines.
This will look for the string ram in the file passy.

```
{127} grep ram passy
tramteke:*:1003:90:Timothy Ramteke:/home/tramteke:/bin/tcsh
```

In the entire passwd file, there are three occurrences of ram.

```
{128} grep ram /etc/passwd
tramteke:*:1003:90:Timothy Ramteke:/home/tramteke:/bin/
tcshrama7441:*:10080:2009:RALPH AMATO:/home/rama7441:/bin/
tcshcram0875:*:12394:2000:CHERYL RAMBERGER:/home/cram0875:/bin/tcsh
{129} grep mat testA
{130} ls
mail         mm.tar       passy
session1     testA        testB
```

In testA, there are no occurrences of the string mat. Remember, UNIX is case sensitive.

```
{131} grep -i mat testA
Matthew    :Henson      :NPole   :1909
{132} grep 19 testA
Matthew    :Henson      :NPole      :1909
Vilhjalmur :Stefansson  :Arctic     :1910
Roald      :Amundsen    :SPole      :1911
Sherpa     :Tenzing     :Everest    :1953
```

Hence, this command is more useful. The -i option tells grep to ignore the case. Now we find the string.
All lines of this file have the string 19 in them.

```
{133} grep [Mm]at testA
grep: No match.
{134} sh
$ grep [Mm]at testA
Matthew    :Henson      :NPole      :1909
$ exit
```

In my tcsh shell, I am looking for either mat or Mat in testA. I don't find it.
If we go into Bourne shell, that same command now works.

Exit the Bourne shell and go back to tcsh.

The tail command here shows the last 4 lines of our 20–line file.

```
{135} tail -4 passy
rjd17:*:1009:10:Richard Doshim:/home/rjd17:/bin—
tcshproblems:*:1012:20:Problem Reports,,,:/home/problems:/usr/local/bin/
pineqwor0666:*:13294:2007:QUENTIN WORTHINGTON:/home/qwor0666:/bin/
tcshjaba6258:*:10000:2004:JOSEPH ABATE:/home/jaba6258:/bin/tcsh
```

The less command is like the more command. It allows you to view one screen at a time, search for strings, and do other operations. Here I have pressed the h key to get help while in less.

```
{136} less /etc/passwd
root:*:0:0:The System Administator,,,:/root:/bin/tcshdaemon:*:1:31:The
```

```
                       SUMMARY OF COMMANDS
Commands marked with * may be preceded by a number.
h       Display this help.
q       Exit.
e       Forward   one  line.
y       Backward  one  line.
f       Forward   one  window.
b       Backward  one  window.
z       Forward   one  window.
```

The sed command allows you to do stream editing. Here it shows all characters, including tabs and carriage returns. Notice, only the first two lines have tabs and no others.

```
{137} sed 'l' testA
Matthew\t\t:Henson\t\t:NPole\t :1909\n$
Matthew           :Henson           :NPole :1909
Vilhjalmur\t:Stefansson\t:Arctic\t:1910\n$
Vilhjalmur :Stefansson    :Arctic   :1910
Roald      :Amundsen      :SPole     :1911\n$
Roald      :Amundsen      :SPole     :1911
Sherpa     :Tenzing       :Everest   :1953\n$
Sherpa     :Tenzing       :Everest   :1953
{138} sort +2 testA
Matthew    :Henson        :NPole     :1909
Vilhjalmur :Stefansson    :Arctic    :1910
Sherpa     :Tenzing       :Everest   :1953
Roald      :Amundsen      :SPole     :1911
```

Here, we are telling the sort command to skip two fields and sort the file on the third field. Notice, Arctic didn't become the first line. Something didn't work right. That is because when we sorted the file on the third field, the sort command interpreted the tab character as the field delimiter. Thus the tab character separates each field. From command 137 we see that only the first two lines have tab characters.

```
{139} sort +2 -t: testA
Vilhjalmur :Stefansson    :Arctic    :1910
Sherpa     :Tenzing       :Everest   :1953
Matthew    :Henson        :NPole     :1909
Roald      :Amundsen      :SPole     :1911
{140} sort +1 testA
Matthew    :Henson        :NPole     :1909
Vilhjalmur :Stefansson    :Arctic    :1910
Roald      :Amundsen      :SPole     :1911
Sherpa     :Tenzing       :Everest   :1953
```

Hence, using the –t option, we tell the sort command to use the colon (:) as the field delimiter and not the tab character. Now notice that Arctic, Everest, NPole, and SPole are in alphabetic order.

Again, sorting past the first field using the tab character as the default field delimiter doesn't work. Amundsen is not on the first line.

```
{141}  sort +1 -t: testA
Roald        :Amundsen     :SPole    :1911
Matthew      :Henson       :NPole    :1909
Vilhjalmur :Stefansson     :Arctic   :1910
Sherpa       :Tenzing      :Everest  :1953
```

However, if we specify the colon as the field delimiter using the –t option, then the column with Amundsen is sorted.

Here are the first three lines of our short password file.

```
{142}  head -3 passy
root:*:0:0:The System Administator,,,:/root:/bin/
tcshoperator:*:2:5:System &:/operator:/sbin/
nologintramteke:*:1003:90:Timothy Ramteke:/home/tramteke:/bin/tcsh
```

We can sort our passy file by using the third field as the sorting field. This file already has colons separating each field. Notice, the third field is in alphabetical order. That is, 0, 10000, 1000, 1001, 1002, etc. are in order.

```
{143}  sort +2 -t: passy
root:*:0:0:The System Administator,,,:/root:/bin/tcsh
jaba6258:*:10000:2004:JOSEPH ABATE:/home/jaba6258:/bin/tcsh
aloiacon:*:1000:20:Anthony Loiacono:/home/aloiacon:/bin/tcsh
wyodlows:*:1001:20:William Yodlowsky,,,:/home/wyodlows:/bin/tcsh
webmaste:*:1002:20:The Webmaster:/home/webmaste:/bin/tcsh
tramteke:*:1003:90:Timothy Ramteke:/home/tramteke:/bin/tcsh
proto:*:1004:10:prototype user:/home/proto:/bin/tcsh
help:*:1006:10:Educational Services Help Line,Educational Services –
Room 240 ,(732) 435-4873,See Hours Below.:/home/help:/bin/tcsh
sga:*:1007:10:Student Government Association:/home/sga:/bin/tcsh
drewtar:*:1008:10:Andrew Mollica:/home/drewtar:/bin/tcsh
rjd17:*:1009:10:Richard Doshim:/home/rjd17:/bin/tcsh
problems:*:1012:20:Problem Reports,,,:/home/problems:/usr/local/bin/pine
majordom:*:102:1:Majordomo Listserver,,,:/usr/majordomo:/nonexistent
qwor0666:*:13294:2007:QUENTIN WORTHINGTON:/home/qwor0666:/bin/tcsh
daemon:*:1:31:The devil himself:/root:/sbin/nologin
operator:*:2:5:System &:/operator:/sbin/nologin
nobody:*:32767:32767:Unprivileged user:/nonexistent:/sbin/nologin
bin:*:3:7:Binaries Commands and Source,,,:/:/sbin/nologin
uucp:*:66:1:UNIX-to-UNIX Copy:/var/spool/uucppublic:/usr/libexec/uucp
```

```
{144}  cut -c1 testA
M
V
R
S
```

This command will display the first character of testA. The file doesn't change.

```
{145}  cut -c2 testA
a
i
o
h
```

Here we cut the second character only of each line.

```
{146}  cut -c1-5 testA
Matth
Vilhj
Roald
Sherp
```

Now we cut the first five characters.

```
```

```
{147} cut -f1 testA
Matthew
Vilhjalmur
Roald        :Amundsen  :SPole    :1911
Sherpa       :Tenzing   :Everest  :1953
{148} cut -f1 -d: testA
Matthew
Vilhjalmur
Roald
Sherpa
{149} cut -f4 -d: testA
1909
1910
1911
1953
{1507} cut -f3 -d: testA
NPole
Arctic
SPole
Everest
{151} cut -f3 -d: passy
0
10000
1001
1002
1003
        (. . . etc.)
{152} cat testA
Matthew    :Henson     :NPole    :1909
Vilhjalmur :Stefansson :Arctic   :1910
Roald      :Amundsen   :SPole    :1911
Sherpa     :Tenzing    :Everest:1953
{153} cut -f1 -d: testA > col1
{154} cat col1
Matthew
Vilhjalmur
Roald
Sherpa
{155} cut -f2 -d: testA > col2
{156} cut -f3 -d: testA > col3
{157} cut -f4 -d: testA > col4
{158} paste col1 col2 col3 col4
Matthew    Henson      NPole     1909
Vilhjalmur Stefansson  Arctic    1910
Roald      Amundsen    SPole     1911
Sherpa     Tenzing     Everest 1953
{159} paste col3 col2 col1
NPole      Henson      Matthew
Arctic     Stefansson  Vilhjalmur
SPole      Amundsen    Roald
Everest    Tenzing     Sherpa
{160} paste col3 col2 col1 > testC
```

We try to cut only the first field. However, it is again the tab character which doesn't give us the result we expect because only the first two lines have these characters.

First we specify that the colon (:) should be used as a field delimiter, and not the tab character, by using the -d option. Then we ask it to cut the first field. Now we get what we expect.

Here we cut the fourth field using the colon as the delimiter, and it works.

Here is the third field.

Here is the third field of passy. Only the first few lines are shown to conserve space.

Here is testA again.

Take the first field and store it in a file called col1. Here is col1.

Similarly, take the second field and store it in col2. The third field is placed in col3, and the fourth field is placed in col4. Using the paste command we can now reconstruct the file using the four "col" files.

They can be pasted together in any order.

The output of the paste can be redirected to a file.

```
{161} cat testC
NPole       Henson          Matthew
Arctic      Stefansson      Vilhjalmur
SPole       Amundsen        Roald
Everest     Tenzing         Sherpa
{162} tr '[A-Z]' '[a-z]' < testC
npole       henson          matthew
arctic      stefansson      vilhjalmur
spole       amundsen        roald
everest     tenzing         sherpa
{163} tr '[a-z]' '[A-Z]' < testC
NPOLE       HENSON          MATTHEW
ARCTIC      STEFANSSON      VILHJALMUR
SPOLE       AMUNDSEN        ROALD
EVEREST     TENZING         SHERPA
{164} tr '[a-z]' '[A-Z]' testC
usage:  tr [-cs] string1 string2
        tr [-c] -d string1
        tr [-c] -s string1
        tr [-c] -ds string1 string2
{165} exit
```

Here we name it testC.

The transpose command does not take a filename as an argument, so a file has to be redirected for input.
All upper–case letters are converted to lower–case letters.

Here the order is different: all lower–case letters are made upper–case. [a–z] means all lower–case letters from a to z, and [A–Z] means all upper–case letters from A to Z.

Here we try to provide the filename, testC, as an argument to the transpose command, and it fails. The file must be provided using the input redirection symbol (<).

That's enough for this unit!

EXPERIMENTS

```
%echo 1111 > file1
%cat file1


%cat file1 > file2
%cat file2


%cat > file3
eric harrison
suzy simon
becky sutphen
martha dear
dwayne Sutter
^d
%ls file*


%cat file3
```

Standard Input and Output

5.1 What does this echo command do when used with the redirection operator? (See Unit 2)
Does it create a file?

5.2 What does this cat command do when used with the redirection operator? If you have to think about it, see Unit 2.

5.3 After you type this command, you will lose your prompt. Notice that no filename is given between the cat and the redirection operator. Type in these names exactly as given, watching for upper–case characters, and terminate the list with a <Ctrl>d. <Ctrl>d is the end–of–file character in UNIX. (In DOS, the end–of–file character is <Ctrl>z.) We will be using this file for a while.
Was a file created?
What is the advantage of creating a file this way over using the echo command? Over using a text editor?
Usually the cat command needs a filename. Since no filename is given right after the cat, the default is taken to be the console. Whatever is typed on the console is the input for cat, whose output is then redirected to file3.
Important! The keyboard has become the input file to the "cat" command. Hence, the keyboard is called *standard input*.

```
%sort file3
```

5.4 Before we look at another example where the input file is taken from the console, explain what this command does.

```
%sort file3 > file4
%cat file4
```

5.5 Instead of having this command show the output, let us redirect it to file4. What is in file4 now?

```
%sort > file5
susan
wendy
bobby
marty
^d
%cat file5
```

5.6 Note the similarity between this experiment and Experiment 5.3. We are sorting a file and we don't provide the input file that is to be sorted, so where is the input file taken for the sort command? To which file is the output of the sort command redirected?

```
%sort < file3
```

5.7 We can also redirect the input. Instead of sorting file3, we do a sort and redirect the input to this command. Where is the input for this command coming from? Is the result of this any different from that of Experiment 5.4?

```
%cat < file3
```

5.8 Where is the input for this command coming from? Is the result of this any different from that of cat file3?

```
%sort < file3 > file4
%cat file4
```

5.9 We can redirect the input as well as the output. Is the result of this any different from that of Experiment 5.5?

```
%sort > file4 < file3
%cat < file1 > file2
%cat file2
```

5.10 Redirecting the input is not used as much as redirecting the output.

```
%cat > file2 < file1
```

5.11 What happens if we don't redirect the output? Where does the output go? This has a simple answer. It is the screen or display. The display is called *standard output*.

```
%cat
eric
eric
tom
tom
becky
becky
^d
```

5.12 Here is an interesting experiment. Type in the three names shown here and terminate the input with a <Ctrl>d. We are executing the cat command but we are not providing the name of the input file. So where is the input taken from? (Fill in the blanks.) It is taken from standard _____. Likewise, since no output file is specified, where does the output go? It is placed in standard _____. This may also be called the console.

```
%sort
```

5.13 Do the same experiment with the sort command. Type in the three names and terminate the input with a <Ctrl>d. Show your screen. Where are the input and output files assumed to be?

wc, grep, and more

```
%wc file3
```

5.14 Now we are ready to cover the concept of pipes. But first, let us explore some more UNIX commands. Using the

Basic File Manipulation

```
%wc -l file3
```

```
%wc -w file3
```

files created thus far, file3 and file5, explain what the following commands and options do. Also, show the result of the display on your left. How can this command help you write an essay?

```
%grep su file3 file5
```

5.15 "grep" stands for global regular expression print. What is the effect of executing these commands? Can you explain them without looking them up? Try other combinations and other files until you can explain these.

```
%grep [sS]u file3
```

```
%sh
$grep [sS]u file3
```

Here we are looking for upper case "S" and lower case "s". Does grep work in csh?
Does it work in Bourne shell?

```
$exit
%grep -i su file3
```

What does the option "i" do?

```
%grep -l su *
```

What does the option "l" do?

```
%grep -li su *
```

```
%grep -ci su *
```

What does the option "c" do?

```
%more /etc/passwd
```

5.16 The /etc/passwd file has information about all the users on the machine. This should be a good-sized file that will help us play with a few commands. While still in more, explain the purpose of each of these keystrokes:

<Return> or <Enter>
<Space>
h
/ler   Do you see this pattern on the top line?
n   Do a couple of "n"s right after the "/ler".
?ler
b
1G
q

```
%grep ramteke /etc/passwd
```

5.17 If you are just looking to see if someone has an account on the system, replace my name with their name here and you won't have to go through more.

```
%tail -4 /etc/passwd
```

5.18 What do these commands do?

```
%head -15 /etc/passwd
```

```
%head /etc/passwd
```

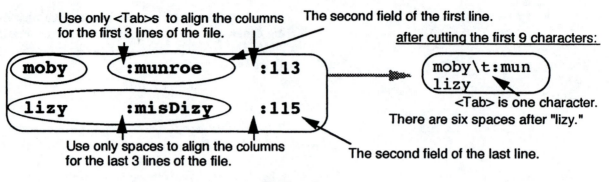

Use only <Tab>s to align the columns for the first 3 lines of the file.

The second field of the first line.

after cutting the first 9 characters:

<Tab> is one character.
There are six spaces after "lizy."

Use only spaces to align the columns for the last 3 lines of the file.

The second field of the last line.

Figure 5.1

5.19 Now create the file called eng1 as shown below using a text editor. For the first three lines use only tabs to separate the columns. For the last three lines use only spaces and not tabs to separate the fields. Because we cannot see whether we used spaces or tabs when we display a file, these experiments will illustrate that whenever a flat file is created it is best to use colons rather just than spaces and tabs to separate the fields. Do not forget the colons. They will determine where the fields begin.

See Figure 5.1. In this file, just before :munroe, and :113, there are <Tab> characters which are not visible on the screen. There are six spaces following lizy but no <Tab>s. If this file were to be sorted by the second field or if the second field were to be extracted from each line, processing would be done on munroe and 115 because fields are separated by the <Tab> characters by default. And these items follow the first <Tab> character on the line on which they are, so they are considered to be the second fields.

If the first nine characters were to be "cut" from each line to create a new file, then the first line would be "moby\t:mun" instead of just "moby   ". This is because the <Tab> character is taken to be one character, although it looks like five spaces on the screen. The last line of the file extracts just the first field, because there are no tabs but spaces here.

In summary, when creating a file that may need some processing, either have the same number of tabs before each field on every line, or use a field delimiter like a colon (:) just before every field. In the following few experiments both ways of file handling will be explored.

This file is called engl:

```
moby            :munroe     :113
serena          :stew       :111
melis           :binde      :112
osie            :stewart    :110
matt            :schaffer   :114
lizy            :misDizy    :115

%sed s/://g engl
```

5.20 Now let us create another file using engl.
sed is a stream editor, that is, it edits whole files at a time. In this command, we substituted every colon with what?
The "g" means to substitute all occurrences of the colon in a line.

```
%sed s/://g engl > eng
%cat eng
```

Does this command show the control characters on your system, like the <Tab>s?
We'll come back to the sed editor.

```
%sed 'l' eng
```

Sorting

5.21 When we sort the file with the colons and the one without the colons by the first set of characters, is there a difference in how they are sorted?

```
%sort eng
```

```
%sort engl
```

```
%sort +2 eng
```

5.22 Is there a difference in the sort of the two files when we sort by the third field? The "–t:" specifies the colon as the delimiter for fields. The default is tab. To use a space for a delimiter, we would use: –t" ".

```
%sort +2 -t: engl
```

If you had to sort files by some field other than the first field, how should you create the file so that the sorting would be easy?

```
%sort +1r -t: engl
```

What does the option of "r" do?
How would you sort the file on the third field?

```
%head -40 /etc/passwd > pass1
%sort +4 -t: pass1 | more
```

5.23 Let us sort part of the passwd file.
See Figure 5.2 for the format of the /etc/passwd file.
Which field number is sorted?

```
%cp eng engx
%sort engx > engx
%cat engx
%ls -l engx
```

5.24 Can you sort a file and redirect the output to itself?
What happens?
What is the file size of engx?

```
%cp eng engx
%sort -o engx engx
%cat engx
```

5.25 What does the sort with the "o" option allow you to do?

How would you have to sort out engx if this option weren't available? List the steps.

```
%cut -c1 eng
```

Cut and Paste

5.26 What do these cut options do?

```
%cut -c1-9 eng
```

```
%cut -c1,3 eng.
```

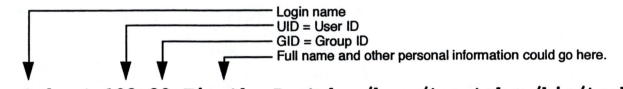

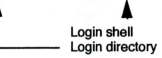

Figure 5.2

```
%cut -f1 eng
```

5.27 When we cut the file with the colons and then without the colons by the first field, is there a difference?
When specifying the field delimiter in the sort command, what option was used?
What option is used with cut?

```
%cut -f1 -d: engl
```

```
%cut -f2 eng
```

5.28 Is there a difference when we cut by the second field?

When specifying the second field in the sort command, what number was used?
What number is used with cut?

```
%cut -f2 -d: engl
```

```
%cut -f2 -d: engl > temp1
%cut -f3 -d: engl > temp2
%paste temp2 temp1
```

5.29 Accurately describe what the paste command does.

```
%paste temp2 temp1 > temp3
%more temp3
```

Transpose and sed

```
%tr '[A-Z]' '[a-z]' < eng
```

5.30 What is happening here? Make sure you use the quote next to the <Return> key. Remember that "[A–Z]" means all upper–case characters.

```
%tr '[A-Z]' '[a-z]' eng
```

Do we have to use input redirection?
Why?

```
%tr '[a-z]' '[A-Z]' < eng
```

```
%tr '\011' ' ' < temp1 > temp2
%more temp2
```

5.31 "\011" is the ASCII code for the <Tab> character. All <Tab>s in temp2 have been replaced by what character?

```
%tr ' ' '\012' < temp2 >temp3
%more temp3
```

"\012" is the ASCII code for the newline character. The file temp3 now doesn't have which two characters? Do the blank lines have any characters?

```
%sed '/^$/d' temp3 > temp4
%more temp4
```

5.32 What did sed do to temp3? The "/d" means to delete lines in sed.

```
%cp temp1 temp2
%sed /binde/d temp1 > temp3
%more temp3
```

5.33 What did this sed command do?

Basic File Manipulation

HOMEWORK

1. Explain what these commands do if they are typed in as shown:
   a. `cut —c3—5 file1`
   b. `sort +2 file1`
   c. `paste file1 file2`
   d. `cat > file1`
   e. `sort file1 > file2`
   f. `cut —d: —f1 /etc/passwd`
   g. `head`

2. Explain the purpose of each field in the /etc/passwd file.
3. When creating a flat file in UNIX, by which character should each field be separated? What can happen if spaces and tabs are used instead?

Standard I/O:
4. Give the command that will accomplish each of the following tasks:
   a. Show the first four characters of the file being typed on the keyboard.
   b. Enter a file from the keyboard and save it as memoA.
   c. Enter a file from the keyboard and immediately display it on the screen. No file is saved.
   d. Display memoA on the screen two ways.
   e. Copy memoA to memoB two ways.
   f. Sort memoA and save the sorted version in memoB.

wc, grep, head, and tail:
5. Give the command that will accomplish each of the following tasks:
   a. Show only the number of lines in memoA.
   b. Show only the lines which have the "bat" pattern in them.
   c. Count the number of lines which have the "bat" pattern in them.
   d. Show only the file names in the current directory which have the "bat" pattern.
   e. Show only the lines which have the "bat" pattern in them, whether it is in lower-case or upper-case letters.
   f. Show the last 10 lines of memoA.
   g. Show the last 20 lines of memoA.
   h. Show the first 8 lines of /etc/passwd.
   i. Show the last 8 lines of /etc/group.

more:
6. Give the keystrokes on your computer to do the following while in more. Some may not work.
   a. Get help.
   b. Quit.
   c. Search for the pattern "bat" forwards.
   d. Search for the pattern "bat" backward.
   e. Go to the beginning of the file.
   f. Scroll one line forward.
   g. Scroll one page forward.
   h. Scroll one page backward.

sort, cut, and paste:
7. Give the command that will accomplish each of the following tasks:
   a. Sort out memoA and save the sorted version into memoA using one command.
   b. Display memoA and memoB side by side on the screen as two columns.
   c. Display memoB and then memoA side by side on the screen as two columns.
   d. Store the output of memoA and memoB side by side as two columns as memoC.

e. Show only the first 10 characters of every line of memoA.
f. Display the second field of memoA, using tabs as field delimiters.
g. Display the second field of memoA, using # characters as field delimiters.
h. Store the third field of memoA in memoB, using <Space> as a field delimiter.
i. Store the sorted version of memoA in memoB, using a colon (:) as a field delimiter and using the second field as the sorting field.
j. Display memoA sorted, using a colon (:) as a field delimiter and using the third field as the sorting field.
k. Display memoA sorted, using the first field as the sorting field, regardless of the delimiting character.
l. Sort out the last 20 lines of the /etc/passwd file using the group ID as the field delimiter. You may need more than one command to do this.
m. Display only the user ID of all accounts who have the "joe" pattern in them, regardless of whether it is upper–case or lower–case. This display should be sorted by their user IDs. Again, you may need more than one command to do this.

sed and tr:
8. Give the command that will accomplish each of the following tasks:
    a. Find out where all the tabs and carriage returns are in memoA.
    b. Convert all lower–case letters of memoA to upper–case letters and save the result in memoB.
    c. Convert all spaces of memoA to carriage returns and save the output to memoB.
    d. Delete all empty lines of memoA and save the output to memoB. These are lines which don't have any characters in them, even spaces.
    e. Delete all lines which have "bat" in them.

LAB ASSIGNMENTS

Create a script file for each assignment by first typing:

```
script lab5.1
```

then do all the following tasks, and do a <Ctrl>D or <Ctrl>C to terminate the script command. After that, find a way to print the file and submit it. You can use WS–FTP to do that or, while in telnet, you can pull down the terminal menu and select start logging. You can name the file telnet.log and save it on the desktop. You can then cat the lab5.1 file in UNIX and copy it in the telnet.log file. Once done, select stop logging from the terminal pull–down menu. Go to the desktop. Using Word or another word processer, open telnet.log and print it through Windows.

1. Using the cat command, create this file called lab1:

```
Marvin Gaye
Hank Williams
Ray Charles
Jimmy Ruffin
Aretha Franklin
```

    a. Show only the last names.
    b. Sort the list by last names.
    c. Create a file called lab2 which has the last name, a comma, and then the first name for each line.
    d. Show the number of characters in the file.

e. Show the lines which have the "in" pattern.
f. Count the lines which have the "in" pattern.
g. Show only the last three lines of the file.
h. Convert all lower–case letters to upper–case letters and save the file in a file called lab3.

2. Create a file called passes that contains the last 30 lines of the /etc/passwd file. Then do all the operations using the passes file. Do not use the /etc/passwd file for the following steps.
   a. Display the entries of users who belong to a particular group.
   b. Show only the full names of these users.
   c. Sort the file in the order of user IDs. Save the sorted file as passes. Do not use any temporary file to do this sorting.
   d. Change all the colons to double colons. Here you may use a temporary file to alter the passes file. Delete the temporary file which you may have created.
   e. Show all lines which have the characters "son" in them, either upper–case or lower–case.

Advanced File Manipulation

CONCEPTS TO LEARN

Filter: A command which takes its input from standard input, performs some operation on that input, and sends the results to standard output is called a filter. For example, the cat command is a filter since it can take its input from the keyboard and show its output on the screen. The echo and the ls commands are not filters since they can't take their input from the keyboard.

Piping: An output from one command can be used as the input to another command. This is done by using the pipe (|) symbol. Using this technique several commands can be used together as if they were one command. Piping also eliminates the need to create temporary files in certain cases. Only filters can be used after a pipe. If you wanted to find out all users in the /etc/passwd file who have "jim" as their name and then sort out those users, one way to do that would be as follows:

```
$  grep —i jim /etc/passwd > tempfile       (Create a file which has all "jim" accounts.)
$  sort  tempfile                           (Sort all "jim" accounts.)
$  rm  tempfile                             (Delete the file which was created to do only this task.)
```

Using a pipe, the same operation can be done more succinctly as follows:

```
$  grep —i jim /etc/passwd | sort
```

Here the output of the grep command, which is a list of all "jim" accounts, is fed directly into the sort command as input. The output of the sort command is then shown on the screen. No temporary file is necessary.

Tape archiving: Using a utility called tar, covered in the following section, several files can be combined as one file. This is useful when you need to handle a group of files as if they were one file, whether you are writing them to an external device or transferring them to another host. This command is not used just for tape drives.

COMMANDS TO LEARN

comm   Compares two sorted files. Three columns are displayed. The first column shows all lines which are unique to the first file, the second column shows all lines which

	are unique to the second file, and the third column shows all lines which are common to both files.
–1	Does not show the first column.
–2	Does not show the second column.
–3	Does not show the third column.
diff	When used with two filenames as arguments, this command shows the lines which are different between the two files. This is a handy command when one needs to find the differences between two files which are almost identical. Also see sdiff.

find ~ –name "filename*"	This command was covered in Unit 3. The paths of files whose names begin with "filename" are printed on the screen. The search is made within the login directory (~). The ~ could also be a dot, meaning the current directory or any other path.
\!	Adding this before the pattern negates the pattern.
–atime 1	This option selects all files which were accessed within the last day.
–exec cat { } \;	This option will execute the cat command on those files which were selected. The cat command could be any command which takes filenames as arguments.
–mtime 1	This option selects files which were modified or created within the last day.
–ok rm { } \;	This option is the same as the exec option, except that the user is prompted for yes and no for each file which is selected. In this example, we will be asked if we want to delete each file that meets the find condition.
–print	This option will simply print the filenames which were selected.
–user ramteke	This selects the files whose owner is ramteke.

ftp	Allows you to transfer files to and from another host. ftp stands for "file transfer protocol."
gzip	Compresses a file. Usually .zip is added as an extension to the file name.
gunzip	Uncompresses a compressed file.
sdiff –s	Similar to the diff command, this command displays lines which are different between two files.

tar	Allows you to create one file out of many. Usually the .tar extension will be added to the file name. All subdirectories are also included, if there are any. After this command, the gzip utility can be used to compress the file.
–c	This creates the tar file.
–t	This option allows one to see the table of contents of the tar file as if one were doing an ls –l.
–x	This will extract the files from a tar file.
–vf	The v for verbose option asks to have messages displayed and the f option indicates that the file name is being provided.

uniq	If a sorted file has duplicate lines, this command will show each line only once.
–u	This option will show only the lines which appear once in the file.
–d	This option will show only the duplicated lines in the file.
whereis	This command looks for executable files in standard binary directories. It shows system commands which are executable by the user. The paths that this looks for are system defined.
which –a	This command looks for executable commands which are available in a user-defined path. The –a option shows all commands and not just the first one.

SAMPLE SESSION

```
% {103} sort > africa1
Casablanca
Lagos
Malange
Bulawayo
^d
% {104} sort > africa2
Lagos
Casablanca
Malange
Kinshasa
^d
% {105} cat africa1
Bulawayo
Casablanca
Lagos
Malange
% {106} cat africa2
Casablanca
Kinshasa
Lagos
Malange
% {107} sort africa1 africa2 > africa3
% {108} diff africa1 africa2
1d0
< Bulawayo
2a2
> Kinshasa
% {109} sdiff -s africa1 africa2
Bulawayo
<
> Kinshasa

% {110} comm africa1 africa2
Bulawayo
                        Casablanca
        Kinshasa
                        Lagos
                        Malange
% {111} comm -2 africa1 africa2
Bulawayo
        Casablanca
        Lagos
        Malange
% {112} comm -3 africa1 africa2
Bulawayo
        Kinshasa
% {113} comm -13 africa1 africa2
Kinshasa
% {114} comm -31 africa1 africa2
Kinshasa
```

Working With Similar Files

Here, we are creating a file called africa1 by providing African cities from standard input. The sort command will sort these names and store them in a file called africa1.

Using the same method we create another file. This one we call africa2.

Here is the content of africa1.

And here is africa2.

africa3 is created by merging africa1 and africa2. We will come back to africa3 later.

Two files which are almost identical can be compared using the diff command. Disregard the 1d0 and the 2a2 codes. They are not important to understand. Remember to use the man command on any of the commands to get more information about them. Here, the sdiff command does the same thing. It shows that Bulawayo appears in africa1 but not in africa2. Also, Kinshasa appears in africa2 but not in africa1.

The comm command shows three columns. The first column, which has Bulawayo in it, gives the lines which occur only in africa1. The second column, Kinshasa, gives the lines which are unique to africa2, and the third column shows all common lines. africa1 and africa2 should be sorted first.

Here, the second column, Kinshasa, is not shown.

The third column with all the common lines is not shown.

Here, the first and the third columns are not shown.

The order of the options, 1 and 3, is not important.

```
% {115} comm -21 africa1 africa2          Columns 1 and 2 are not shown.
Casablanca
Lagos
Malange
% {117} cat africa3                       In command 107, we created africa3 using africa1 and africa2.
Bulawayo                                  Here is its content. Notice, the common lines are duplicated.
Casablanca
Casablanca
Kinshasa
Lagos
Lagos
Malange
Malange
% {118} uniq africa3                      The uniq command shows all lines only once, even if they are
Bulawayo                                  duplicated.
Casablanca
Kinshasa
Lagos
Malange
% {119} uniq -d africa3                   The –d option will show only the lines which are duplicated.
Casablanca
Lagos
Malange
% {120} uniq -u africa3                   And the –u option will show only those lines which are
Bulawayo                                  unique, or that appear only once.
Kinshasa
```

More on the Find Command

```
% {121} mkdir dir1 dir2
% {124} mv africa1 dir1
% {125} pwd
/home/tramteke
```

We looked at this useful command in Unit 3. Let us look at it again. We first create two directories called dir1 and dir2 and move the africa1 file to dir1. Currently we are in the login directory.

```
% {126} find ~ -name "africa*" -print
/home/tramteke/africa2
/home/tramteke/africa3
/home/tramteke/dir1/africa1
% {129} ls -1
total 16
-rw-r--r--    1 tramteke    africa2
-rw-r--r--    1 tramteke    africa3
-rw-r--r--    1 tramteke    courses.txt
drwxr-xr-x    2 tramteke    dir1
drwxr-xr-x    2 tramteke    dir2
drwx------    2 tramteke    mail
% {130} find ~ -name "africa1" -print
/home/tramteke/dir1/africa1
```

This find command starts looking in the login directory because of the tilde (~). Because the –name option specifies all file names which begin with africa, our three africa files are selected. africa2 and africa3 are in the login directory and africa1 is in dir1. The –print option displays these filenames and their paths on the screen.

The ls command shows that africa2 and africa3 are still in the login directory, while africa1 is not here.

This find command shows again that africa1 is in dir1.

```
% {133} find ~ -name "africa2" -exec cat {} \;
Casablanca
Kinshasa
```

Here file africa2 is searched. All the selected files, in this case only africa2, are placed in the braces { } by the system. The –exec option executes the cat command on the files

```
Lagos
Malange
```

which are in the braces. Finally, the semicolon terminates the command with the backslash acting as a quote for the semicolon.

```
% {134} find ~ -name "africa*" -ok cat {} \;
"cat  /home/tramteke/africa2"? n
"cat  /home/tramteke/africa3"? n
"cat  /home/tramteke/dir1/africa1"? y
Bulawayo
Casablanca
Lagos
Malange
```

With "africa*", all the africa files are selected. And with the –ok option, only those files for which a y is entered are printed out because of the cat command provided.

```
% {135} find ~ \! -name "africa*" -print
/home/tramteke
/home/tramteke/courses.txt
/home/tramteke/mail
/home/tramteke/.history
/home/tramteke/.login
/home/tramteke/dir1
/home/tramteke/dir2
```

Here we find that all files which do not begin with "africa" are selected. The \! symbols indicate negation.

```
% {143} find ~ -mtime 1 -print
/home/tramteke
/home/tramteke/.history
/home/tramteke/africa2
/home/tramteke/africa3
/home/tramteke/dir1
/home/tramteke/dir1/africa1
/home/tramteke/dir2
```

The –mtime 1 option finds all files which were modified or created within the last day. The .history file is automatically updated whenever we enter a new command. The africa files and the directories were created in this session.

```
% {144} find ~ -atime 1 -print
/home/tramteke
/home/tramteke/mail
/home/tramteke/.cshrc
/home/tramteke/.history
/home/tramteke/africa2
/home/tramteke/.login
/home/tramteke/africa3
/home/tramteke/dir1
/home/tramteke/dir1/africa1
/home/tramteke/dir2
```

The –atime 1 option finds all files which have been accessed within the last day. All the files from the –mtime 1 option are shown here because files which were created or modified within the last day also had to be accessed. The .login and the .cshrc files were accessed by the system when we first logged in.

Piping

Here, we have who is logged on our system. The IP addresses or host addresses in parentheses are where each person is logged in from. I am tramteke and I am logged in from the computer called ann.com.

```
% {150} who
brancone   pts/0   Sep    4  08:50   (TURBO.Kean.EDU)
anderman   pts/1   Sep    4  08:39   (207.207.219.131)
damiller   pts/2   Sep    4  09:55   (146.203.2.135)
kkaplan    pts/4   Aug   25  09:22   (margarita.njin.net)
samkim     pts/5   Aug   29  21:10   (babbage-asy-1.rutgers.edu)
tramteke   pts/8   Sep    4  11:03   (ann.com)
```

Advanced File Manipulation

```
        ┌──► brancone pts/0 Sep  4 ─┐                    ┌► brancone pts/0 Sep   4
        │    anderman pts/1 Sep  4  │                    │  anderman pts/1 Sep   4
 who ───┤    damiller pts/2 Sep  4  ├─► grep Sep ───────►│  damiller pts/2 Sep   4
        │    kkaplan  pts/4 Aug 25  │                    └► tramteke pts/8 Sep   4
        │    samkim   pts/5 Aug 29  │
        └──► tramteke pts/8 Sep  4 ─┘
```

% {151} **who | grep Sep**
```
brancone pts/0 Sep   4 08:50  (TURBO.Kean.EDU)
anderman pts/1 Sep   4 08:39  (207.207.219.131)
damiller pts/2 Sep   4 09:55  (146.203.2.135)
tramteke pts/8 Sep   4 11:03  (ann.com)
```

As shown in the figure above, the who command lists all the users who are currently logged on. We use the pipe symbol (|) to feed this output into the grep command to find out who has logged on in the month of September. Then only those lines are displayed.

% {152} **who | grep an**
```
brancone pts/0 Sep   4 08:50  (TURBO.Kean.EDU)
anderman pts/1 Sep   4 08:39  (207.207.219.131)
kkaplan  pts/4 Aug 25 09:22  (margarita.njin.net)
tramteke pts/8 Sep   4 11:03  (ann.com)
```

This pipeline shows all the lines which have the characters "an" in them from the output of who.

% {153} **who | cut -c1-9**
```
brancone
anderman
damiller
kkaplan
samkim
tramteke
```

Here, the output of the who command is fed into the cut command to select columns 1 through 9. The rest of the columns are not displayed.

% {155} **who | cut -f1 -d(**
```
Too many ('s.
```

% {156} **who | cut -f1 -d"("**
```
brancone pts/0 Sep   4 08:50
anderman pts/1 Sep   4 08:39
damiller pts/2 Sep   4 09:55
kkaplan  pts/4 Aug 25 09:22
samkim   pts/5 Aug 29 21:10
tramteke pts/8 Sep   4 11:03
```

Oops! This message means that I need quotes around the parentheses. Here, the output of the who command is piped into the cut command. The cut command selects the first field using the (as the field delimiter. Hence, all the characters up to the first (become the first field. This field is then displayed.

% {157} **who | sort**
```
anderman pts/1 Sep   4 08:39  (207.207.219.131)
brancone pts/0 Sep   4 08:50  (TURBO.Kean.EDU)
damiller pts/2 Sep   4 09:55  (146.203.2.135)
kkaplan  pts/4 Aug 25 09:22  (margarita.njin.net)
tramteke pts/8 Sep   4 11:03  (ann.com)
samkim   pts/5 Aug 29 21:10  (babbage-asy-1.rutgers.edu)
```

The output of who becomes the input of the sort command. Notice, all lines are sorted using the first characters of each line as the sorting field.

% {158} **who | sort +1 -t"("**
```
damiller pts/2 Sep   4 09:55  (146.203.2.135)
anderman pts/1 Sep   4 08:39  (207.207.219.131)
brancone pts/0 Sep   4 08:50  (TURBO.Kean.EDU)
tramteke pts/8 Sep   4 11:03  (ann.com)
samkim   pts/5 Aug 29 21:10  (babbage-asy-1.rutgers.edu)
kkaplan  pts/4 Aug 25 09:22  (margarita.njin.net)
```

Here, the sorting field is the host address or IP address which follows the parenthesis. The +1 indicates to skip the first field and sort on the second.

Advanced File Manipulation

```
                              who
      brancone  pts/0 Sep   4 08:50  (TURBO.Kean.EDU)
      anderman  pts/1 Sep   4 08:39  (207.207.219.131)
      damiller  pts/2 Sep   4 09:55  (146.203.2.135)
      kkaplan   pts/4 Aug  25 09:22  (margarita.njin.net)
      samkim    pts/5 Aug  29 21:10  (babbage-asy-1.rutgers.edu)
      tramteke  pts/8 Sep   4 11:03  (ann.com)

                          sort +1 -t"("

      damiller  pts/2 Sep   4 09:55  (146.203.2.135)
      anderman  pts/1 Sep   4 08:39  (207.207.219.131)
      brancone  pts/0 Sep   4 08:50  (TURBO.Kean.EDU)
      tramteke  pts/8 Sep   4 11:03  (ann.com)
      samkim    pts/5 Aug  29 21:10  (babbage-asy-1.rutgers.edu)
      kkaplan   pts/4 Aug  25 09:22  (margarita.njin.net)

                        cut -f2 -d"("

           (146.203.2.135)
           (207.207.219.131)
           (TURBO.Kean.EDU)
           (ann.com)
           (babbage-asy-1.rutgers.edu)
           (margarita.njin.net)
```

```
% {161} who | sort +1 -t"(" | cut -f2 -d"("
146.203.2.135)
207.207.219.131)
TURBO.Kean.EDU)
ann.com)
babbage-asy-1.rutgers.edu)
margarita.njin.net)
```

Studying the figure above, we see that in this command the output of who becomes the input to the sort command. The sort command again sorts out the field with host names and addresses. The output of the sort command is then piped into the cut command which shows only the second field.

```
% {162} who | cut -f1 | sort
anderman  pts/1 Sep   4 08:39
brancone  pts/0 Sep   4 08:50
damiller  pts/2 Sep   4 09:55
kkaplan   pts/4 Aug  25 09:22
tramteke  pts/8 Sep   4 11:03
samkim    pts/5 Aug  29 21:10
```

With this command, the first field is cut. No field delimiter is provided, so the tab character is used as a field delimiter by default. The first tab character on each line appears after the time field and hence those characters are treated as the first field. The output of that field is then sorted.

```
% {163} who | cut -f1 -d" " | sort
anderman
brancone
damiller
kkaplan
tramteke
samkim
```

Here we cut the first field and then sort it. The first field is specified up to the first space denoted by " ".

Advanced File Manipulation

```
% {164} who | sort | cut -f1 -d" "
anderman
brancone
damiller
kkaplan
tramteke
samkim
```

Here we do the same operation as in command 163, but in reverse order. We first sort the output of the who command and then cut the first field.

```
% {165} who | grep an | sort | cut -f1 -d" "
anderman
brancone
kkaplan
tramteke
```

First, all lines with "an" are selected. tramteke, who is logged on from ann.com, is selected. Then those lines are sorted and cut.

```
% {166} who | sort | cut -f1 -d" " | grep an
anderman
brancone
kkaplan
```

Here, the order is different and tramteke is not selected because by the time grep looks for the "an", the field containing it is cut off.

```
% {167} who | sort | cut -f1 -d" " | grep an > file1
% {171} cat file1
anderman
brancone
kkaplan
```

The output of a pipeline can be redirected to a file, such as this one.

```
% {172} who | sort | tee file2 | cut -f1 -d" " | tee file3 | grep an
anderman
brancone
kkaplan
```

This command is illustrated in the following figure:

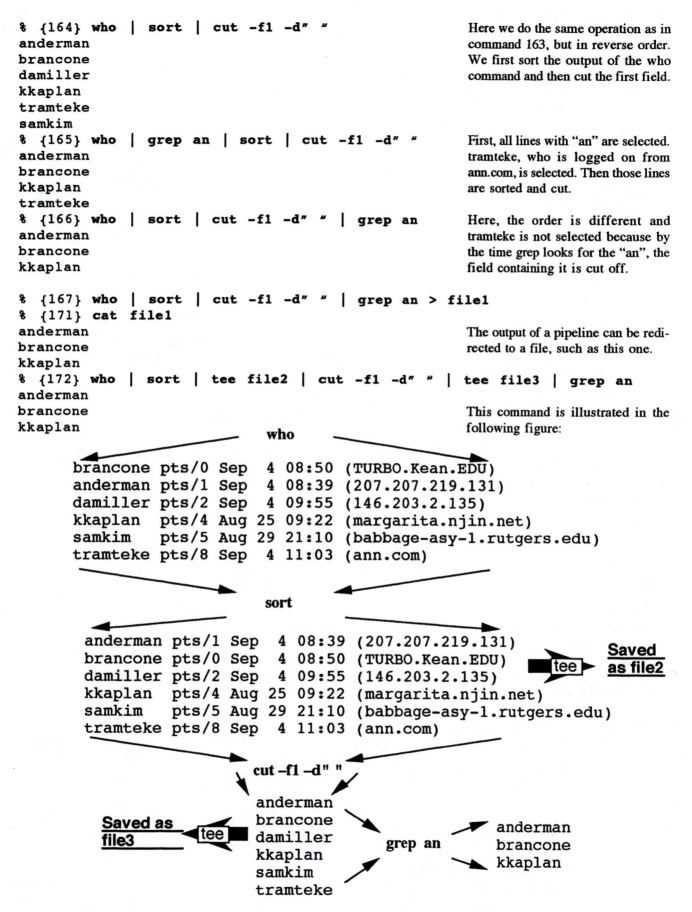

```
% {173} cat file2
anderman  pts/1 Sep   4 08:39 (207.207.219.131)
brancone  pts/0 Sep   4 08:50 (TURBO.Kean.EDU)
damiller  pts/2 Sep   4 09:55 (146.203.2.135)
kkaplan   pts/4 Aug  25 09:22 (margarita.njin.net)
samkim    pts/5 Aug  29 21:10 (babbage-asy-1.rutgers.edu)
tramteke  pts/8 Sep   4 11:03 (ann.com)
% {174} cat file3
anderman
brancone
damiller
kkaplan
samkim
tramteke
```

The output of the who command is sorted. The output of the sort command becomes the input to the cut command. However, because of the tee option, this intermediate result is stored in file2. Similarly, the output of the cut command is saved in the file called file3 and piped into the grep command. When we print out file2 and file3, we confirm that those intermediate results were indeed saved there.

More Piping Examples

```
% {176} who | head -5
brancone  pts/0 Sep   4 08:50 (TURBO.Kean.EDU)
anderman  pts/1 Sep   4 08:39 (207.207.219.131)
damiller  pts/2 Sep   4 09:55 (146.203.2.135)
kkaplan   pts/4 Aug  25 09:22 (margarita.njin.net)
samkim    pts/5 Aug  29 21:10 (babbage-asy-1.rutgers.edu)
```

Here the output of who is piped into the head command to show the first five lines.

```
% {177} who | head -5 | tr '[a-z]' '[A-Z]'
BRANCONE  PTS/0 SEP   4 08:50 (TURBO.KEAN.EDU)
ANDERMAN  PTS/1 SEP   4 08:39 (207.207.219.131)
DAMILLER  PTS/2 SEP   4 09:55 (146.203.2.135)
KKAPLAN   PTS/4 AUG  25 09:22 (MARGARITA.NJIN.NET)
SAMKIM    PTS/5 AUG  29 21:10 (BABBAGE-ASY-1.RUTGERS.EDU)
```

The result from the head command is now piped into the transpose command to convert all lower-case letters to upper-case letters.

```
% {208} history | head
1   11:49    rm session1
2   11:49    cat testA
3   11:50    cat testB
4   11:50    rm testB
5   11:50    ls
6   11:50    cat testC
7   11:50    rm testC
8   11:50    cat u
9   11:50    more u
10  11:50    ls
```

The output of history is piped into the head command.

```
% {209} history | head | grep cat
2   11:49    cat testA
3   11:50    cat testB
6   11:50    cat testC
8   11:50    cat u
```

The output of the head command is piped into the grep command to show the times when the cat command was used.

```
% {212} ls -l
total 6
-rw-r--r--   1 tramteke    africa2
-rw-r--r--   1 tramteke    africa3
-rw-r--r--   1 tramteke    courses.txt
```

An ls -l will provide a long listing of the current directory.

Advanced File Manipulation

```
drwxr-xr-x    2  tramteke    dir1
drwxr-xr-x    2  tramteke    dir2
drwx------    2  tramteke    mail
% {210} ls -l | wc -l
7
% {211} ls
africa2         africa3         courses.txt
dir1            dir2            mail
% {214} ls | wc -w
6

% {216} ls | wc -c
43

% {217} date
Fri Sep  4 11:24:16 EDT 1998
% {218} date | cut -f2 -d" "
Sep
% {219} date | cut -f5 -d" "
11:25:37
% {220} echo la la la | wc -c
9
% {221} uptime
11:26AM   up 2 days, 21:15, 3 users

% {222} ls | uptime
11:26AM   up 2 days, 21:15, 3 users
```

If we pipe this listing into wc –l, we will count the number of lines that were in the output of the long listing. Here we have 7. This is approximately the number of files in our directory.

Another way to count the number of files in the current directory is to do a simple ls and then pipe that into wc –w, which counts the number of words. In this case, it would be the number of files. There are 6 in this case. This example counts the number of characters in the output of ls, which is not that useful.

If we cut the second field from the output of date, given the space (" ") as the delimiter, we get only the month.

Similarly, if we cut the fifth field, we get only the time.

We can count the number of characters in the output of an echo command.

uptime will show how long the UNIX server has been running since it was last rebooted.

uptime can't get its input from standard input, so it doesn't make any sense to pipe the output of ls into it. You see only the output of uptime here. All the commands previously used after the pipe symbol are not like uptime. They were filters. We should use only filters after a pipe. uptime, echo, date, ls, are all examples of non–filters which can't be used after a pipe. Piping ls into cat makes sense because cat is a filter.

```
% {223} ls | cat
africa2
africa3
courses.txt
dir1
dir2
mail
% {224} cat africa2 | ls
africa2         africa3         courses.txt
dir1            dir2            mail
% {225} ls | date
Fri Sep  4 11:27:33 EDT 1998
```

However, piping the output of cat into ls doesn't make sense. Only the output of ls is shown.

date is also a non–filter.

Handling of Many Files

Many times you will need to perform a certain operation on large files. Backing up files is one instance. In those cases, it is more convenient to handle a group of files as if they were one file. In the following example, we will get all our "africa" files into one directory. Then we will create what is called a tar file, which will combine all those files into one. Then we will compress the tar file so it takes less space to store. Then using the ftp command, we will transfer that compressed tar file to another host where I have an account. Then we will telnet to that host, uncompress that file into the tar file, and extract the "africa" files from it.

First, let us find the africa1 file and move it to the current directory.

```
% {227} find . -name "africa1" -exec mv {} . \;
% {228} ls
africa1         africa3         dir1
africa2         courses.txt     dir2
```
Now we have all three africa files in our current directory.

```
% {229} cd dir1
```
Let us go to the dir1 directory.

```
alankay:dir1 {130} ls
alankay:dir1 {131} mv ../af* .
```
Move the africa files there.

```
alankay:dir1 {132} ls
```
Here they are.

```
africa1 africa2 africa3
alankay:dir1 {133} tar -cvf $HOME/africa.tar .
.
./africa1
./africa2
./africa3
```
This tar command will create (using the –c option) the tar file in the login directory ($HOME/). The name of the file, following the –f option, is africa.tar. The –v option, for verbose, shows the filenames as they are archived into the tar file. The last dot is very important! It specifies the directory which is to be archived — the current working directory.

```
alankay:dir1 {134} cd
% {236} ls -l
total 32
-rw-r--r--   1 tramteke     africa.tar
-rw-r--r--   1 tramteke     courses.txt
drwxr-xr-x   2 tramteke     dir1
drwxr-xr-x   2 tramteke     dir2
```
Since the tar file was created in the home directory, let us change our directory to that directory. An ls –l shows the tar file that we just created.

The output of the ls –l is simplified so it doesn't take much space to show.

```
% {235} tar -tvf africa.tar
drwxr-xr-x   2 tramteke     .
-rw-r--r--   1 tramteke     ./africa1
-rw-r--r--   1 tramteke     ./africa2
-rw-r--r--   1 tramteke     ./africa3
```
Here we do a tar command on africa.tar. This time we use the –t option for table of contents. This command shows what is archived in the tar file as if it were a long listing.

```
% {237} gzip africa.tar
```
Then we compress the tar file using gzip.

```
% {238} ls -l
total 14
-rw-r--r--   1 tramteke africa.tar.gz
-rw-r--r--   1 tramteke courses.txt
drwxr-xr-x   2 tramteke dir1
drwxr-xr-x   2 tramteke dir2
```
Here, the .gz extension is added, and if the entire output of the ls –l were shown, you would see that the zipped file takes up less storage space.

```
% {239} ftp pilot.njin.net
Connected to tolip.njin.net.
220 tolip.njin.net FTP server (Rutgers Version 4.3) ready.
Name (pilot.njin.net:tramteke): ramteke
331 Password required for ramteke.
Password:
230 User ramteke logged in.
Remote system type is UNIX..
ftp> hash
Hash mark printing
ftp> put africa.tar.gz
#
226 Transfer complete.
```
Now let us transfer this file to my account on a host named pilot. We use ftp for that.

My login name is ramteke on pilot, not tramteke, so I give my correct login name. I enter my password.

I ask the ftp program to place a hash mark at fixed intervals as the data is transferred.

Now we transfer the africa.tar.gz file from our machine to pilot. A hash mark indicates that some data was

Advanced File Manipulation

```
267 bytes sent in 0.03 seconds
(8.91 KB/s)


ftp> quit
221 Goodbye.
% {240} telnet pilot.njin.net
Trying 165.230.224.139...
Connected to pilot.njin.net.
SunOS 5.6

login: ramteke
Password:
% {001} mkdir afr
% {002} ls
afr          africa.tar.gz
% {003} cp africa.tar.gz afr
% {004} cd afr
~/afr% {005} ls
africa.tar.gz
~/afr% {006} gunzip africa.tar.gz
~/afr% {011} ls -l
total 10
-rw-------   1 ramteke   africa.tar
~/afr% {012} tar -xvf africa.tar
.
./africa1
./africa2
./africa3
~/afr% {013} ls -l
total 13
-rw-------   1 ramteke   africa.tar
-rw-------   1 ramteke   africa1
-rw-------   1 ramteke   africa2
-rw-------   1 ramteke   africa3
~/afr% {014} rm africa.tar
~/afr% {015} cat africa1
Bulawayo
Casablanca
Lagos
Malange
~/afr% {016} logout
Connection closed by foreign host.
```

transferred. For a large file transfer this indication is nice to have so you know that something is happening and that the hosts are not idle. The final message indicates that the file transfer is complete and specifies the amount of data that was sent. Now, let us quit ftp.

Now let us log into pilot using telnet. We will first confirm that the file was transferred and then uncompress and extract the files.

Before we extract the files, let us create a directory called afr and extract and store the files in it. Notice, the file which was transferred is in the login directory for pilot.

Copy the file africa.tar.gz into the afr directory.
Change the working directory to the afr directory.
The ls command confirms that the file is there.

First, we must uncompress the file using the gunzip utility. Here, it is unzipped.

Using the –x option, extract the files from africa.tar.
Here they are listed because of the –v, or verbose, option.

We have the original tar file and the three extracted files.

Now that the files are extracted, we don't need the tar file. Voila! The africa1 file is as we had first entered it at the beginning of this session.

Log out of pilot.

EXPERIMENTS

```
%cat > temp1
harmonies
legato
rhythm
staccato
sharp
^d
```

Working with Similar Files

6.1 Create a file called temp1 as shown in Figure 6.1.

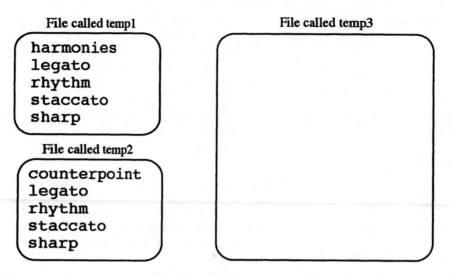

File called temp1

```
harmonies
legato
rhythm
staccato
sharp
```

File called temp2

```
counterpoint
legato
rhythm
staccato
sharp
```

File called temp3

Figure 6.1

```
%cat > temp2
counterpoint
legato
rhythm
staccato
sharp
^d
%sort —o temp1 temp1
%sort —o temp2 temp2
%sort temp1 temp2 > temp3
%more temp3
```

6.2 Similarly, create the file called temp2.

6.3 Make sure that they are sorted.

6.4 Create a file called temp3 using temp1 and temp2. Write down its contents in Figure 6.1.

Which name does temp1 have that temp2 doesn't?

Which name does temp2 have that temp1 doesn't?

```
%uniq temp3
```

6.5 What does the uniq command do?

```
%uniq —d temp3
```

What does the —d option do?

```
%uniq —u temp3
```

What does the —u option do?

```
%diff temp1 temp2
```

6.6 Disregard those cryptic numbers in the output of this command. What do the "greater than" and "less than" symbols and the output next to them indicate?

```
%sdiff —s temp1 temp2
```

What does "sdiff —s" do?

```
%comm temp1 temp2
```

6.7 Files should already be sorted when using the comm command. diff and sdiff don't require that.
What is shown in the first column of the output?

What is shown in the second column?

What is shown in the third column?

```
%comm -1 temp1 temp2
```

6.8 Which column is NOT printed?

```
%comm -2 temp1 temp2
```

Which column is NOT printed?

```
%comm -12 temp1 temp2
```

Which column IS printed?

```
%
```

6.9 How would you get a list of names that are in the temp1 file but not in the temp2 file?

```
%
```

6.10 How would you get a list of names that are in the temp2 file but not in the temp1 file?

Looking for Files

```
%cd

%find ~ -name "temp*" -print
```

6.11 Go to the login directory. Let us suppose we don't know where the "temp" files were located. How does the find command help us locate them?

What does the tilde (~) specify?

What does the "-name" option specify?

The "-print" option specifies to print the response on the screen.

```
%find ~ -user ramteke -print
```

Replace my login name with yours.
What does the "-user" option help you find?

```
%cd
%find ~ -mtime 1 -print

%find ~ -atime 1 -print

%find ~ -name "*" -print
```

Try these two options from your home directory. Can you tell which one specifies the files that were accessed in the last day and which one specifies the files that were modified in the last day?

```
%find ~ —name "*" —ok cat {} \;
```

6.12 Once you find the files you were looking for in the directories, you may want to execute a command on these files. What does this do? You may enter "y" or "n."

In spite of this strange syntax "–ok" is a very powerful option. cat is the command we want to perform on the files which are selected. The set of braces means to include all the files that are found and the semicolon means that this is the end of the command to be executed on the files. The backslash, covered in the next unit, is needed before the semicolon to remove the special meaning of the semicolon.

```
%
```

6.13 Now write down, but do not execute the command to delete all files that start with "temp".

```
%whereis temp1

%whereis cat

%whereis cd

%whereis file3
```

6.14 This is a simpler form of the find command, but how is it limited? Try all of these commands. Which ones work? Can you determine in what cases whereis is helpful? In what cases find is helpful?

Piping

Now let us look at piping. This feature of UNIX allows us to combine many commands into one without creating temporary files as we have been doing up to this point. The symbol for the piping operation is "|". The pipe is used to combine two commands into one. However, the command that comes after a pipe must be a *filter*. A filter is a command which can take its input from standard input, perform some operation on it, and send the result to standard output.

```
%grep '^s' temp1
```

6.15 Going back to the temp1 file used in Experiment 6.19, try the grep command. It will find all lines in the file temp1 which begin with an "s".

```
%cat temp1 | grep '^s'
```

Now try this one. Is there any difference in the output of these commands using a pipe symbol and that of the grep command alone? No. The output of the cat command, instead of going to standard output or the screen, becomes the input for the grep command. There is no pipe after the grep command, so the output is placed in standard output, that is, the screen.

```
%cat temp1 | grep '^s' | sort
```

6.16 Instead of getting the output on the screen, we can feed the output to another command.

```
%cat temp1 | grep '^s' | sort > temp
%cat temp
```

6.17 Instead of seeing the sorted output on the screen, we could redirect the output to a file.

```
%cat temp1 | grep '^s' | tee temp | sort
```

6.18 Or we could save an intermediate result in a file as well by using the "tee" option.

Advanced File Manipulation

```
%cat  temp
```

In Experiment 6.17, does any output go on the screen from the piping command? What about in Experiment 6.18? Does a sorted list go in temp in Experiment 6.17? What about in Experiment 6.18?

```
%head  /etc/passwd
```

6.19 Okay, it's not fair for me to get to do all the playing. For the following set of experiments, I'll let you write commands using pipes. You should have a file called passwd in the /etc directory. Redo this command so that you see only one screen at a time.

```
%head  −20  /etc/passwd

%
```

6.20 Write the equivalent of this command using a pipe.

```
%head  -20  /etc/passwd > mypass
```

6.21 Create a file called mypass which we will use to do the following experiments.

```
%cut  −f5  −d: mypass
%cat  mypass
```

6.22 Write the equivalent of this command starting with "cat mypass".

```
%sort  +4  −t:  mypass
%cat  mypass
```

6.23 Write the equivalent of this command starting with "cat mypass".

```
%
```

6.24 Using the syntax of Experiments 6.22 and/or 6.23 and two pipes, cut the fifth field of mypass and sort it.

```
%
```

6.25 Rewrite Experiment 6.24. Create a file called cutpass which stores the file which was cut before it was sorted.

```
%
```

6.26 Write the equivalent of Experiment 6.24 using only one pipe.

```
%cat  mypass
```

6.27 Starting with "cat mypass", find all the lines in the file which begin with the letter b, upper–case or lower–case.

```
%cat  mypass
```

6.28 Starting with "cat mypass", find all the lines in the file which have the character string "lan".

```
%cat  *
```

6.29 Starting with "cat *", find all the lines which have the character string "lan" in the files of your current directory.

```
%
```

6.30 Remember that "wc −l" counts the number of lines in a file. Find a string which appears in more than one file. Write a pipeline to find out the number of lines in your files which have that string.

```
%
```

6.31 Now rewrite Experiment 6.30 without using a pipe.

Advanced File Manipulation

97

Using the tar Command

```
%ls
```

6.32 From the beginning of the experiments, make sure you have temp1, temp2, and temp3 files in your current working directory. If not, create these files with text in them.

```
%tar —cvf $HOME/temps.tar  .
```

6.33 When doing this command, please don't forget the dot at the end!

```
%cd
%ls —l temp*
```

6.34 Are your original temp files still available?

What is the size of the temps.tar file which is in the home directory?

```
%gzip temps.tar
```

6.35 If the system cannot find gzip, do whereis gzip. This will show you the path where gzip is available. Then execute the command again, using the given path. If you still cannot do the gzip command, omit this part for now and also later on when you are told to use the gunzip command. (That will be in Experiment 6.38.)

What is the size of the temps.tar.gz file?

What did the gzip utility do to the tar file?

Is temps.tar still in existence?

```
%mkdir dump
%mv temps.tar.gz dump
%cd dump
```

6.36 Create a directory called dump and move the temps.tar.gz file there. Then change your directory.
Now let us do everything in reverse order.

```
%ls —l
```

6.37 How many files are there in dump? Which ones?

```
%gunzip temps.tar.gz
%ls —l
```

6.38 What do you think gunzip does?
Is the .gz file still there? If not, what became of it?

```
%tar —tvf temps.tar
```

6.39 What does the —t option do with the tar command?

```
%ls —l
```

6.40 Did the —t option recreate or extract the original files?

```
%tar —xvf temps.tar
```

6.41 What does the —x option do with the tar command?

```
%ls —l
```

HOMEWORK

comm, diff, sdiff, and uniq:
1. Give the commands to do the following tasks:
   a. Sort a file called notes and save the sorted contents in the same file.
   b. Find all lines which are duplicates in a sorted file called notes.
   c. Find all lines which appear only once in a sorted file called notes.
   d. Display all lines once in a sorted file called notes. Even duplicate lines should be displayed only once.
   e. Find the lines which are in fileA, but not in fileB, and vice versa. Do this two ways.
   f. Find only the lines which are in fileA but not in fileB.

find vs. whereis:
2. Give the command which will find the location of each of the following files and commands:
   a. the sort command
   b. the head command
   c. the files whose owners are ramteke in your own login directory
   d. the telnet command
   e. the files which were modified within the last day in your own login directory
   f. the files which have the character string "file" anywhere in their name
   g. the files which begin with an "aj" and their names
   h. the files which belong to the owner "kristen"
3. How are find and whereis different?

–exec vs. –ok using find:
4. Give the version of the find command to do the following operations on files in your own login directory:
   a. Delete all files which have the character string "file" anywhere in their name. Do this operation on all files.
   b. Copy all files which have the character string "file" anywhere in their name to a directory called bum. The directory called bum is under the login directory. Do this operation on a selected file by prompts for yes and no.
   c. Display the contents of all files whose user is not yourself. Be able to select the files by entering yes and no.
   d. Move all files which have been modified in the last day to the directory called bum.
   e. Move all files that have not been accessed in the last 2 days to the "/tmp" directory.

Working with Many and/or Large Files. Also, Logging in and File Transfers:
5. Give the appropriate command to do the following tasks.
   a. Remotely log into a host called hardees.
   b. Set up a login session where you will be able to login to a host called hardees.
   c. See the contents of a tape archive file called test.tar.
   d. Uncompress a file called test.tar.gz.
   e. Create a tape archive file called test.tar using all the files in the directory called bum. Store this file in the login directory.
   f. Compress a file called test.
6. Which of the following are filters?

   who, cat, grep, date, cut, tail, wc, sort, uptime, cp, echo, ls

Piping:
7. A pipeline command is a set of commands separated by pipe symbols. Give the pipeline command for each of the following:

a. Find out all users in the passwd file that have 'bash' characters. (These are the users who use the bash shell after logging in.) Then sort these users.
b. Using the pipeline of Homework 7a, show only the first 10 users of the sorted list.
c. Using the pipeline of Homework 7a, show only a count of the users who use the C shell.
d. Out of all the people that are currently logged on, show who has a user name that has 'ma' anywhere in it.
e. Write a pipeline to count the number of files in the current directory.
f. Show only the first 6 characters of the user names those who are currently logged in.
g. Do a man page of the who command and pipe that into a grep command which will find all lines that contain the word "example". Then "tee" that into a file called "temp" and display on the screen the number of lines that were selected.
h. Show how many people are currently logged in.
i. From the previous commands that you did, show which used the wc command. Use a pipeline.
j. Using a pipeline, change all upper–case letters of file engl to lower–case letters.

LAB ASSIGNMENTS

1. Using the script command given in the Lab Assignment section of Unit 3 make a record of your session. You should have no errors in this session. Save the script file as lab6.1.
Move the last 20 lines of the /etc/passwd file into a file called localpass. Then using one pipeline do all of the following:

Sort the file on the 4th field where each field is delimited by a colon (:). Store this file as sortfile. Then cut the 5th field and save this file as cutfile.
Now select only the lines which have the characters na in them and store them in a file called lastfile.
Finally, display the outputs of each of the files in the reverse order of how they were created.

2. Create a script file called lab6.2.
Create a file called sportsA which has four of your favorite sports players using the sort command. Copy sportsA to sportsB. Using the sed command from Unit 5, delete one player from sportsB and save the file into temp. Then using the echo command, add a brand new player to the end of temp. Now rename temp as sportsB. Using the sort command, combine sportsA and sportsB files into sportsC. Many of the players will be duplicated here.
Show all players in sportsC once, whether they appear once in the file or not.
Show only the duplicate players once.
Show the players which are in sports A and not in sportsB in one column. Next to that column, show the players which are in sportsB and not in sportsA. Finally, in the last column show all the players which are in both files.

3. If you have a shell account on another host, use your own hostname and user name instead of hardees and stephen, respectively, in this lab. If you don't have an account on another host, then write down the commands as they would be done and seen on your screen.
Remotely log into the host called hardees.com. Assume your login name is stephen. Create a directory called myfilesystem and copy all your files and directories from your login directory into this directory. Make sure you don't end up trying to copy the myfilesystem directory into itself recursively. This will create an infinite loop and make you run out of hard disk space. Now go into the myfilesystem directory. Create a tar file called system.tar which will go into the login or $HOME directory. (Don't forget the dot at the end of this command!) Go back into your login directory. Compress the system.tar file then log out of the remote host.

Advanced File Manipulation

From your local host, do an ftp to hardees.com. Using get instead of put, transfer the compressed tar file to your local host. Then quit out of ftp.

Now in your local host create a directory called mysystemfile. Move the transferred file into it. Show the table of contents after you uncompress the file. Then extract the files as they were stored in the tape archive file.

Unit 7

Working in C Shell and tcsh

CONCEPTS TO LEARN

What Is a Shell:

An analogy may be helpful here. When I go to the printer to get copies of my work, I give the original papers to Jose, the operator of the copying machine. The machine is complicated and I don't know which buttons to push and how to make the copies. And I don't want to know. Jose is my interface to the copier. I give him a task, he does it, and returns back to me what I had requested him to do. Similarly, the UNIX operating system uses what is called a shell to provide an interface between us and the operating system. We are considered users of the operating system. Just like I find Jose to be a friendly interface to the copier, users can pick their own shells on the basis of how user–friendly they are.

The Bourne shell (sh), C shell (csh), and "teesh" (tcsh) are some of the shells that are available on the UNIX operating system. As seen in Figure 7.1, it doesn't matter what kind of UNIX one is working with: the shell provides a consistent interface to the operating system over various platforms. The kernel is the central part of the operating system that interacts directly with the CPU and it is in RAM.

The shell acts as a command interpreter. Whatever command you feed it, the shell will provide it to the operating system in a form it can understand. On the other hand, when the operating system responds, the shell presents that information to the user in a form that we humans find easy to

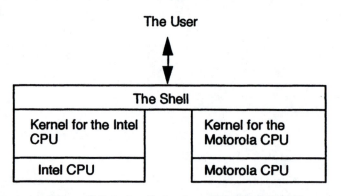

Figure 7.1 A simplistic view of the UNIX shell

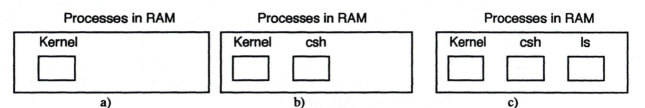

Programs on the Hard Drive

csh	ls	cat

Processes in RAM

Kernel

Processes in RAM

Kernel	csh

Processes in RAM

Kernel	csh	ls

a)   b)   c)

Figure 7.2 a) Before you log on, basically only the kernel is running and the other programs are still on the hard drive. b) Once you log on, a copy of the shell is made for you from the hard drive. c) When you give a command to the shell, that program is copied for you from the hard drive.

understand. If a user enters a command with an error, it doesn't even reach the kernel because the shell "returns" that command back to the user as an error. For instance, I can't tell Jose to give me color copies when all he has available is the black and white copier.

On the other hand, I could give Jose a number of jobs to do that are a bit involved. This is similar to the shell acting as a programming language. The shell also provides a whole working environment under which the user becomes familiar over time.

What Else Is a Shell:

Actually, the shell is just like any other UNIX command or program. As seen in Figure 7.2a, when the UNIX system is first started, only the kernel is running and all the UNIX commands or programs are stored on the hard drive. When you first log on, a copy of the shell, in this case csh, is made for you in RAM. See Figure 7.2b. Then the shell is given control and it waits for you to enter a command. If you enter a command with a syntax error, the shell will tell you. Otherwise, the shell will find the program on the drive and give control to the kernel which loads the program in RAM, in this case ls. This is shown in Figure 7.2c. Then while the csh process is not doing anything, the ls process runs, shows the output on the screen, and gets erased from RAM. Now we are back to Figure 7.2b. Here, the csh process awaits for you to type in the next command.

The shell then is not just a command interpreter: it also executes programs as illustrated above. The shell can also redirect your input and output: it can pipe the output of one process into the input of another one. The shell can also define the environment under which you are working. It can define aliases to commands: long commands can be aliased into short and simple ones. Programs can be written to be executed under a shell. This will be covered in Unit 9. In summary, the shell provides UNIX users with many facilities which they take for granted.

Choosing Your Shell:

Throughout this unit, I assume that you are working in C shell (csh). However, since tc shell (tcsh) is becoming more popular, at the end of the unit I will give you the major differences between the two shells. Most operations in these two shells are the same so the differences will not be pointed out until then. If you have a choice, you should pick tcsh to work with because of its benefits. The most notable benefit is being able to use the up and down arrow keys to select a previously used command. Also, the right and left arrows can be used to edit the command on the command line.

User–Defined Shell Variables:

A variable can be defined in a shell to contain a certain value. Later that value can be changed. To get the value of a variable, place a $ in front of its name. For example:

```
%set name = bobo
%echo name is $name
name is bobo
```

System–Defined Shell Variables:

The UNIX operating system needs to keep track of certain things, such as who the user is, what his or her login shell is, and so on. These items are stored in special system–defined shell variables. Here are a few of them:

history	The number of commands to display every time the history command is executed.
filec	The file completion shell variable that, when set, allows you to type only part of the filename and then press <Esc> twice or <Tab>. The system will complete the filename for you if it is uniquely identifiable. The tcsh shell doesn't use this variable. It is always set.
	If you enter some characters for a filename and press <Esc> to have the filename completed, but it can't be completed because there is more than one file which begins with those characters, press <Ctrl>d to see all the filenames which start with those characters. Then you can provide the additional characters necessary for the shell to figure out which file you are requesting.
noclobber	If this shell variable is set, you can't destroy an already existing file by redirection (>).
path	The path variable contains the set of paths which should be searched whenever looking to execute a command that is not internal to the shell. There are a few internal commands that are defined in the shell which are always available regardless of whether the path is set correctly or not.
prompt	This shell variable contains the information of how each prompt should be displayed.
term	The type of the terminal in use is stored here. Typically, it is vt100.
unalias	Removes the definition of an alias.
user	This variable contains the login name of the user.

System–Defined Environment Variables:

Environment variables are set for your login session and are usually static. For example, if you change your working shell, the environment variable called SHELL doesn't change, but the shell variable called shell will change. Environment variables are checked by other processes that need to know what your settings are. When you invoke vi, vi will check the environment variable called TERM to see what terminal type you are using. If you are running a mail program and it allows you to go into an editor, the mail program will look at the EDITOR variable to see which editor you usually use.

Environment variable names are typically in upper–case characters and shell variable names are in lower–case characters. Here are some of the typical environment variables and the types of information they contain:

EDITOR	your default editor
HOME	login directory
MAIL	mail directory
PATH	set of directories where commands are to be searched
SHELL	type of shell being used
TERM	type of terminal being used
USER	login name of the user

Quotes:

double quotes (")	Characters placed inside a pair of double quotes are displayed exactly as they are, except for $, `, and \. These three characters don't lose their special meaning inside double quotes.
Single quotes (')	All characters placed inside a pair of single quotes in an echo command are displayed exactly as they are given.
Back quotes (`)	When a UNIX command needs to be executed inside an echo command, that command has to be placed in back quotes.
Backslash (\ )	The character placed directly after a backslash has the effect of being quoted. That is, if the backslash is placed outside of double quotes.
	In Bourne shell, if the backslash is placed inside double quotes, then all characters lose their special meaning if they have one. And with $, *, `, and \ the backslash is not printed, but with all other characters, the backslash is printed.

Some Characters with Special Meanings:

$	A shell variable preceded by $ provides the value of that variable.
`	A command placed between back quotes in an echo statement will actually execute that command instead of displaying the characters of the command.
'	All characters placed within a pair of single quotes are displayed exactly as they are in an echo statement. There are no exceptions.
>	The redirection symbol is usually used to store the output to a file.
|	The pipe symbol is used to direct the output of one command to the input of another one.
\	To place a single character inside quotes, you would normally need two quotes, one before and one after the character. With a backslash, however, you only need to place it once in front of a character to assign it a special meaning.

COMMANDS TO LEARN

alias	If there is a command which you use often, you can abbreviate that command by giving it a shorter name called an alias. Long commands or sets of commands can be defined by using a simple alias. It's like me setting a signal between myself and Jose, the copy room operator. I could tell him up front that if I ever place a blue sticker on my print request, he should use three-hole paper and staple each set of copies. Here is an example that defines an alias called nou which displays the number of users currently logged on the UNIX server:

```
alias nou 'who | wc -l'
```

alias	Displays all the aliases which have been defined.
printenv	Displays all the environment variables, if used by itself. Otherwise, this command can be used to display an environment variable.
set	Displays all the shell variables, both system-defined and user-defined, if used by itself. Otherwise, this command can be used to set a variable.
setenv	Displays all the environment variables, if used by itself. Otherwise, this command can be used to set an environment variable.
source	When it is given a filename, this command will execute the file.

SAMPLE SESSION

```
% {106} set item = pen
% {107} echo item
item
% {108} echo $item
pen
% {109} set item = ball point pen
% {110} echo $item
ball
%{111}set item = "ball point pen"
% {112} echo $item
ball point pen
% {113} set new_item = $item
% {114} echo $new_item
ball
% {115} echo $item
ball point pen
% {116} set new_item = "$item"
% {117} echo $new_item
ball point pen
% {119} echo "item = $item"
item = ball point pen
% {120} echo "new_item = $new_item"
new_item = ball point pen
% {121} echo $old_item
old_item: Undefined variable.
% {123} set d = "pwd"
% {124} $d
/home/tramteke
% {130} set qty = 5
% {131} echo $qty
5
% {132} $qty
5: Command not found.
% {133} echo $qty + 1
5 + 1
% {134} expr $qty + 1
6
% {135} expr $qty * 3
expr: syntax error
% {136} expr $qty "*" 3
15
% {137} echo *
a.out africa.tar.gz cis238.csh
% {138} 5 + 1
5: Command not found.
```

```
% {139} mkdir unit7
% {140} cd unit7
% {141} ls
% {142} echo 11111 > fileL
```

Shell Variables

We are defining a variable called item to the shell. We don't have to give its data type as we do in the C programming language. If we echo item, then the word item is displayed. However, if we want to see the value stored in item, the shell variable we just defined, then we need to put a $ before it. Let us redefine the value of item to be "ball point pen." However, only "ball" was assigned to item, our shell variable, since we left off the quotes.

Here we provide the quotes so that the spaces can be included.

And they are.

A new variable called new_item is defined here which is given the same value as item. When echoing the value of new_item, we again lose our last two words.

Let us check item again. It still has three words.

If we use quotes around $item, we then get all three words assigned to new_item.

Now both variables have the same value.

If we try to echo the value of a variable called old_item, which hasn't been defined, we are told so.

Here, we assign a UNIX command to d, a new shell variable. If we simply enter $d, the value of d which is pwd is executed as a command. Our working directory is printed.

We can also assign numbers to shell variables. qty is assigned the character 5 and the echo command displays this character.

We cannot enter $qty as we entered $d in command 123. $qty, which is 5, is not a UNIX command.

We can echo the value of qty, but it is taken as a character and is not added to 1.

The expr command will evaluate the arithmetic as we would expect it.

However, if we want to multiply numbers with the expr command, we must use quotes around the multiplication sign.

This is because the asterisk (*) symbol refers to all the filenames that are in the current working directory.

5 is not a command. To evaluate an arithmetic expression, use the expr command.

Quotes

Before we experiment with the various types of quotes available in UNIX, let us create a few files in a directory of their own.

```
% {143} echo qqqqq > fileQ
% {144} echo ppppp > fileP
% {145} echo *
fileL fileP fileQ
% {146} ls
fileL fileP fileQ
% {147} ls -l
total 6
-rw-r--r--   1 tramteke   fileL
-rw-r--r--   1 tramteke   fileP
-rw-r--r--   1 tramteke   fileQ
% {148} set | grep item
item        ball point pen
new_item    ball point pen
% {149} echo item
item
% {150} echo $item
ball point pen
% {151} echo $item "*" > fileT
% {152} ls
fileL fileP fileQ fileT
% {153} cat fileT
ball point pen *

% {154} echo "$item *" > file1
% {155} cat fileT
ball point pen *

% {156} echo "$item * > " file1
ball point pen * >   file1

% {157} cat fileT
ball point pen *
% {158} echo * > fileT
% {159} cat fileT
file1 fileL fileP fileQ fileT
```

We have now created fileL, fileQ, and fileP in the unit7 directory.

An asterisk means all the filenames in the current directory. Hence, the command echo * gives the same result as doing an ls.

Here is a long listing, but I have shortened the display to save space on the page.

Double Quotes: All characters except for $, `, and \ lose their special meaning inside double quotes.

The simple set command will give all the shell variables which have been defined. To see the ones which have item in them, we pipe the output of the set command into grep item. Echoing item will simply display item.

Echoing $item will display the value of the shell variable item.

Here, the value of item and * is redirected to fileT. Since * is quoted, it loses its special meaning of substituting all the filenames. The output of ls shows that fileT was created.

The content of fileT has the value of item, which is "ball point pen" and the asterisk.

Does placing the dollar sign ($) inside double quotes make it lose its special meaning, that is, of giving the value of the shell variable?

No, the dollar sign preserved its special meaning inside quotes, but the asterisk didn't.

What about the redirection arrow?

It lost its special meaning. The output of echo wasn't redirected.

Here is the content of fileT again.

If we substitute all filenames in place of the asterisk, they are redirected into fileT.

Here is the content of fileT.

```
% {160} echo ls
ls
% {161} echo `ls`
file1 fileL fileP fileQ fileT
% {162} echo "ls: `ls`"
ls: file1 fileL fileP fileQ fileT
% {163} echo "number of logged users: `who | wc -l`"
number of logged users: 4
% {164} who
tramteke  ttyp1   (204.142.106.7)
bgat2249  ttyp2   (204.142.106.3)
ksch6907  ttyp3   (204.142.106.3)
cgay1455  ttyp4   (204.142.106.3)

% {165} echo number of logged users: `who | wc -l`
number of logged users: 4
```

Back Quotes: Commands placed between back quotes are executed.

Echoing ls will simply display ls.

However, placing ls inside a pair of back quotes executes that command and shows its output. Even if the back quotes are placed within a pair of double quotes, the ls command is executed.

Here, we place the command who | wc -l within back quotes and it is executed, giving us the number of users who are logged on at this time.

Next, we do the same echo command, but without the double quotes, and we get the same result.

Working in C Shell and tcsh

```
% {166} echo `fileP`
fileP: Permission denied.
```

Placing a filename or any other random characters within a pair of back quotes doesn't make sense because they are not valid UNIX commands.

```
% {167} echo `cat fileP`
PPPPP
```

fileP is not executable, but cat fileP is executable.

Backslashes: To place a single character inside quotes, a single backwards slash can be used. Placing backslashes inside double quotes in Bourne shell makes the characters following the backslashes lose their special meaning. We will not explore that here.

```
% {168} echo \$item
$item
```

The dollar sign lost its special meaning because of the backslash.

```
% {169} echo \$item = $item
$item = ball point pen
```

Without the backslash, the dollar sign provides us with the value of the shell variable.

```
%{170}echo \$item's value: $item
Unmatched '.
```

The quote is not displayed. UNIX is expecting quotes to come in pairs.

```
%{172}echo \$item\'s value: $item
$item's value: ball point pen
```

Here the backslash comes in handy to place the quote as if itself were in quotes.

```
% {173} echo \*
*
```

Placing a backslash in front of an asterisk, displays it.

```
% {174} echo *
file1 fileL fileP fileQ fileT
```

Of course, without the backslash, we get all the filenames.

```
% {175} echo > fileT
```

The redirection arrow places nothing in fileT.

```
% {176} cat fileT
```

The file has nothing in it.

```
% {177} echo \> fileT
> fileT
```

However, placing a backslash in front of the redirection arrow makes it lose its special meaning and the line is echoed on the screen.

```
% {178} cat fileT
```

Notice that fileT still has nothing in it.

```
% {181} echo Fine Time | more
Fine Time
```

Here, the pipe symbol pipes the output of the echo command to more.

```
% {182} echo Fine Time \| more
Fine Time | more
```

With the backslash the pipe is not a pipe symbol anymore. It's echoed just like any other character.

Single Quotes: There are no exceptions to the following rule: all characters placed within single quotes are displayed exactly as they are given.

```
% {183} echo '$item'
$item
```

Single quotes prevent the value of a shell variable from being displayed.

```
% {184} echo '*'
*
```

They also prevent an asterisk from substituting all the filenames in its place.

```
% {185} echo '`date`'
`date`
```

Single quotes even prevent us from executing a date command which is inside back quotes.

```
% {186} echo '`date`' is date
`date` is date
```

The date command isn't executed in either case here. The first time it is in single quotes and the next time it isn't in back quotes.

```
% {187} echo '`date`' is `date`
`date` is Fri Sep 11 12:20:29
```

When date is inside only back quotes, the command is executed.

```
% {188} echo "date is `date`"
date is Fri Sep 11 12:21:13
```

Placing back quotes inside of double quotes will still execute the command.

```
% {190} echo '$item' = \'$item\'
$item = 'ball point pen'
```

Here, $item is printed as it is because it is in single quotes the first time. However, the second time, the backslashes in front of the single quotes make the single quotes lose their special meaning. They are displayed on the screen instead.

```
% {212} echo $path
/home/tramteke/bin  /bin  /usr/bin
/usr/host  /usr/local/bin
%tramteke  {213} whereis ls
/bin/ls
%tramteke  {214} whereis cat
/bin/cat
%tramteke  {215} whereis date
/bin/date
%tramteke  {216} whereis whereis
/usr/bin/whereis
%tramteke  {217} whereis head
/usr/bin/head
%tramteke  {218} whereis whoami
/usr/bin/whoami
%tramteke  {219} whereis clear
/usr/bin/clear
%tramteke  {220} ls
africa.tar.gz    mail    unit7
%tramteke  {221} cd unit7
% {222} ls
fileL fileQ file1 fileP fileT
% {223} cat file1
ball point pen *
% {224} date
Sun Sep 13 04:52:06 EDT 1998
% {225} head file1
ball point pen *
% {226} whoami
tramteke
% {227} clear
% {228} set path = ( )


% {229} ls
ls: Command not found.
% (229.1} /bin/ls
fileL fileQ file1 fileP fileT
% {230} cat file1
cat: Command not found.
% {231} date
date: Command not found.
% {232} pwd
pwd: Command not found.
% {233} head file1
head: Command not found.
% {234} whoami
whoami: Command not found.
```

The path Shell Variable

The UNIX shell which you are running under defines a special shell variable called path. The directories defined in that variable determine which directories the shell will search for executable commands when requested to execute them. On the left is the value of the special shell variable called path. It was set when we first logged on.

Let us locate some executable commands in our system. We find that most commands are located in /bin and /usr/bin. The following figure shows which commands are in which directories.

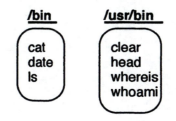

Since the path is set according to command 212, ls is executable. The ls command is available under /bin.

If we change the directory, the ls command is still executable since the path shell variable is not dependent on which directory you are under.

As the path is set originally, all these commands are available for us to execute.

Now let us make the path null so that when we try to execute a command, the shell will not look in either the /bin or the /usr/bin directories.

When trying to do the ls command, we get an error message saying that the ls command is not found.

However, we can still execute the ls command by explicitly giving the directory where it is located.

Since the path is null, we can't do the cat command or any of these commands either: date, pwd, head, whoami, and whereis.

```
% {235} whereis sort
whereis: Command not found.
% unit7 {236} cd ..
%tramteke {237} cd ..
% home {238} cd /bin
% bin {239} cd
%tramteke {240} echo hello Mars
hello Mars
% {241} set path = ($path /bin)
%tramteke {242} ls
africa.tar.gz    mail    unit7
%tramteke {244} cd unit7
% unit7 {245} cat file1
ball point pen *
% unit7 {247} date
Sun Sep 13 04:56:28 EDT 1998
% unit7 {248} pwd
/home/tramteke/unit7
% unit7 {249} head file1
head: Command not found.
% {250} whoami
whoami: Command not found.
% {251} whereis pwd
whereis: Command not found.
% {252} clear
clear: Command not found.

%{253}set path = ($path /usr/bin)
% {254} ls
fileL fileQ file1 fileP fileT
% {255} cat file1
ball point pen *
% {256} pwd
/home/tramteke/unit7
% {257} date
Sun Sep 13 04:58:41 EDT 1998
% {258} head file1
ball point pen *
% {259} whoami
tramteke
% {260} whereis cat
/bin/cat
% {261} echo echo You are Wonderful > encouragement
% {262} cat encouragement
echo You are Wonderful
% {263} encouragement
encouragement: Command not found.

% {267} ./encouragement
./encouragement: Permission denied

% {264} ls -l encouragement
-rw------- tramteke encouragement
% {266} chmod 700 encouragement
```

However, we can execute the cd command even if the path is null. That is because the cd command is internal to the shell. We are running in csh, and while we are running that shell the cd command comes with it. It is a command built in the shell.

echo is also available with the shell.

Now let us take the current path which is denoted by $path and add /bin to it. The ls command which is in /bin is now executable because the path specifies to the shell to look in this directory also when executing a command.

Going to the unit7 directory, we can use the cat command.

The date and pwd commands are also in the /bin directory, so we can execute them.

However, the following commands as shown in the figure of command 217 are in /usr/bin. Hence, they cannot be found.

Now let us add the /usr/bin directory to the current path and all these commands will be available to us.

Let us create our own command called encouragement.

Here is the content of the file.

However, we cannot execute it because it is not found. The path variable tells the shell to look only in /bin and /usr/bin, not the current directory.

Hence, we place ./ in front of the file or command name and the shell finds the file. However, we don't have executable permission.

If we look at the permissions, we see that we can only read and write the file, not execute it.

We alter the permissions to include write permission. ls

Working in C Shell and tcsh

```
% {268} ls -l encouragement
-rwx------ tramteke encouragement
% {265} ./encouragement
You are Wonderful

% {271} encouragement
encouragement: Command not found.
% {272} set path = ($path .)
% {273} encouragement
You are Wonderful

% {274} ls
fileL fileQ fileL fileP fileT
% {275} head file1
ball point pen *
% {276} encouragement
You are Wonderful
% {277} echo $path
/bin /usr/bin .
% {278} csh
% {11} echo $path
/home/tramteke/bin /bin /usr/bin
/usr/host /usr/local/bin
```

shows in the long listing that we did it correctly. This is seen by the x.

We can now execute our file. We have given the directory in which to find it, specifically, the current directory shown by ./. We have also made it executable for the owner. However, we still must provide ./ to execute it.

If we append the current directory to the current path by adding a dot, then we don't need to specify ./ when executing the file.

Now all commands work from /bin, /usr/bin, and the current directory (.).

Here is our path now.

Our path is reset by a start-up file called .cshrc if we go into another shell.

System-Defined Shell and Environment Variables

The set command will give all the shell variables specified both by the system and by the user. Here are their meanings:
Current Working Directory.
File Completion.
The last 1000 commands are displayed with history.
The login directory for the user.
<Ctrl>D will not log you off.
The name of the machine.
The path which is set at the start-up of the shell

```
% {12} set
cwd        /home/tramteke/unit7
filec
history 1000
home       /home/tramteke
ignoreeof
mch        alankay
path       (/home/tramteke/bin  /bin
/usr/bin  /usr/host  /usr/local/bin)
prompt     alankay:unit7  {!}
shell      /bin/csh
term       ansi
user       tramteke
```

The prompt setting.
The current shell.
The type of the terminal.
The name of the user.

Environment variable names are usually in all upper-case letters. The shell variables are specific to the shell you are under, but the environment variables are specific to your login session.

The setenv gives the environment variables as they are defined.

```
% {13} setenv
TERM=ansi
HOME=/home/tramteke
SHELL=/bin/tcsh
LOGNAME=tramteke
USER=tramteke
PATH=/home/tramteke/bin:/bin:
/usr/bin:/usr/host:/usr/local/bin:
HOSTTYPE=i386
OSTYPE=bsd44
MACHTYPE=i386
PWD=/home/tramteke/unit7
GROUP=prof
HOST=alankay
```

Working in C Shell and tcsh

```
TERMCAP=ansi:u6=\E[%
% {14} printenv
TERM=ansi
HOME=/home/tramteke
     (etc.)
% {15} printenv HOST
alankay
% {16} echo $HOST
alankay

% {19} alias
cd        cd !*; prompt
df        (df -k)
du        (du -k)
f         finger
h         history -r | more
prompt    set prompt =
"$mch:q"":$cwd:t {!} "
  (etc.)

% {20} set history = 3
% {21} history
19   alias
20   set history = 3
21   history
% {22} h
22   h
21   history
20   set history = 3
% {23} set history = 5
% {24} h
24   h
23   set history = 5
22   h
21   history
20   set history = 3

% {25} ls
encouragement fileL        fileQ
file1    fileP             fileT
% {26} unset filec
% {27} cat en^[^[^[^[
cat: en: No such file or directory

% {28} set filec

% {29} cat en <ESC> couragement
echo You are Wonderful
```

The printenv and setenv commands give the same output. (Here the output is shortened to save space.)

To see the value of an environment variable, such as HOST, you can use printenv.
Using the echo command and the dollar sign, you can see how an environment variable is set.

The alias command by itself shows all the commands as they were set up by the start-up files. Many have been deleted to save space.

history:
The history shell variable is set to 3.
When we do a history, we get only the last three commands which were entered.

Since the history command has an alias of h, from command 19, we could just type an h and get the same result.

Here we are setting the history shell variable to 5.
Now we will see the last 5 commands that we entered.

filec:
Here are the files in the current directory.
In csh, there is a shell variable called filec. If it is unset and we partially type the filename, the shell can't complete the filename for us.
If we press the <Esc> key repeatedly after typing en, the shell doesn't complete the spelling for the encouragement file.
Once the file completion shell variable is set, all we have to do is type the first few characters of the filename which are unique in the current directory. Then when we press <Esc> once or twice, the shell completes the filename for us. What a time saver! With tcsh, you always have this feature.
If there is more than one filename which starts with the characters entered, press <Ctl>d and the shell will show the names of those files for you from which you can choose.

```
% {30} cat file1
ball point pen *
% {31} set noclobber
% {32} echo 111111l > file1
file1: File exists.
% {33} unset noclobber
% {35} echo 111111 > file1
% {36} cat file1
111111


% {37} echo $prompt
%  !
% {38} echo $cwd
/home/tramteke/unit7
% {39} echo $user
tramteke

% {40} alias | grep cd
cd         cd !*; prompt
% unit7 {41} unalias cd
% unit7 {42} alias | grep cd
% unit7 {43} cd ..
% unit7 {44} cd /
% unit7 {45} pwd
/

% unit7 {46} alias setp 'set prompt = "$cwd :"'
% unit7 {47} alias cd 'cd \!*; setp'
```

noclobber:
This is the content of file1.

We are setting the noclobber shell variable.
If we try to clobber file1 by redirecting something to it, we are prevented from doing so.
Here, we unset the noclobber shell variable.
Then we are allowed to redirect output to it and write over the file. Notice, now file1 is destroyed and all 1's have been written over it.

Other Shell Variables:
prompt is another shell variable which is set as shown.

The current working directory (cwd) stores the directory at the present time.
The $user variable stores the value of the login user.

Setting the Prompt to Show $cwd:
Included in the currently defined aliases is an alias for cd. This alias shows the working directory at each prompt.
Let us clear the alias for cd.
Notice that it's not there.
If we change the directory to any other directory, the prompt doesn't show the current directory. It still shows that we are in unit7, when a pwd confirms that we are actually in root.

Let us reset our prompt so that it shows the current working directory (cwd) every time we change directories. Commands 46 and 47 do this for us in csh. The way we do that is by creating an alias for setp first which shows the value of cwd. Then we create an alias for cd which does the cd command and then does the setp alias.

The following figure shows how a command, cd /bin, is converted to "cd /bin; setp" and then sets the prompt to the value of cwd. The \!* is the place where the argument for the cd command is substituted. In this case, it is /bin. Then the alias for setp is expanded to show the prompt as $cwd. We will see later that this is much simpler in tcsh.

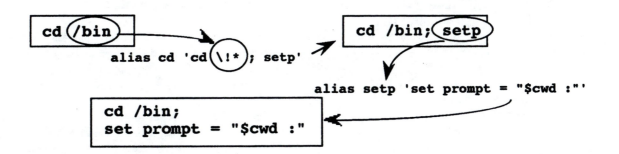

```
% unit7 {48} cd ..
/ :pwd
/
/ :cd
/home/tramteke :pwd
/home/tramteke
/home/tramteke :cd ..
/home :cd /bin
/bin :cd


% echo $HOME
/home/tramteke
%tramteke {66} echo $MAIL
MAIL: Undefined variable.
% {67} echo $TERM
ansi
% {68} echo $PATH
/home/tramteke/bin:/bin:
/usr/bin:/usr/host:/usr/local/bin:
% {69} set path = ""
% {70} echo $path
% {71} echo $PATH
% {72} setenv PATH /bin
% {73} printenv PATH
printenv: Command not found.
% {74} echo $PATH
/bin
% {75} echo $path
/bin
% {76} setenv SHELL sh
% {77} echo $SHELL
sh
% {78} echo $shell
/bin/csh


% {8} ls -a | grep .csh
.cshrc
.cshrc.orig
% {9} more .cshrc
# .cshrc initialization
alias cd          'cd !*; prompt'
alias df          (df -k)
alias du          (du -k)
alias f           finger
alias h           'history -r | more'
prompt  set prompt =
   "$mch:q""":$cwd:t {!} "
set path = (~/bin /bin /usr/
   {bin,host,local/bin,games} .)
if ($?prompt) then
   # An interactive shell
   set filec
   set mch = 'hostname -s'
   alias prompt 'set prompt =
```

Here we change our directory.
Now we are in root.

If we go to our home directory, the correct directory is displayed for the prompt. A pwd confirms that.

If we go up to /home, the prompt shows us that we did. And if we go down to /bin, our prompt shows us that too.

Environment Variables:
$HOME shows the value of the HOME environment variable.

Apparently, MAIL is not set.

The terminal type is ansi.

And the path value for the environment is the same as that for the shell.

If we set the shell variable, path, it also changes the environment variable, PATH.

We use the setenv command to set environment variables. Since we nulled out the path in command 69, we can't use the printenv command without specifying its directory.
We'll use the echo command instead.
We see that setting the environment variable, PATH, also changes the corresponding shell variable, path.

However, if we change the environment SHELL variable, it doesn't change the corresponding shell variable called shell.

Start–up Files

When you first log on, if your start–up shell is csh or tcsh, the system looks for the .cshrc file to execute. This is a very special file and if it gets damaged, you might not be able to log in at all. Notice that we have .cshrc.orig and .cshrc files. When you first alter the .cshrc file that comes with your system, it is best that you save it as an .orig file. This way, if you end up damaging the .cshrc file, you will still be able to copy from the .cshrc.orig file.

Here I have shown parts of the .cshrc file. It has defined some aliases. It has defined the prompt for tcsh and other items.

The $? prompt checks to see if there is some value given to the prompt variable. It has a value, which means that we are running an interactive shell. Some other variables also get set here.

```
     "$mch:q"":$cwd:t {\!}  "'
  alias cd 'cd \!*; prompt'
  umask 22
endif
        (etc.)
% {12} alias nou 'who | wc -l'
% {13} nou
2

% {14} cd ..
% home {15} nou
2

% home {16} who
tramteke ttyp1          (204.142.106.7)
fbha6183 ttyp3          (204.142.106.3)
% home {17} csh
% home {7} nou
nou: Command not found.
% {8} cp .cshrc .cshrc.backup
```

Now let us create an alias called "nou" for number of users. If we type nou, it executes the command given for the nou alias and shows the number of users logged on.
If we change the directory, the alias still works.

We have two users logged on.

However, if we change our shell,
the alias is not defined in that new shell. What we need to do is to define the alias in the .cshrc file so that it is available every time we log in and every time we change the shell. Before we alter the .cshrc file in any way, let us back it up in case we need to revert to the previous one. The .cshrc.orig file already exists. Let us not overwrite it.

```
%{10}echo "alais nou 'who | wc -l' " >> .cshrc
```

This command places the definition of nou at the end of .cshrc.

```
% {12} source .cshrc
alais: Command not found.
% {15} pico .cshrc
Incomplete termcap entry
% {18} vi .cshrc
  du du -k
```

Before you try it out, run the .cshrc file by using the source command. Apparently, I typed the word "alias" incorrectly! If I try to go into the pico editor to correct the spelling, I can't. This shows the difficulty involved in altering this file.
If I try to go into vi, my display screen goes out of sync.

```
% {19} tail .cshrc
umask 22
endif
alais nou 'who | wc -l'
% {22} source .cshrc
alais: Command not found.
% {25} csh
alais: Command not found.
% {26} sed /alais/d .cshrc
```

The last few lines of the .cshrc file show that I did spell alias incorrectly.
At this time, we could use our backup file to overwrite the existing .cshrc file, but let's not.
Try running the .cshrc file again. It still doesn't work!

Try going into another shell again. That doesn't work either.

This command will delete the line which contains the word, "alais." We are assuming that no other lines contain this character string.

```
% {27} source .cshrc
alais: Command not found.
% {29} sed /alais/d .cshrc > temp
% {30} mv temp .cshrc


% {31} source .cshrc
```

However, it didn't change the .cshrc file.

We delete the proper line and save the new file into a file called temp. Then we move it back to .cshrc.
We try to run the .cshrc file and it works! No error messages are given. Then we have the nerve to re-enter the alias into the .cshrc file correctly.

```
%{32}echo "alias nou 'who | wc -l' " >> .cshrc
```

```
%  {33}  source  .cshrc
%  {34}  nou
2
%  {34}  csh
%  {1}  nou
2
%  {2}  exit
%  {3}  telnet  alankay

%  {1}  nou
3
%  {2}  logout
%  {4}  logout
```

This time it works. No error messages.
Does our alias work?
Yes.
Let us go into another shell and see if the .cshrc file redefines the nou alias.
Yes, it does.
We come back to the original shell.
We telnet back into our own machine.

Here we check and see that not only were we able to log back in, but the nou alias still works here. Now that we are satisfied that we can log in as well as go into other shells without problems, we log out.

Using tcsh

The tcsh shell also executes the .cshrc file, if it exists. With tcsh, you can use the left and right arrow keys to edit the command line. The up and down arrow keys can be used to scroll through previous commands. These features are good enough reason to switch your default shell to tcsh.

```
tramteke  {89}  cd  /
{90}  cd  /usr
usr  {91}  cd  /bin
bin  {92}  cd  ~/unit7
unit7  {93}  cd  -
bin  {94}  cd  -
unit7  {99}  set  prompt  =  ""
pwd
/home/tramteke
```

Suppose you are changing between two different directories: using cd – will switch you back to the previous directory without having to give the path.

Here we go back to the previous directory, which was /bin.
Here we go back to ~/unit7.
Now we set our prompt to null.
Now no prompt is shown at all. We type pwd and see that we are in our login directory.
When we set the prompt, we get an error message because I forgot to place a space on both sides of the equal sign.

```
set  prompt  ="\!  :  "
set:  Variable  name  must  begin  with  a  letter.
set  prompt  =  "\!  :  "
104  :
```

Here, setting the prompt worked. The \! characters give the command number in history which you are currently entering. The colon gets printed as shown. It doesn't have any special meaning associated with it.

```
104  :  echo  hello  Mars
hello  Mars
105  :  pwd
/home/tramteke
105  :  set  prompt  =  "%~%  :"
~%  :cd  ..
/home%  :cd  /bin
/bin%:set  prompt  =  "%m:%/%  {\!}"
alankay:/bin%  {111}cd
alankay:/home/tramteke%  {112}cd  ..
alankay:/home%  {113}cd  /
```

If we type in a command, the command number increases from 104 to 105.

If we set the prompt to %~%, we will see the directory we are in each time. This is so much easier than what we had to do in csh.

Here we are setting the prompt to first show the name of the machine or server by using %m. That is alankay, in our case. Then a colon follows that. After the colon %/% shows the entire path. The short path using the login directory as the base directory is not shown here as it was with %~%. Finally, {\!} shows the command number within braces.

```
%set correct = cmd
%ct file1
CORRECT>cut file1 (y|n|e|a)e
%cat file1
```

EXPERIMENTS

```
%csh
%set path = ($path .)


%whereis csh

%cat > lm
#! /bin/csh
ls -l | more
^d




%chmod 600 lm
%ls -l lm

%lm

%chmod 700 lm
%ls -l lm

%lm

%cat lm


%echo lm

----lm-file------



%lm


%cd /
%lm

%~/lm

%cd
```

If the variable called correct is set to cmd, for command, then whenever you misspell a command, such as cat, the shell will prompt you with the command it thinks you want. If you enter Y, that means that you accept the correction. If you enter N, that means that the command will be executed just as you typed it. An E will allow you to edit the command and an A will allow you to abort the command.

Command Files

Type csh to get into the C shell.
Before we start, set the path as shown here. This command will be explained later on in this unit. If you have to stop doing these experiments midstream and log out, remember to do these two commands before you continue.
Also, find out where the csh program is located. On my system it is "/bin/csh". Hence, in the file "lm" that we need to create has that path given. If your path is different, then enter that path instead in the "lm" file.

7.1 Let us say that I find myself doing "ls -l | more" over and over again and I want to make it into a new command that is short, like "lm."

First, make sure that lm is not executable.
Notice how the permissions are set.

Try executing it. Does it work?

Change the mode so that it is executable.
Notice how the permissions are set.

Try executing it. Does it work?

Remember what this does?

And this?

7.2 Now edit the "lm" file so that after it displays the listing it also displays your working directory, who you are, and the number of people who are currently logged in. Write down what your "lm" file looks like here. You have just created your own UNIX command!

Does this command work from other directories?

Or do you also have to specify that the command is found in the home directory? The squiggle before the slash means get the command from the home directory. Now go back home.

Aliases

```
%rm −i lm
%alias lm 'ls −l | more'
%cd /
%lm

%cd
%lm
```

7.3 What if I don't want to keep this "lm" file floating around in my directory? Here is an alternative. It is called creating an alias. The shell remembers the meaning of "lm".

Does "lm" work from any directory?

```
%cat lm
```

What happens if you try to print it?

```
%echo lm
```

```
%find ~ −name "lm" −print
```

Is there now a file called "lm"?

```
%alias
```

List all the aliases. Is "lm" listed there?

```
%echo $SHELL
```

7.4 I am assuming that you are using C shell. Let us confirm that.

```
%ps
```

```
%csh
%lm
```

Now start another shell. Just type "csh".
Does the new shell know that "lm" is an alias?

```
%alias
```

Is "lm" listed as an alias in the list for this new shell?

CAUTION: DO NOT PROCEED WITH EXPERIMENTS 7.5 THROUGH 7.8 UNTIL YOU GET YOUR INSTRUCTOR'S PERMISSION. And even then, proceed with these steps correctly and slowly. You could end up not being able to log back in!! If you would rather do this section some other time, you can skip to Experiment 7.9 without losing continuity.

```
%cp .cshrc .cshrc.orig
```

7.5 When you first log in or start a new shell, the .cshrc file is executed. We need to place our lm alias in this file so that that alias is available every time we log in. First, make a copy of your old .cshrc file and give it the extension "orig". This way, if you butcher the ".cshrc" file, you will still have the ".cshrc.orig" file to go back to. This is a very important step whenever you are editing a sensitive file.

```
%vi .cshrc
```

7.6 Do a ":set showmode". Find the place where the aliases are defined. Type an "o" to create a line under the current one. Enter "alias lm 'ls −l | more'", keeping the columns lined up with the other aliases. Did you mess up? Then, after an escape, type :q! This will quit your vi session without doing a save. Now try again. When you have the file as you want it, enter :wq

```
%source .cshrc
```

7.7 Don't start a new shell or log out yet! Run your ".cshrc" file first by using the source command. Do you get any errors? If you do, then use vi to correct this file until the command runs without errors. If you still can't get it to work,

```
%lm
%csh
%lm


%alias

%unalias  lm
%lm

%alias  lm  'ls —l | more'
%lm  /bin




%unalias  lm
%alias  lm  'ls —l \!* | more'
%lm  /bin



%
```

then restore your original file by using this command: "cp .cshrc.org .cshrc".

7.8 Did you come through this experiment with flying colors? Congratulations! Now let us test our new ".cshrc" file. Is the alias "lm" recognized every time you start a new shell? Is it recognized every time you log out and then log back in? You are starting to create your own working environment!

7.9 Is "lm" defined as one of the aliases?

7.10 What does this do?

7.11 What if we want to do an ls —l not of the current directory but of some other directory, like "/bin"? Can we add this argument to our alias? (An argument is something that you provide an alias or a command to act upon. Here the argument is "/bin".)

7.12 No. This would have worked if we hadn't placed a more command at the end of our alias.
Redefine "lm" with a "\!*" just before the pipe. This is where all the arguments for the alias will get substituted. The backslash is considered to be a type of a quote and the bang-star stores all the arguments. You will learn more about quotes later.

7.13 Rewrite the complete ls command as it is interpreted by the shell when using the "lm" alias with the "/bin" directory as an argument.

User—Defined Shell Variables

7.14 That's enough play: let's get back to work! The shell allows us to create variables which can be changed on the fly.

```
%set  name  =  "soundhog"
%echo  name

%echo  $name

%set  last  =  $name
%echo  $last

%set  name  =  "tim bo"
%echo  my  first  name  is  $name

%echo  $last  is  my  last  name.

%echo  middle  name  is  $middle

%set  com  =  "who"
%set  nxt  =  "wc —l"
%$com  |  $nxt


%
```

In C shell, what command is used to assign a value to a variable? The Bourne shell doesn't use any command. You would just enter name="tim bo".
Do you have to declare the variable as in C programming?

Can C shell tell if a variable wasn't assigned a value?
How do you see what is stored in the variable "name"?

7.15 Create a new variable called "full". Use the values stored in the "name" and the "last" variables and assign the full name to "full". Then display it. Of course, you should show your steps.

Working in C Shell and tcsh

```
%
```

7.16 Assign "/bin" to the variable called "loc". Assign the command "cd" to the variable called "command". First using only the "loc" variable then using both of these variables, change the directory to "/bin" and confirm that.

```
%set age = 17
%echo age
```

7.17 Does the shell distinguish between integers and characters?

```
%echo $age
```

```
%echo $age + 2
```

7.18 Are all values stored in variables treated as characters?

```
%17 — 4
```

7.19 What do you need to do if you want to do a calculation?

```
%expr 17 — 4
```

```
%expr $age * 2
```

7.20 Are quotes necessary for doing multiplication?

```
%expr $age "*" 3
```

7.21 What does the asterisk stand for if no double quotes are used?

```
%echo *
```

Four Kinds of Quotes!

```
%cd
%mkdir unit7
%cd unit7
%touch f1 f2 f3
%ls —l
```

7.22 UNIX has four kinds of quotes, enough to make anyone confused! But on the other hand, they allow you to do practically anything you want. Characters placed within a set of **double quotes** (") are interpreted just as they are without any special meaning. For instance, echo "*" will simply print the asterisk and not print the names of all the files in the current directory. For this rule, the only exceptions are $, `, and \. These characters don't lose their special meanings. (The touch command creates files or updates the date and time–stamp on it.)

```
%echo *
```

```
%echo * > f1
%cat f1
```

```
%set name = bobo
%echo $name * yes
```

```
%echo "$name" "*" ">"
```

From these experiments, did the $ lose its special meaning? Did the asterisk?

```
%echo "i am in `pwd`"
```

Did the back quote lose its special meaning here?
Were the characters "pwd" printed as well as "i am"?

```
%echo "$name >" file1
```

Did the $ lose its special meaning, that is, the value of the shell variable?
Did the > lose its special meaning of redirection?

```
%echo "$name" > file1
%cat file1
```

In this instance, did the > lose its special meaning? Why or why not?

```
%echo '$name' '*'
```

7.23 All characters placed within a pair of **single quotes** (') are interpreted just as they are. There are no exceptions.

```
%echo 'i am in `pwd`'
```

Working in C Shell and tcsh

```
%echo '$name >' file1
```

```
%echo \* \> f1
```

```
%echo hello | more
```

```
%echo hello \| more
```

```
%echo \$name
```

```
%echo '$name' = \'$name\'
```


```
%sh
$name=bobo
$echo "\$name" "\*"
```

```
$echo "i am in \`pwd\`"
```

```
$echo "$name \>" f1
```

```
$echo "`cat f1` \|" f1
```

```
$echo "'$name' = \'$name\'"
```

```
$echo '"$name" = \"$name\"'
```

```
$echo "\"$name\""
```


```
$exit
```


```
%echo `cat f1`
```

```
%echo "cat f1"
```

```
%echo "Here's f1: `cat f1`"
```

```
%echo `f1`
```


```
%
```


```
%
```

Which characters kept their special meaning inside single quotes?

7.24 The **backslash** (\) is used to quote single characters only. It removes the special meaning of any character that follows it.

Which of the following lose their special meaning if followed by a backslash outside double quotes?

*	> (redirection)
| (pipe)	' (full quote, don't expand)

7.25 Ask your instructor if you can skip this step. Use the Bourne shell for testing the **backslash inside double quotes**. Since you have changed shells, you must redefine the name shell variable. In Bourne shell, that is done without the set command and with no spaces before and after the equals sign. Inside double quotes the backslash removes the special meaning from all characters. However, with $, ", `, and \ the backslash is not printed and with all others, it is printed.

Inside double quotes, which of the following lose their special meaning when used with (\)?

$	|	'
*	>	`

Inside double quotes, with which of the following is the (\) not printed?

$	|	'
*	>	`

Return to the C shell.

7.26 Only commands should be placed inside a pair of **back quotes** (`) because they will get executed at that point.

If any input besides a command is placed inside back quotes, you will get an error since this input is not a command.

7.27 Give the echo command that will print a statement showing the correct number of files and the correct working directory. You will need to review piping and the wc command for this.

7.28 Give the echo command that will print a statement giving the current date. You will need the cut command for this.

Establishing Your Environment using System–Defined Shell Variables

In Experiment 7.14 we introduced shell variables which were defined by the user. In this section, we will explore some of the shell variables which are predefined by the system and carry special meanings. Changing the values of these variables will affect the environment under which you work and play. Figure 7.3 summarizes the categories of shell variables.

There are two types of predefined variables. These are environment variables and shell variables. The environment variables use all upper–case letters. The value of the environment variables are available to any program that may need them. For instance, another program which you are running may need to know what terminal type you are using. In that case, that program will access the TERM environment variable.

Shell variables, on the other hand, are known only to the shell in which they are defined. If you change the shell they disappear, unless you defined them. However, the environment variables are common to all the shells and programs which you may be running. Some environment variables are named the same as the shell variables.

Binary shell variables are either set or not set. They don't take any other values. Regular variables take arbitrary values. Let's start playing with them.

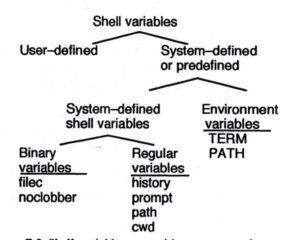

Figure 7.3 Shell variable types with some examples.

Shell Variables

```
%set
```
7.29 Display all the shell variables that are defined. Are "filec" and "noclobber" defined here?

```
%mkdir unit7
%cd unit7
%pwd
```
7.30 Create a directory called "unit7". Do the following experiments in that directory so I can keep track of the files that you have.

```
%echo some stuff > flile.for.testing
```

```
%set filec
%cat fl<esc>
```
7.31 Set the "filec" shell variable. This one is used only in csh. In tcsh, it is always set.

Type "cat fl" and then press the <Esc> key twice. In tcsh, you may have to press <Tab>. Does the shell complete the name of the file? If it does, just hit <Return> and the command is done. This is called the "filec" shell variable. If there are several files which begin with a given character string, press <Ctrl>d to find out those filenames.

```
%unset filec
%cat fl<esc>


%set filec


%set noclobber
%echo more > fl<esc>

%cat fl<esc>

%unset noclobber
%echo more > flile.for.testing


%cat fl<esc>

%set history = 4
%history


%set history = 6
%history


%csh


%set


%logout

%echo $prompt

%set prompt = "$user :"

    :ls


    :alias setp 'set prompt = "$cwd: "'
    :alias cd 'cd \!*; setp'


        :cd ..


        :ls

        :cd /


        :exit
```

7.32 After unsetting the filec variable, does your shell complete the name for you? If your filenames are not uniquely identifiable, then this feature doesn't help.
For now you can set your file completion variable and use this feature whenever you don't want to type the entire filename.

7.33 Here's another binary–type shell variable.
Can you clobber the "file.for.testing" file by redirecting an output to it?

What about now? After you unset the "noclobber" shell variable, can you overwrite a file by redirecting output to it?

7.34 "history" is a nonbinary type of shell variable to which you can assign a numeric value. What does it do?

7.35 Let us go into another shell and see if the previous variables kept their original values.

Did your previous shell variables, "noclobber", and "history," keep the same values they had in the last shell?

7.36 Incidentally, can you log out from a shell that wasn't your log–in shell?
Let us stay in the same shell.

7.37 What does the shell variable "prompt" store?

Show your new prompt here. What does the shell variable "user" store?

In csh, you would set your prompt to show the current directory by defining these two aliases. In tcsh, it is easier. You would simply enter set prompt = "%/%".
Check your .cshrc file to see how the prompt is set.
Show your new prompt. What does the shell variable "cwd" store?

Get back to your original shell and prompt.

```
%printenv
%setenv
```

Environment Variables:
7.38 Is there a difference in the information given by either of these commands?

```
___ HOME
___ SHELL
___ PATH
___ MAIL
___ TERM
___ USER
```

Can you match these variables with their meanings?
A. Path of where the shell is located
B. Directory of the mail program
C. Type of terminal in use
D. Path of the login directory
E. The person logged on
F. Directories to be searched when running a program

```
%printenv TERM
%echo $TERM

%echo $term

%set term = sewing_machine
%echo $term

%echo $TERM

%vi file1

%set term = vt100
```

7.39 How can you display the value of the TERM or terminal type environment variable?
Write down the value of your terminal type because we'll be changing it. Mine is "vt100".

7.40 When the shell variables, term, path, and user are changed, the environment variables, TERM, PATH, and USER are also automatically changed. Is that true for "term"?

What terminal type error message do you get?

If the terminal type is changed to your original terminal type, can you get back into "vi"? (Substitute your terminal type in place of the "vt100" that I got.)

```
%setenv TERM sewing_thing

%printenv TERM

%echo $term

%setenv TERM vt100
```

7.41 Does changing the environment variable change the shell equivalent? Your answer should be no. Notice that when you change the environment variable, the "setenv" command is used and no equal sign is used.

Reset your TERM variable to what it was in Experiment 7.39.
Can vi recognize your terminal type?

```
%vi file1
:q!
```

The "path" variable.
7.42 Find out where the following commands are stored.

```
%whereis ls

%whereis cat

%whereis sort

%whereis tail

%whereis pwd
```

    ls
    cat
    sort
    tail
    pwd

My ls, cat, and pwd commands are stored in /bin and the other two commands are in /usr/bin.

Working in C Shell and tcsh

```
%csh
%echo $path
```

7.43 First get a new shell.
Write down your default path.

```
%set path = ""
%echo $path
```

Then null your path.

```
%ls
```

7.44 Does the ls command work? If not, what error message do you get?

```
%pwd
%sort
```

What about these commands?

```
%echo hello
```

7.45 If these commands work, then they are part of the shell. They don't have their own man pages, but are described in the man page of csh. Are the echo, ls, and cd commands internal to the shell?

```
%cd ..
```

```
%echo $cwd
```

```
%ls −l
```

```
%man csh
```

7.46 Are the commands, which you determined to be internal, described in the man page of csh?

```
%ls −l
```

7.47 With the path still set to null, go to the home directory. Does ls work here?

```
%/bin/ls −l
```

Run the ls command by preceding it with the path to the directory where it is located. Refer to Experiment 7.42. I found it in "/bin" in my system. If you find it in a different directory, then replace my path with the path where you found ls.

```
%echo stuff > file1
%tail file1
```

7.48 Create file1. Does tail work?

```
%/usr/bin/tail file1
```

What happens if you provide the path to where tail is found on your system?

```
%set path = (/bin)
%ls −l
```

7.49 Now set the path to where ls is stored.
Do we need to provide the path for ls as we did in Experiment 7.47?

```
%cat file1
```

Does cat work?

```
%tail file1
```

Do you need to provide the path for tail as we did in Experiment 7.47?

```
%/usr/bin/tail file1
```

I still had to provide the path. This command was found in "/usr/bin" and the path variable told the system to look only in "/bin" if a command is to be executed.

```
%set path = ($path /usr/bin)
%echo $path
```

7.50 Append the path for tail to the existing path.

```
%ls ..
```

7.51 Your path should now contain the directories where ls and tail are found.

```
%tail file1
```

Does ls work by itself?

Does tail work also without having to give the path each time?

```
%unalias lm
%cat > lm
#! /bin/csh
ls −l | more
^d
```

7.52 Unalias "lm" if it was an alias before.
Create the file called "lm" if you don't have it in the current directory.

```
%chmod 700 lm
```

Make lm executable.

```
%lm
```

Can you execute lm? You shouldn't be able to.

```
%./lm
```

What if you tell it where the command is found? Here, we specify the path to be the current directory. Does it work now?

```
%set path = ($path .)
```

```
%echo $path
```

Now set the path to what it was before and add the current directory. Now all three commands should work without having to give the path where they are found each time. Plus, once the path is set, we don't have to remember where all the commands are kept.

```
%ls
```

```
%tail file1
```

```
%lm
```

```
%cd ..
```

7.53 Does your lm command work from any directory? If not, then change your path so that all three commands can work from any directory. This time you are on your own.

```
%lm
```

```
%exit
```

Lastly, exit back into your login shell. Now your environment is reset the way it was originally.

.cshrc and .login scripts
7.54 When you first log on, the .cshrc script and then the .login script are executed. Every time you go into another shell the .cshrc script is executed. Typically, the .login script defines your environment variables and the .cshrc file defines the shell variables. There may also be a .logout script that is executed when you log out.
Type out your .cshrc.
Which lines make sense?
Which lines did we not cover?
Also, type out and examine your .login script.

```
%ls −al | more
%more .cshrc
```

```
%more .login
```

7.55 In Experiments 7.5 through 7.8 you may have changed your .cshrc file. If you did, then you are in a position to create your own working environment by implementing the ideas you learned here. If you do decide to change your .cshrc or .login files, first make a copy of the originals and label them as such. Then ask your instructor for advice, and follow the steps described in Experiments 7.5 through 7.8.

Working in C Shell and tcsh

HOMEWORK

1. Identify the term being described.
    a. A command interpreter used in UNIX.
    b. A shortcut used for commands.
    c. A dollar sign ($) is used preceding it to evaluate it.
    d. A type of variable that is set using the setenv command.

2. Describe the various facilities that a shell provides.

3. Identify the **shell variable** being described.
    a. Allows you to use long descriptive names for files without having to type the entire filename.
    b. When looking at the previous commands in your session, this variable determines how many of them will be shown by default.
    c. If you are poor at typing, this variable, if set properly in tcsh, will try to correct your mistakes in entering commands.
    d. This variable doesn't allow files to be overwritten by redirection.
    e. This variable contains the current working directory.

4. Identify the **environment variable** that
    a. contains the type of terminal being used.
    b. contains the set of directories to be searched when executing commands.
    c. contains the login name of the user.
    d. contains the login shell of the user.
    e. stores the directory of the mail program.

5. Do the following commands dealing with **aliases**.
    a. Create an alias called ll which does ls –l.
    b. Delete the alias called ll.
    c. Show all aliases.
    d. Create an alias called s which shows the date on the screen.
    e. Create an alias called look which takes a string for an argument and displays the lines in the /etc/passwd file which contain that string, whether upper–case or lower–case. For example, if I enter look bob, the command will print all lines in the file which contain bob.

6. Give the name of the file being described.
    a. The file used only by tcsh as a start–up file.
    b. The file used by either csh or tcsh as a start–up file when starting a new shell.
    c. The file used when first logging in but not when starting a new shell.
    d. The file that should be saved before you edit the .cshrc file which came with your system.

7. Give the command for each task.
    a. Run the .cshrc file without starting a new shell.
    b. Subtract 2300 and 743 and display the answer.
    c. Do an ls without using the ls command.
    d. Display all shell variables.
    e. Give two methods to display all environment variables.
    f. Set the path to null.
    g. Set the path to whatever the path is currently and add /sbin and /usr/sbin to the path.
    h. Find out in which directory the ping command is stored.

Quotes:

8. Suppose that the following files are in the current working directory: fileX, fileY, and flile; the content of flile is "Yes me!"; the current directory is /home; and the following variables are set:

```
set my = *
set his = "*"
set its = `echo *`
```

Show the output for each command.

a. echo my

b. echo *

c. echo $my

d. echo $his

e. echo cat flile is `cat flile`

f. echo its $its

g. echo "$my * \>" flile

h. echo '"$my * \>" flile'

i. echo \`pwd\` `pwd` "pwd"

j. echo `pwd` * * > \| fileX'

9. Give the command for each task in order.
   a. Create a variable called disk and assign "me oh my" to it.
   b. Store the value of disk, the string which you just stored in it, to a file called f1.
   c. Create a variable called tape and assign it the contents of file f1.
   d. Show the value of tape using this format:

```
tape = me oh my
```

   e. Show the value of disk using this format:

```
"disk =" me oh my
```

   f. Show the contents of f1 using this format:

```
f1 = 'me oh my'
```

LAB ASSIGNMENTS

1. Show your entries for these steps in order and save the script of your session.
   Create a command file called pp which will do these commands: ps, pwd, and printenv.
   Then set the permissions so that the file can be executed.
   Then give the command which will confirm that the permissions are set correctly.
   Now go to the root directory and execute the pp file from there.

2. Create a file called mystuff. In this file create an alias called nypl, which stands for New York Public Library. This alias should do this command: telnet nyplgate.nypl.org
   When you test this out, enter nypl for the login name.
   Then add the current directory (.) to your path.
   Then create a shell variable called bobs which counts the number of times that "bob" appears in /etc/passwd, regardless of case.
   Then set your prompt so that it shows the current directory regardless of the directory you are in. Do this with the assumption that you are running csh.
   Then set the term shell variable to your default terminal type. Typically, it is vt100.
   Finally, display the following items using the formats shown:

```
'HOME' is /home/tramteke
```

   Your HOME variable will be different. Use printenv to get the value of HOME.

```
My PATH is set to > /bin /usr/bin   etc. . .
```

   Do not use the printenv command to get the value of your PATH.

```
The current date and time is:
```

   Have the output of date displayed at the end of this line and not below it.

```
35 * 3 is "105"
```
Have the shell calculate this product.

```
The alias for nypl is set to "telnet nyplgate.nypl.org"
```
You have to figure out how to print the value of the alias of nypl. Don't just type it in.

```
Number of bob's who have accounts is 4
```
Display the output after running the bobs variable declared above. It may not be 4 in your case.

Now execute this file and test all its parts to show that they work by creating a session script to keep a record of what you did.

UNIX Networking

CONCEPTS TO LEARN

.forward This file is used to send all incoming mail to the specified complete address. This prevents one from having to check all servers on which you may an account to check your mail. By forwarding mail from all servers, except for one, to a single server, mail has to be checked only at that single server.

.plan The content of this file is displayed every time someone does a finger on the user. This is a crude way to communicate what your current projects are in case someone else may be working on something which may benefit both of you.

.signature The content of this file is sent at the end of each mail which you send. Usually, this contains your full name, address, phone number, and anything else you may want to include at the end of your mail. It could be your favorite quote.

Network cards: In order to be connected to a LAN, a host must have a NIC (Network Interface Card) inside of it. The NIC provides an interface between the host and the physical network. Each NIC has a unique address called the hardware or physical address. Whenever a NIC has to communicate with another NIC over a LAN, it must know that NIC's physical address. NIC addresses are stored in a table called the ARP table. If an address is not in this table then the NIC can search for it.

COMMANDS TO LEARN

arp –a The ARP (Address Resolution Protocol) table can be seen by entering this command. It is maintained dynamically by the UNIX host. It contains the network card address of each IP address on your local area network.

finger This command will allow you to get information about a person on the UNIX server.

ftp File Transfer Protocol allows you to transfer files between the server on which you are logged on and the server to which the ftp is done. A get command brings a file *from* the server from which the ftp was done and a put command transfers a file *to* the server to which the ftp is done. You cannot enter commands as if you were logged in using telnet.

ifconfig Given the interface, this command will show you how that interface is configured.

mesg y This command will allow you to receive messages from others. If no one can talk or write to you, then do this command to see if it helps.

netstat –nr	This command shows the routing tables. The n indicates to show the entries using the IP numbers. Without the n, host names would be shown instead.
netstat –ain	This will show the status of all (a option) the interfaces (i option) in numeric (n option) format.
ping	Allows you to see if the remote server is up and running. This is the first test you should do if no connection can be established with the remote site.
talk	This will allow you to chat with someone else. Do a <Ctrl>d or <Ctrl>c to terminate the session. Both parties can type simultaneously. The messages don't appear on the same line on the screen, but rather the screen is split to separate the two transmissions. See the mesg and write commands.
telnet	Allows you to log into a server remotely. Usually, you need an account on the server. Then you can enter all commands as if you were at the server's console.
traceroute	Shows the hops through which IP packets are routed when accessing a remote server.
w	Similar to the who command, this command shows how long the server has been up and what time it is.
write	This command will allow you to talk with someone else. Do a <Ctrl>d or <Ctrl>c to terminate the session. This method unfortunately will garble up what you type and what the other person types on the same line unless you take turns typing. See the talk and mesg commands.

SAMPLE SESSION

telnet and Commands Relating to Users

```
tramteke {9} hostname
alankay
```

First, let us see the name of the server we are on.

Then let us see who is logged on our server. The IP address of where I am logged from is 204.142.106.7.

```
{10} who
tramteke ttyp0 Sep 30 10:43 (204.142.106.7)
mrah0620 ttyp1 Sep 30 10:21 (204.142.106.3)
dnoc0993 ttyp2 Sep 30 10:35 (204.142.106.3)
```

204.142.106.4   204.142.106.7
alankay ← My PC

The w command gives us what the other users are doing as well as the current time and the amount of time the server has been up. Notice, mrah0620 is running tcsh and dnoc0993 is running pine.

```
{11} w
10:45AM   up 14 days,   1:48,  3 users,  load averages: 0.09, 0.14, 0.13
USER      TTY FROM             LOGIN@  IDLE WHAT
tramteke  p0  204.142.106.7    10:43AM    0 w
mrah0620  p1  204.142.106.3    10:21AM    0 -tcsh
dnoc0993  p2  204.142.106.3    10:35AM    0 (pine)
```

I could log back into alankay from alankay; then I would be logged twice, once from my PC and once from alankay.

```
{12} telnet
alankay.nj.devry.edu
Trying 204.142.105.4...
Connected to
alankay.nj.devry.edu.
login: tramteke
```

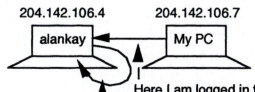

204.142.106.4   204.142.106.7
alankay ← My PC

Here I am logged in from 204.142.106.7
And here I am logged in from 204.142.106.4

```
Password:
Welcome  to  OpenBSD.
```
Here, we see that my second login is confirmed.
```
{13} who
tramteke  ttyp0  Sep  30  10:43  (204.142.106.7)
mrah0620  ttyp1  Sep  30  10:21  (204.142.106.3)
dnoc0993  ttyp2  Sep  30  10:35  (204.142.106.3)
tramteke  ttyp3  Sep  30  10:46  (204.142.106.4)
```

I can now log into a server on the Internet on which I have an account. Its name is pilot.njin.net.
You would need a shell account with your ISP in order to do a login on your ISP's UNIX server.

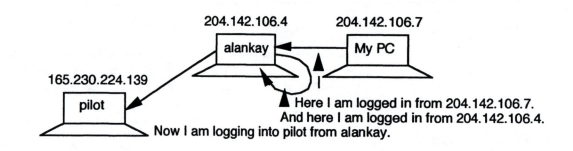

Here I am logged in from 204.142.106.7.
And here I am logged in from 204.142.106.4.
Now I am logging into pilot from alankay.

```
{19} telnet pilot.njin.net
Trying 165.230.224.139...
Connected to pilot.njin.net.
Escape character is '^]'.
SunOS 5.6
login: ramteke
Password:
Last login: Wed Sep 30 10:24:07 from adminb.nj.devry.
New Jersey Intercampus Network, Inc.
%who
ramteke  pts/8  Sep  30  10:14  (alankay.nj.devry.edu)
kkaplan  pts/3  Sep  24  13:56  (margarita.njin.net)
%telnet alankay.nj.devry.edu
Trying 204.142.105.4...
Connected to alankay.nj.devry.edu.
login: tramteke
Password:
Welcome  to  OpenBSD.
{11} who
tramteke  ttyp0     Sep  30  10:43  (204.142.106.7)
mrah0620  ttyp1     Sep  30  10:21  (204.142.106.3)
dnoc0993  ttyp2     Sep  30  10:35  (204.142.106.3)
tramteke  ttyp3     Sep  30  10:46  (204.142.105.4)
tramteke  ttyp5     Sep  30  10:49  (pilot.njin.net)
{12} logout
Connection closed by  foreign  host.
~%logout
Connection closed by  foreign  host.
{20} hostname
alankay
```

My login name on that server is ramteke and
there is only one other person logged in pilot at this time.

And from pilot, I could log back into alankay.

I am now logged into alankay from three locations:
once from my PC, once from alankay, and once from pilot.

This login is from my own PC.

This one is from alankay itself.
This one is from pilot.

Here I am logging out of alankay which puts me back
into pilot.

Now I am logging out of pilot which places me back
into alankay.

Sure enough, I'm now in alankay.

```
{21} who                              A who confirms that I am logged into alankay only twice now.
tramteke  ttyp0  Sep 30  10:43  (204.142.106.7)
mrah0620  ttyp1  Sep 30  10:21  (204.142.106.3)
dnoc0993  ttyp2  Sep 30  10:35  (204.142.106.3)
tramteke  ttyp3  Sep 30  10:46  (204.142.105.4)
{22} logout
Connection closed by foreign host.
{23} who                              Another logout leaves me with only one login session with alankay.
tramteke  ttyp0  Sep 30  10:43  (204.142.106.7)
mrah0620  ttyp1  Sep 30  10:21  (204.142.106.3)
dnoc0993  ttyp2  Sep 30  10:35  (204.142.106.3)
```

If we want to know the full name of mrah0620, we can simply look for that string in the /etc/passwd file. Similarly, we look for dnoc's full name.

```
{24} grep mrah /etc/passwd
mrah0620:*:10370:2001:Marian  Rahman:/home/mrah0620:/bin/tcsh
{25} grep dnoc /etc/passwd
dnoc0993:*:12073:2002:DAVID  NOCK:/home/dnoc0993:/bin/tcsh
```

Let us try to talk with David Nock. He is currently refusing messages. Otherwise, we could chat with him. A <Ctrl>d would have let us quit the talk session.

```
{26} talk dnoc0993
[Your party is refusing messages]
[No connection yet]
```

I try to tell David to enter the mesg y command so I can chat with him. But the write command doesn't work either for the same reason.

```
{27} mesg y
{28} write dnoc0993
write: dnoc0993 has messages disabled
{29} finger               Here, this command gives the full names of those who are logged on.
Login      Name              Tty   Idle   Login Time
dnoc0993  DAVID NOCK         *p2    -     Wed 10:35
mrah0620  Marian Rahman      *p1    1     Wed 10:21
tramteke  Timothy Ramteke    *p0    -     Wed 10:43
```

Doing the finger command on David not only gives David's full name, but also his login directory and shell, from where he logged in and when, and the last time he read his mail. The output also says that his messages are off, indicating that we can't chat with him using talk or write. It gives the last time he read his mail, so that if you sent mail to him after that time, you know that hasn't seen it yet. Lastly, it also gives the plan or project which he may be working on.

```
{32} finger dnoc0993
Login: dnoc0993
Name: DAVID NOCK
Directory: /home/dnoc0993
Shell: /bin/tcsh
(messages off)
On since Wed Sep 30 10:35 (EDT) on ttyp2 from 204.142.106.3
Mail last read Wed Sep 30 10:35 1998 (EDT)
Plan:
I plan to put and keep my best foot forward no matter what
{33} finger tramteke         If I do a finger on myself, I see that I don't have a plan given. That is
Login: tramteke              because I don't have a .plan file in my login directory. (Only part of the
Name: Timothy Ramteke        output of this command is shown in order to save space.)
. . .
No plan                      Let us create a .plan file and see if it appears in the output of finger.
{34} echo I am working on UNIX > .plan
```

```
{35} cat .plan
I am working on UNIX
{36} finger tramteke
Login: tramteke              Name: TimothyRamteke
Directory: /home/tramteke   Shell: /bin/tcsh
On since Wed Sep 30 10:43 (EDT) on ttyp0 from 204.142.106.7
Mail last read Fri Sep 11 14:25 1998 (EDT)
Plan:I am working on UNIX
```

Here is the content of the .plan file and the output of the finger command.

```
{38} chfn
Permission denied.
```

The chfn (change finger) command allows you to change information which is shown in the finger command. This information is also available in the user's entry of the /etc/passwd file.

```
{41} more .signature
: No such file or directory
{42} cat > .signature
Timothy Ramteke
Professor, CIS Dept.
ramteke@alankay.nj.devry.edu
Phone: 732 555 1212
^d
```

It seems that I don't have a .signature file in my login directory. Here I am creating one. Now, every time I send mail, this file will be attached to the end of it. This way, I don't have to enter the same items every time at the end of every message.

```
{43} cat > .forward
ramteke@pilot.njin.net
^d
{44} cat .forward
ramteke@pilot.njin.net
```

I want only to check if I got any email from pilot. Others might send me mail to different hosts, but I want to log into only one host to check my mail. Hence, I create a .forward file in my alankay account which will forward all mail I receive there to pilot. Now I only need to log into pilot to check my mail.

ftp

Let us now start transferring files between UNIX hosts. First, I log into pilot to see what is there.

```
{45} telnet pilot.njin.net
Trying 165.230.224.139...
Connected to pilot.njin.net.
login: ramteke
Password:
Last login: Wed Sep 30 10:49:30 from alankay.nj.devry
~%ls
```

Here are the files which I have in my login directory.

```
#t#       courses.txt    reap.sh
#test#    file1          reap.sh~
~%cat file1
anderman
brancone
kkaplan
smundane
~%logout
Connection closed by foreign host.
```

Let us see what I have in file1.

Let us log out and try to transfer the file1 file from pilot to alankay. Now we are back in alankay.
Here we start the ftp program.
A question mark gives all the commands which are available us. I have shown only a few here.

```
{46} ftp
ftp> ?
Commands may be abbreviated.
! disconnect mdelete preservesend
account exit mget prompt   site
ascii    ftp  mls    put    status
bell     get  mode   pwd    struct
```

```
binary    gate      modtime  quit      sunique
close     lcd       nmap     restart   user
```

If we precede a command with the help command, we get a short description of what it does.

```
ftp> help quit
quit   terminate ftp session and exit
```

quit will terminate the ftp session and exit the ftp program.

```
ftp> help open
open  connect to remote ftp server
```

The open command will make a ftp connection to a remote host.

```
ftp> help user
user  send new user information
```

The user command will let us log on to the host to which we are connected.

```
ftp> help close
close terminate ftp session
```

close will only close a connection.

```
ftp> help get
get   receive file
```

get will transfer a file from the other site to the current site, which is alankay in our case.

```
ftp> user
Not connected.
```

We are not connected yet, so we can't log on.

```
ftp> open pilot.njin.net
Connected to pilot.njin.net.
Name (pilot.njin.net:tramteke): ramteke
331 Password required for ramteke.
Password:
230 User ramteke logged in.
Remote system type is UNIX.
Using binary mode to transfer files.
#
ftp> get file1
```

This open command will allow us to connect to pilot. Now I am logging on.

Here we are transferring file1, which we saw on pilot, to alankay.

```
local: file1 remote: file1
227 Entering Passive Mode (165,230,224,140,247,244)
150 Opening BINARY mode data connection for file1 (35
bytes).
100% |###################|
35            00:00 ETA
226 Transfer complete.
35 bytes received in 0.00 seconds (8.15 KB/s)
```

And here we are transferring a file in the other direction. The put command will transfer the t.cc file from alankay to pilot. The hash marks (#) tell us that data is being transferred.

```
ftp> put t.cc
local: t.cc remote: t.cc
227 Entering Passive Mode (165,230,224,140,249,6)
150 Opening BINARY mode data connection for t.cc.
100% |##############################################|
1206          00:00 ETA
226 Transfer complete.
1206 bytes sent in 0.10 seconds (12.15 KB/s)
#
ftp> close
221 Goodbye.
```

The close disconnects us from pilot.

```
ftp> logout
?Invalid command.
```

Oops! logout isn't recognized.

```
ftp> quit
221 Goodbye.
```

quit allows us to get out of the ftp program.

```
{51} ls
africa.tar.gz dir1  t.cc
cis238.csh    dir2  jj
courses.txt   file1 unit7
{52} cat file1
anderman
brancone
kkaplan
smundane
```

The ls command shows us that file1 was transferred using the get command of ftp.

Here is the content of file1. It is as we had seen it in pilot. See command 45.

One way you can transfer files between your PC and a UNIX server like alankay is by using a ftp program for Windows 98. WS–FTP is such a program. From Windows, you open this application and it asks you to enter some of the fields shown in this diagram:

Profile Name:	
Host Name/Address:	alankay.nj.devry.edu
Host Type:	Automatic Detect
User ID:	tramteke
Password:	

The name of the host is the host on which you have an account, and the user ID is your login name. Usually, the host type should be kept at automatic detect and then, after entering the password, you will be logged in. Here I am logged into alankay to do file transfers:

Local System

C:\Prog Files\WS_ftp

```
[ | | ]whatsnew.txt
[ | | ]toby.doc
[-a-]
[-b-]
```

◄
►

Remote System

home/tramteke

```
[ | | ]t.cc
[ | | ]file1
```

Messages

On the left side the local system or the PC is shown, and on the right–hand side the remote system or alankay is shown. On the local system, we are in the C drive which has two files in it, whatsnew.txt and toby.doc. We can change the drive to A or B by double–clicking on it. If we highlight a file and click on the right arrow, then we would be doing a put, or placing the file into alankay. If we were to highlight t.cc and click on the left arrow, we would be doing a get, or transferring the file from alankay to our PC. The box on the bottom shows any messages the application may want to convey to us.

Network Interfaces and Routing

To find out what interfaces alankay has, we enter the netstat command. The –i option stands for interface. There is really only one physical interface to the network or the LAN on our NIC. It is called ep0. This is an Ethernet interface. The first ep0 entry gives the hardware address of the NIC and the second entry shows that all traffic going to the 204.142.105 subnet should be directed via 204.142.105.4. The lo0 interface is a local loopback interface which always has an address of 127.0.0.1.

```
{56} netstat -ain
Name    Mtu      Network         Address
lo0     32768    127/8           127.0.0.1
ep0     1500     <Link>          00:a0:24:d5:9a:ce
ep0     1500     204.142.105     204.142.105.4
{57} ifconfig lo0
ifconfig: Command not found.
{60} whereis ifconfig
/sbin/ifconfig
{61} set path = ($path /sbin )
{62} ifconfig lo0
lo0:  flags=8009<UP,LOOPBACK,MULTICAST>
inet 127.0.0.1 netmask 0xff000000
{63} ifconfig ep0
ep0:  flags=b863<UP,BROADCAST,NOTRAILERS,
RUNNING,SIMPLEX,LINK0,LINK1,MULTICAST>
inet 204.142.105.4 netmask 0xffffff00
broadcast 204.142.105.255
```

The ifconfig command is not in our path. Hence, by using the whereis command we find out where it is and add it to our path.

Now we can enter the ifconfig command and ask it to show how the lo0 interface is configured. The server is up and its address is 127.0.0.1.
Here is how the Ethernet interface is configured.

The ping command shows if the distant host is up. To terminate the pinging, use <Ctrl>C. It looks like pilot is up. Any other host on the Internet can also be checked whether you have an account on it or not.

```
{64} ping pilot.njin.net
PING pilot.njin.net (165.230.224.139): 56 data bytes
64 bytes from 165.230.224.139: icmp_seq=0 ttl=239 time=48.687 ms
64 bytes from 165.230.224.139: icmp_seq=1 ttl=239 time=21.198 ms
64 bytes from 165.230.224.139: icmp_seq=2 ttl=239 time=31.302 ms
64 bytes from 165.230.224.139: icmp_seq=3 ttl=239 time=43.323 ms
pilot.njin.net ping statistics —
5 packets transmitted, 4 packets received, 20% packet loss
round-trip min/avg/max = 21.198/36.127/48.687 ms
```

If the ping were unsuccessful, then you could do a traceroute to see where the transmission is getting lost. Here we are doing a traceroute to a host in Germany. The de domain stands for Deutschland. Notice how the time to go from Washington to Frankfurt jumps from 28 milliseconds to 147 milliseconds.

```
{66} traceroute monad.swb.de
to monad.swb.de (193.175.30.33), 30 hops max, 40 byte packets
1    204.142.105.1 (204.142.105.1)  2.419 ms   2.317 ms   2.270 ms
2    nbw-devry.jvnc.net (130.94.52.33)  5.839 ms   5.566 ms   5.808 ms
3    T3-pri-nbw.jvnc.net (130.94.14.249)  7.23 ms   5.877 ms   5.895 ms
4    pdl-prn-45M.jvnc.net (130.94.40.101)  9.540 ms   8.582 ms   8.537 ms
5    fe5-0-0.phl1.verio.net (205.238.53.241) 10.35ms   9.413 ms   11.259 ms
6    core3-hssi1-0.WestOrange.cw.net (204.70.1.9) 38.81ms 26.95ms 13.86ms
7    bordercore3.Washington.cw.net (166.48.40.1) 16.46ms 15.92ms 16.503ms
8    dfn.Washington.cw.net (166.48.41.250)  28.296 ms  29.512ms 26.16ms
9    ZR-Frankfurt1.DFN.DE (188.1.144.77) 147.12ms 137.41ms 149.581ms
```

```
10    *  TU-Darmstadt2.WiN-IP.DFN.DE (188.1.11.114) 186.320ms   165.412ms
11    cisco.TU-Darmstadt.DE (188.1.11.18) 147.44ms 159.26ms   131.587 ms
12    cis4181c.hrz.tu-darmstadt.de (130.83.128.8)   146.21ms  *   165.324 ms
13    ingate.tu-darmstadt.de (130.83.47.100) 162.31ms 160.71ms 162.70ms
14    swbgate.swb.de (193.175.30.2)   198.310 ms  *   441.833 ms
15    zahara.swb.de (193.175.30.9)   198.616 ms   193.725 ms   176.970 ms
16    monad.swb.de (193.175.30.33)   214.824 ms   211.415 ms  *
```

Next, comes the netstat command with the –r option. The –n option shows addresses in numeric format; otherwise, netstat shows the addresses as hostnames. We basically have only two interfaces over which to route packets: the lo0 or the local loopback interface, and the ep0 or the Ethernet interface. Any addresses given in the Destination column are routed through the address given in the Gateway column using the interface shown on the far right. A flag of U means that a route is up. A flag of H means that a route is going through a host. The default route is chosen if an address is not specified in the routing table. Other information can be obtained by doing a man netstat.

```
{53} netstat -nr
Routing tables
Destination         Gateway           Flags   Refs   Use         Mtu    Interface
default             204.142.105.1     UGS     11     54109795    -      ep0
127/8               127.0.0.1         UGRS    0      0           -      lo0
127.0.0.1           127.0.0.1         UH      4      176331      -      lo0
204.142.105/24      link#1            UC      0      0           -      ep0
204.142.105.1       0:0:a2:cc:35:ce   UHL     1      3           -      ep0
204.142.105.4       127.0.0.1         UGHS    1      96563       -      lo0
224/8               link#1            UCS     0      0           -      ep0

{54} netstat -r
Routing tables
Destination         Gateway           Flags   Refs   Use         Mtu    Interface
default             204.142.105.1     UGS     12     54109929    -      ep0
loopback            localhost         UGRS    0      0           -      lo0
localhost           localhost         UH      6      176374      -      lo0
204.142.105/24      link#1            UC      0      0           -      ep0
204.142.105.1       0:0:a2:cc:35:ce   UHL     1      3           -      ep0
alankay.nj.devry.e  localhost         UGHS    1      96563       -      lo0
BASE-ADDRESS.MCAST  link#1            UCS     0      0           -      ep0
```

```
{55} telnet pilot.njin.net
Trying 165.230.224.139...
Connected to pilot.njin.net.
SunOS 5.6
login: ramteke
Password:


~%arp -a
Net to Media Table
Device     IP Address                    Phys Addr
le0        busch-gw.rutgers.edu          00:60:3e:04:f8:02
le0        tolip                         08:00:20:7a:01:f4
hme0       wakko-x.rutgers.edu           08:00:20:83:40:87

~%ping babbage.rutgers.edu
```

Now, let us go over to pilot and see how things are set up there.

The ARP (Address Resolution Protocol) table shows which hosts have which physical addresses. All these hosts have to be on the same LAN. Since tolip's and wakko's physical addresses begin with the same six hex digits, they are made by the same manufacturer. Pilot's le0 interface is a 10Mbps Ethernet LAN and the hme0 is a 100Mbps Ethernet interface.

I just happen to know that babbage is on the same LAN segment as pilot. If we ping to it, pilot will first look for its physical address in its ARP table. Since babbage is not there, it will search for it. How it finds the address is simple, but let us not worry about that now.

Now if we look at the ARP table, we find the entry for babbage. Its vendor is some other vendor than that of the other cards.

```
~%arp -a
Net to Media Table
Device      IP Address                  Phys Addr
le0         babbage.rutgers.edu         00:c0:49:02:0a:79
le0         busch-gw.rutgers.edu        00:60:3e:04:f8:02
le0         tolip                       08:00:20:7a:01:f4
hme0        wakko-x.rutgers.edu         08:00:20:83:40:87
```

Here are the routing tables of pilot.

```
~%netstat -r
Routing Table:
Destination               Gateway                  Flags   Ref   Use      Interface
165.230.224.128           pilot                    U       3     5935     le0
net-165.rutgers.edu       pilot-x.rutgers.edu      U       2     327      hme0
BASE-ADDRESS.MCAST.NET    pilot                    U       3     0        le0
default                   busch-gw.rutgers.edu     UG      0     727835
localhost                 localhost                UH      0     206      lo0
```

Here are all its interfaces.

```
~%netstat -ain
Name   Mtu    Net/Dest        Address           Ipkts     Ierrs   Opkts     Oerrs
lo0    8232   127.0.0.0       127.0.0.1         9032      0       9032      0
hme0   1500   165.230.196.64  165.230.196.77    3068272   1       6148268   23
le0    1500   165.230.224.128 165.230.224.139   126       107     27138     209
```

We can see how each interface is configured, but first we have to find out where ifconfig is located and use that path to run the ifconfig program.

```
~%ifconfig lo0
ifconfig: Command not found.
~%whereis ifconfig
ifconfig: /sbin/ifconfig /usr/sbin/ifconfig
~%/sbin/ifconfig lo0
lo0: flags=849<UP,LOOPBACK,RUNNING,MULTICAST> mtu 8232
inet 127.0.0.1 netmask ff000000
~%/sbin/ifconfig hme0
hme0: flags=863<UP,BROADCAST,NOTRAILERS,RUNNING,MULTICAST> mtu 1500
inet 165.230.196.77 netmask fffffc0 broadcast 165.230.196.127
~%/sbin/ifconfig le0
le0: flags=863<UP,BROADCAST,NOTRAILERS,RUNNING,MULTICAST> mtu 1500
inet 165.230.224.139 netmask fffffc0 broadcast 165.230.224.191
```

Here we log out of pilot.

```
~%logout
Connection closed by foreign host.
{56} logout
```

Then we log out of alankay.

EXPERIMENTS

Basic Communications

`%who`

8.1 You can get two lists about users. One is a list of users who have an account on the system but are not necessarily currently logged on. The other is a list of users who are currently logged on. Which list does the who command give?

`%`

Write down the command that shows the other list.

`%grep tramteke /etc/passwd`

`%chfn`

`%grep tramteke /etc/passwd`

8.2 The "/etc/passwd" file shows information about each user. The chfn command will place you in vi. Add or change information about yourself. If you can't quit vi, you may have done something wrong in the file. Either correct it or do a ":q!" which will quit without making any changes. chfn doesn't work on all systems. Were you able to change your entry in the "/etc/passwd" file?

`%w`

8.3 The w command gives more information about the users. The first line gives information about the system.
How long has the system been up?

How many users are currently logged on?
The load average gives you the average number of programs that were waiting to be executed in the last minute, 5 minutes, and 15 minutes.
Which user hasn't pressed any key on the keyboard for a while?

What program are you running?

When did you log into the system?

`%finger ramteke`

8.4 Replace my name with your user name in this command. What does the finger command do?
Using vi, create a file called ".plan". Write in it something nice that you are planning to do.
Then do a finger on yourself.

`%finger ramteke`

`%finger ramteke`

Do a finger on someone else on your system.

`%talk ramteke`

8.5 Use the who command to find out who is logged on. Pick with whom you want to communicate and replace my name with their user name. If that person wants to talk to you, they will respond with a talk using your user name. When you are done, type "bye" and then do a <Ctrl>d.

`%write ramteke`

8.6 On some systems talk will not work, but write will. With write, you can do a UNIX command while communicating, but with talk, you can talk to someone else on the Internet. With write you need to take turns talking. Type "(o)" when you want the other person to respond, and type "(oo)" when you are "over and out." Use a <Ctrl>d to terminate the session.

```
!pwd
```

What does the "!" before any shell command do while you are in write?

Internet Applications

telnet

8.7 Replace "route1" with your own UNIX server name. Can you log into your account twice?

```
%telnet route1
```

Does who show that you are logged in twice?

Go to another terminal and telnet to your server again. Does who show that you are logged in twice?

8.8 telnet to "nypl." For the login name, use "nypl." It should not ask for a password.
What does "nypl" stand for?

```
%telnet nyplgate.nypl.org
login: nypl
```

What kind of information is available here?

If you have an account on another computer, you should be able to telnet to it.
What are the advantages of telnet?

SMTP (Simple Mail Transfer Protocol)

8.9 Create a file called ".signature". In it, place your name as if you were signing it. Also place in it your address and/or a nice quote or a clean joke. Then find out someone's email address and send a test message to that person. Send mail through pine, if you have it. You could send mail to yourself or do a "cc" to yourself. While constructing your message, where did your ".signature" file appear? What is its purpose?

```
%vi .signature
```

```
%pine
```

8.10 Here is an old–fashioned way to send mail. Replace my name with an address you know. If it is someone on the Internet, then provide the full address.
Replace "jones" with your own user name.

```
%mail -v ramteke
Subject: Just testing
1 2 3
~c jones
This here is a test.
^d
%
```

Can you tell what the "~c" command does?

Test out the "–v" option. What does it do?

8.11 To read your mail, simply type mail then the number that corresponds to the message number. Use "?" to see a list of commands.
When done, type "q".

```
%mail
```

ftp (file transfer protocol)

8.12 With ftp, you can only transfer files. You can view them only after you get back into your account. Create a file called "file1" with anything in it, if you don't have one already. See if you can ftp to "athos.rutgers.edu". For the login name you can type "anonymous", and for the pass-

```
%ftp athos.rutgers.edu
Name: anonymous
Password: ramteke@route1.edu
ftp>?
```

```
ftp>pwd

ftp>cd rfc
ftp>ls fyi*


ftp>get fyi-index


ftp>put file1


ftp>quit
%ls -l fyi*


%more fyi-index


%rm fyi-index
```

word, type in your full address. Now you should see the "ftp>" prompt. What does the "?" do?

Look for a filename and use the get command to retrieve the file into your working directory.

Can you place "file1" into athos?

Is the file that you retrieved in your working directory? Can you look at it?

Now delete the file so it doesn't use up your allocated space.

8.13 If you are running from a personal computer that has TCP/IP support and has a ftp client, then do this step; otherwise, skip it.

First log out and exit your telnet client.

```
%ftp alankay
login: ramteke
password:

ftp>?
ftp>ls
ftp>get file1
ftp>quit
```

Place a diskette in your local drive. Click on the ftp client icon and do an ftp to your UNIX server. My UNIX server is called "route1". The ftp client program should ask you for your user name and password. Then get a file from your home directory.

```
%whereis netstat
```

`netstat`

8.14 Using the whereis command, find out where these commands are in your system: netstat, ifconfig, traceroute, ping, and nslookup. Then add those directories to your existing path.

```
%netstat -ain
```

8.15 Using this command, find out the names of the interfaces on your machine.

In the space provided below write down the name of each interface, the network address it is connected to, and the address of the IP interface. Disregard the other numbers on the right. On alankay, you will need to do "8.17" before you can answer the following questions.

name	Mtu	Network	Address	Ipkts (etc.)

```
%netstat -ai
```

name	Mtu	Network	Address	Ipkts (etc.)

a) Locate your loopback interface. Usually it is labeled "lo0". What is your loopback interface labeled as?

b) To what network is your loopback interface connected?

c) What is the IP address of your loopback interface?

d) What is the name of your first network interface?

e) To what network is your first network interface connected?

f) What is the IP address of your first interface?

g) Any packet sent to network _____ (fill in the network address) is sent to interface _____ (fill in the IP address).

h) Answer questions "d" through "f" for each of the additional interfaces you have.

8.16 The "a" stands for "all" interfaces, the "i" for "interfaces", and "n" for "numeric" rather than host names. How does the result of the netstat –ai command differ from that of the previous one?

ifconfig

`%ifconfig <interface number>`

8.17 Now do an ifconfig on your loopback interface. Enter your loopback interface number. For me this would be:
ifconfig lo0

From this printout, fill in the following:
Internet address:

Netmask:

`%ifconfig <interface number>`

8.18 Now do an ifconfig on your first interface. Enter your interface number. For me this would be:
ifconfig eth0

From this printout, fill in the following:
Internet address:

Netmask:

Broadcast address:

What class of address is this?
Subnetting is done using how many bits?

`%arp –a`

8.19 Now view your ARP table. Show only the first three entries.

`%`

What command will count how many entries there are in your ARP table?

```
%
```

Using one of the entries you copied down, answer this question: When sending data to an IP address of _____ the MAC layer will place _____ in the address field.

```
%netstat -nr | head -5
```

Routing Tables
8.20 Let us now look at the routing tables. Write down about three entries either in the numeric form or the hostname form.

```
%netstat -r | head -5
Destination
```

<u>Gateway</u>   <u>Flags</u> <u>Interface</u>

What option for netstat means to show the routing tables?

What is one of the IP addresses of the local host?

Does this address end with a non-zero number?
If it does, then it is a host.
What host is listed next in your routing table?

Which flag means that the host is up and running?

Which flag means that that the host is a gateway to other subnets?

If the address is not found in the routing tables, where are the packets sent?

```
%ping pilot.njin.net

%ping    .    .    .


%
```

ICMP packets
8.21 Find out the IP address of this host.
You can break out of it by doing a <Ctrl>c.

Do a ping again of pilot, except using the IP address you found above. This time do not use "pilot.njin.net". Does it work? Remember to do a <Ctrl>c to stop the pinging.

Is pilot up at this time?

```
%ping central.murdoch.edu.au

%ping    .    .    .
```

8.22 Now ping central in Australia.

Ping again using the IP address instead.

Is central.murdoch.edu.au up and running?

```
%ping    .    .    .
```

8.23 Skip this step if you are not logged on a PC. Find the IP address of your PC and do a ping from the UNIX server you are logged onto.

```
%traceroute      .    .    .
```
Put the IP address of your PC here.
How many hops did you go through?
What is the approximate time it took to reach your PC?

```
%traceroute  pilot.njin.net
```
8.24 How many hops did you go through to get to pilot?

What is the approximate time it took to reach pilot?

```
%traceroute  central.murdoch.edu.au
```

HOMEWORK

1. Give the command you would enter to do each of the following tasks:
   a. Find the list of NIC addresses on the LAN which are currently being accessed.
   b. Find the list of interfaces which are available to the UNIX host by using host addresses and not numeric format.
   c. List the routing table for the UNIX host using the numeric format.
   d. Cause all mail to be forwarded to craig@mond.sweb.in.
   e. Find a host address on the Internet and find out how many hops are used to get there from where you are.
   f. For the host address you found in part e of this question, find out if the host is turned on and connected to the network.
   g. Find out if a user named "joe" has an account on your UNIX server.
   h. Find out who is playing Tetris on your UNIX server currently.
   i. Find out when a user named johnson last read her email.

2. Name each file described here.
   a. This file is appended to all your outgoing email.
   b. This file contains the names of the users who have accounts on your server.
   c. This file contains the address where all your email should be forwarded.
   d. This file contains the current projects you are working on.

3. When you are logged on a PC and you do an ftp to some site, what command is used to place a file from the site onto your PC? Is the site a local system?

4. Run the ftp client on your server and give the command to do each of the following:
   a. Find out which commands are available.
   b. Find out what the exit command does.
   c. Download a file called fileX from the connected host.
   d. Close the connection but don't exit the ftp client.
   e. Get connected to a host called wazu.la.uk.
   f. Log on as ramteke as the user.

LAB ASSIGNMENTS

1. Find some anonymous ftp sites on the Internet and try to download some files. You may have to do some searching to find such sites.

2. If you have a ftp client for your PC, such as WS–FTP, download the first 30 lines of the /etc/passwd file onto your diskette. You could also try to use the Windows 98 ftp client.

3. If you have a shell account on another UNIX server, create a script file to show how you can telnet between the two servers several times.

4. For your server, display the ARP table and the routing table, and do a traceroute to a certain site out of the country. Do this on two different days. From these three listings obtained on two different days, state which entries are the same and which ones are different.

Programming in Bourne Shell

CONCEPTS TO LEARN

Bourne Shell programming is important to know for those who want to learn Perl and UNIX systems administration. Writing shell scripts in Bourne is much more common than writing scripts in csh or tcsh. The results of Bourne scripts are more consistent over various systems than those of other shells. When writing this unit, I was tempted to include many concepts. However, I tried keep them to a minimum. Handling double quotes is always a problem with shell programmers, so I spend some time on that topic. You might want to review the different types of quotes from Unit 7 before doing this unit. Other topics which are not covered in this unit will be much easier to master once you have a foundation in what is covered here.

Relational operators: These are given in Table 9.1 and Table 9.2. They are mostly used when writing an if statement or setting up a loop.

Shell variables: In Bourne shell, shell variables are assigned values without the set command as in csh and tcsh. The shell variable for your working shell is not available to shell programs when you run them, unless you use the export command.

Special Shell Variables:

$1	The value of the first parameter passed to a shell program.
$2	The value of the second parameter passed to a shell program.
$*	The list of all the parameters passed to a shell program.
$#	The number of parameters passed to a shell program.
"$@"	List of parameters passed to a shell program. It is similar to the $* variable, except that here the parameters given in quotes do not lose their quotes.
$?	Contains the value of the exit status of the last command. 0 means that the last command was successful and non-zero means that it wasn't.

Rules for Substitution:

1. Outside double quotes: First comes variable name substitution. Then comes filename substitution. For example:

```
$x='file*'
$echo $x
file1 file2
```

Table 9.1 Relational Operators for Integers	
i −eq j	Does i equal j?
i −ne j	Does i not equal j?
i −gt j	Is i greater than j?
i −ge j	Is i greater than or equal to j?
i −lt j	Is i less than j?
i −le j	Is i less than or equal to j?

Table 9.2 Relational Operators for Strings	
string1 = string2	Are the two strings equal?
string1 != string2	Are the two strings not identical?
−z string1	Is the string null?
−n string1	Is the string not null?

In the echo command, the variable name substitution is done first so the command becomes:

```
echo file*
```

Then the filename substitution is done, giving you the names of the files in the current directory which begin with file.

2. Inside double quotes: There is only variable name substitution done. No filename substitution occurs. For example,

```
$x='file*'
$echo "$x"
file*
```

Notice that here the value of the x is substituted, giving us variable name substitution, but no filename substitution is done. If you want to display the substituted characters as they are without interpretation for their meanings, then enclose the variables in double quotes.

Rules for double quotes:
1. Enclose shell variables with double quotes if you are not sure whether the string is null or not. Then if the variable is null, the shell will accept the null value and not give you an error message saying that an argument is expected. For example, this code:

```
string=
if [ $string = "UNIX" ]
```

will be interpreted this way:

```
string=
if [   = "UNIX" ]
```

giving the shell nothing to compare "UNIX" against. However, if the $string is enclosed in double quotes, then it will interpret it this way:

```
string=
if [ "" = "UNIX" ]
```

Here no error is given.

2. If you are sure that the string is not null, then you probably want to omit the quotes. For example if the value of string were " UNIX", then the statement

```
if [  "$string"  =  "UNIX"  ]
```

would be false because " UNIX" has leading spaces and "UNIX" doesn't. On the other hand, with the statement

```
if [  $string  =  "UNIX"  ]
```

the shell would remove the leading spaces and thus make the condition true.

COMMANDS TO LEARN

case

```
case  "$name"
in
    "yes" )  echo  "YES";;
    "no"  )  echo  "NO";;
    *     )  echo  "MAYBE";;
esac
```

In this case statement, if the value of name is yes, then YES will be displayed, and if it is no, then NO will be displayed. For any other value of name case will display MAYBE. The case statement is not a loop but can be used inside of one.

export x   This will export the shell variable called x to any other shell programs that will be executed. There is no way you can return a shell variable value from a subshell to the parent or working shell.

if

```
if [  string1  =  "UNIX"  ]
then
    echo  "Right on!"
else
    echo  "Go back"
fi
```

If the value of string is UNIX then "Right on!" will be displayed. Otherwise, "Go back" will be displayed. The fi is necessary to terminate the if statement. The else is optional.

for   The for loop below will be done four times.

```
for i in 1 2 3 4
do
    echo i
done
```

Adding "> file" after the done will store all output to the file listed.
Adding "2> file" after the done will store all error messages to the file listed.

read x y   The read statement is used to read from the keyboard. The first item entered up to the first space becomes the value of x and all the rest of the words up to the carriage return become the value for y. Always precede the read with an echo command so that the user knows what to type in when the program pauses.

shift	This command will shift all the parameters from right to left. That is, the tenth parameter becomes the ninth, and the ninth becomes the eighth, and so on. The first parameter vanishes because the second one takes its place.
shift 2	This will shift the parameters twice.

Running Bourne Shell Programs

```
~% sh
$ ls -l
$ cat > p1
echo $a
a=51
echo $a
$ cat p1
echo $a
a=51
echo $a
$ p1
sh: p1: not found
$ ls -l
total 2
-rw-r--r--   1 tramteke   p1
$ chmod 700 p1
$ p1
sh: p1: not found
$ ./p1

51
$ echo $PATH
/bin:/sbin:/usr/bin:/usr/sbin:
/usr/local/bin:/usr/contrib/bin
$ PATH=$PATH:.
$ p1

51

$ a=24
$ echo $a
24
$ p1

51

$ echo $a
24




$ export a
```

Here we go into the Bourne shell.

Notice that the prompt changes to $. There are no files yet.

Let us create a shell program called p1. Many times a .sh is added to the filename to remind others that it is a shell program. We will not use that naming convention here.

Here is our file. First, we display the value of the shell variable called a. The $a does that for us. No spaces are used on either side of the equals sign. Then we assign 51 to it. Last, we display the value of the a variable again.

Let us now run the program.

Oops! The system notifies us that it can't find the file.

Let us see which files we have in our current directory.

p1 is there, but the x or executable bit is not set. That explains it.

Let us set the executable bit and then run it again.

Again, the file is not found.

Let us specifically say to run it from the current directory. Now it works. First, the value of a is displayed, which is null. Then a is set to 51 and displayed again.

Let us check the path.

Here the current directory is not in the path.

So let us add it to the path by adding the dot. Colons are used to separate the directories in Bourne shell.

Now p1 works without having to explicitly specify that the file is located in the current directory.

Let us set a to 24 and see if p1 has access to a.

From our working shell, the value of a is 24 as we just set it.

However, when p1 is executed, another copy of the shell is made just for the p1 process since it has no knowledge of a from the working shell.

The p1 process sets its a variable to 51. Does the working shell know that a is 51? NO! The working shell's a variable is still 24, as before. These two variables are different variables, even though they have the same name. It's like having two students in two different classrooms with the same name. Even though the classrooms may be close together, they do not know that the other is in the adjacent room. If you make one happy, it doesn't mean that you make the other happy. The working shell is called the parent shell and the shell to run p1 is called a subshell. These shells don't share variables unless we use the export command.

Now the value of a which is 24 is exported from the working shell to the subshell. The 24 gets displayed.

Programming in Bourne Shell

```
$ p1
24
51
$ echo $a
24
```

However, the 51 from the subshell cannot be returned to the parent shell, where the value of a is still 24.

Types of Substitution

```
$ echo Lovely day! > file1
$ ls
file1 p1
$ a=*
$ echo *
file1 p1
$ echo '*'
*
$ echo $a
file1 p1

$ echo "*"
*
$ echo "$a"
*
$ echo '$a'
$a

$ echo Lovely          day!
Lovely day!


$ echo "Lovely
>         day
> !"
Lovely
     day
!
$ a="Lovely
>         day
> !"
$ echo $a
Lovely day !
$ echo "$a"
Lovely
   day
!
```

Create another file.
Now we have two files.

The value of a is *.
If we display *, we do a filename substitution and display the filenames.
Using single quotes, we display the *.

Here, we first do a variable name substitution, that is, we change $a into *. Then we do a filename substitution, that is, we change * into the filenames.
No filename substitution is done inside double quotes.

However, inside double quotes, variable name substitution is done, but again, no filename substitution is done.
With single quotes, no substitution is done at all.

When the shell sees this command with extra spaces, it replaces them with a single space. In fact, all whitespace characters which are spaces, new line characters, and tabs are replaced by single spaces by the shell.
Here, the whitespace characters, tabs and carriage returns, are enclosed in double quotes so the shell can't get to them.

The variable a is now set with those characters.

If we display $a, then the shell replaces all the spaces, tabs, and carriage returns by single spaces.
However, if we send "$a" to the shell it can't get to the whitespace characters and they are shown exactly as they were assigned. See Figure 9.1.

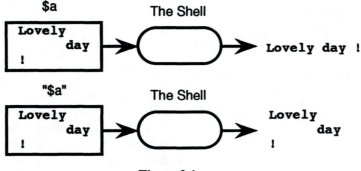

Figure 9.1

Passing Arguments

```
$ cat > p2
echo $1
echo "$1"
$ p2 Lovely
Lovely
Lovely
$ p2


$ p2 "Lovely"
Lovely
Lovely


$ food=fish
$ echo $food
fish
$ echo $fish

$ if [ $food = fish ]
> then
>        echo "It's fish!"
> fi
It's fish!
$ food=eggs
$ if [ $food = fish ]
> then
>        echo "It's fish!"
> else
>        echo "No fish today"
> fi
No fish today
$ food="   "
$ if [ $food = "" ]
> then
>        echo Null
> fi
sh: [: : unexpected operator

$ if [ "$food" = "" ]
> then
>        echo Null
> fi
$ if [ "$food" = "" ]
> then
>        echo "It's null"
> else
>        echo "Not a null value"
> fi
Not a null value
$ pico p3


$ cat p3
```

Many times it is very helpful to send arguments or parameters to a shell program. The shell program here called p2 displays the first argument passed to it twice. The $1 variable stores the first argument, the $2 stores the second argument, and so on all the way up to the ninth argument. Lovely is passed to the shell program so it is displayed twice.

Here nothing, or null, is passed to the program, so nothing is printed. The blank lines are printed because the echo command itself adds a new line character at the end of the statement.

The if Statement

Let us create a shell variable called food and assign it the value of fish.

We never defined a shell variable called fish, so its value is null. In csh, you would have received an error message. Anyway, if the value of food is fish, then "It's fish!" is displayed. This is true. Notice the spaces surrounding the brackets and the special words: then and fi.

If food is assigned the value of eggs, then the same condition will be false, which it is. This time we added an else clause to the if statement and because of it "No fish today" is displayed. Notice that the else clause is optional with the if statement.

Here, we have assigned three spaces to the value of food and we get an error message! The if statement checks to see if the value of food is null or nothing. That is confirmed, but now $food becomes spaces and the shell ignores the whitespace characters. The if statement gives an error because it is seen to be: if [= ""].

By adding double quotes around $food, we don't lose the three spaces to the shell. No error is now displayed because the statement is seen to be: if ["   " = ""]. Also, "Null" is not displayed either because the spaces are not equal to "".

In this if statement we have added an else to confirm that the if condition is indeed false.

Let us now go into pico and create a shell program called p3. It is tiring to enter the if statement each time we want to test something new.

The program begins on the next page.

```
# Program to check double quotes
if [ "$1" = "" ]
then
   echo No food!
else
   if [ $1 = fish ]
   then
      echo "It's fish"
   else
      echo "No fish today"
   fi
fi
$ p3
No food!
$ p3 fish
It's fish

$ p3 "fish    "
It's fish


$ p3 "    fish"
It's fish
$ p3 eggs
No fish today
$ p3 "   eggs"
No fish today
$ p3 'eggs'
No fish today
$ p3 fries
No fish today
$ p3 "   "
./p3:[: fish: unexpected operator
No fish today

$ pico p3
$ p3 "   "
No fish today
$ p3 "fish"
It's fish
$ p3 "   fish"
No fish today


$ cat p4
# Program to test parameters

echo "First parmameter:  " $1
echo "Ninth Parameter: "$9
echo "Tenth parameter?   " $10

echo "\nInitially..."
echo "param list       : " $*
echo "number of parms : " $#
```

Everything after the pound sign (#) is taken as a comment. First, we check to see if the first argument ($1) is null. If the quotes weren't around $1 and its value were null, then the shell would interpret the statement to be: if [= ""]. Then we would get an error message as before.

As long as we know that the first argument is not null, we should omit the quotes. Then if the value of the first argument were "fish " or " fish", the shell would "eat up" the leading and trailing spaces and interpret the statement to be if [fish = fish] and make the condition true. Let us test it out.

p3 is given no argument. The first argument is null, the first if statement becomes true, and no error message is given.

Here we give fish as an argument. The first if checks the argument to make sure it is not null and the nested if confirms that it is fish.

The trailing spaces in the first argument are lost and the nested if becomes true. If the nested if were written with double quotes around $1, then it would have been evaluated as false.

Providing leading spaces in the argument gives the same result.

If the argument is something other than fish, then "No fish today" is displayed.

Omitting the double quotes around the first argument in the nested if will give us an error here.

Let me go back to p3 and add the double quotes so that the nested if becomes: if ["$1" = fish].
Now no error message is displayed because the spaces are preserved when evaluating the if statement.
This works.

Because of the quotes, however, the spaces here are preserved and the condition ends up false.

Parameter Lists

Here is a new program which experiments with more than one parameter.

First, we will display the first parameter or argument.
Then we will display the ninth argument.
However, this will not display the tenth argument. We will see what it does when we run it.
The "\n" displays a blank line for readability.
The special variable called $* displays all the arguments.
And the $# variable displays the number of arguments.

```
parm_list="$*"
shift
echo "\nAfter shifting once"
echo "parm list      : " $*
echo "number of parms : " $#

shift
shift
echo "\nAfter shifting twice"
echo "parm list      : " $*
echo "number of parms : " $#

shift 5
echo "\nAfter shifting 5 times"
echo "parm list      : " $*
echo "number of parms : " $#

echo "\n $parm_list"
$ p4 a b c d e f g h i j k l
First parameter:   a
Ninth Parameter:   i
Tenth parameter?      a0

Initially...
param list:a b c d e f g h i j k l
number of parms :   12

After shifting once
parm list:  b c d e f g h i j k l
number of parms :   11

After shifting twice
parm list:  d e f g h i j k l
number of parms :   9

After shifting 5 times
parm list        :  i j k l
number of parms :   4

a b c d e f g h i j k l


$echo "a\nb c\td"
a
b c      d
$echo 'a\nb c\td'
a
b c      d
$echo a\nb c\td
anb ctd

$i=8
$i='expr $i + 5'
```

We can save the parameters in a variable called parm_list.
The shift command will make the first argument disappear, and make all the others move up by one.
This will show the new list of arguments.
The number of arguments will become one less than before.

Here we shift arguments twice so we now lose the first three arguments including one from before.

Now we shift another five arguments.

And finally, we display the original list of parameters.
Let us run the program now with these arguments.
The first argument is 'a'.
The ninth one is i, but we cannot access the tenth argument.
The $10 is interpreted as $1 which is the character 'a' with a zero tacked after it.
Initially, we have these twelve arguments.
Here is $*.
And here is $#.

After shifting once, the twelfth argument becomes the eleventh, and so on. Now, 'b' becomes the first argument and the 'a' disappears.

After shifting twice, 'd' becomes the first argument.
And now we end up having only nine arguments left.

This time we shift five times.
Here is our new parameter list.
Only four parameters are left.

The original list is still available through parm_list.

Loops and More on Double Quotes

When we display \n inside double quotes, we get a carriage return.
When we display \t, we get a horizontal tab.
Using single quotes, it's the same.

The \n and \t are called escape characters and the slashes act like quotes for single characters outside quotes.

i is set to 8.
Here we add 5 to the value of i.

```
$echo $i
13

$ pico p7.1
$ cat p7.1
echo '$#= ' $#
i=0
for parm in $*
do
    echo $parm
    i='expr $i + 1'
done
echo "Loop was done $i times."
$ p7.1 'a
> b' "c          d"
$#=  2
a
b
c
d
Loop was done 4 times.
```

This makes the value of i equal to 13. We need to know these items to understand the following seven programs.

Here is a program called p7.1.
First we display the number of parameters.
Then we set i to 0.
Now we start a for loop and the shell variable called parm is used to step through the loop. The values for parm are taken from the parameter list or $*. Each time, the value of parm is displayed. i is incremented each time, and after the loop is finished it is displayed, indicating the number of times that the loop was executed. Notice the do and done words which are required with the for loop. Now we run the program and pass two parameters to it. Notice that the value of $# is 2. However, the loop was executed four times!

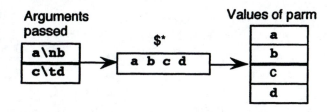

As shown in the diagram above, "a\nb" and "c\td" are passed as parameters. The parameter list, $*, becomes "a b c d" and the values of parm become a, b, c, and d. Every time echo is executed, a carriage return is done.

Here is program p7.2. The only thing we added were the quotes around the $* which are shown in bold. We pass it the same parameters as before and see that the loop was done only once.

```
$ pico p7.2
$ cat p7.2
echo '$#= ' $#
i=0
for parm in "$*"
do
    echo $parm
    i='expr $i + 1'
done
echo "Loop was done $i times."
$ p7.2 'a
> b' "c          d"
$#=  2
a b c d
Loop was done 1 times.

$ pico p7.3
$ cat p7.3
echo '$#= ' $#
i=0
for parm in "$*"
do
    echo "$parm"
    i='expr $i + 1'
done
echo "Loop was done $i times."
```

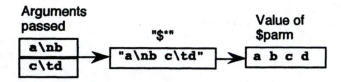

As shown in the diagram above, the quotes prevent the shell from "eating up" the \n and the \t characters. However, when "$*" is assigned to parm, these whitespace characters are replaced by single spaces by the shell. This is because parm is not in quotes.

Well then, let us add quotes around $parm as well. The expression is shown in bold.

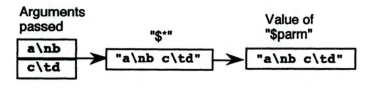

```
$ p7.3 'a
> b' "c            d"
$#=   2
a
b c               d
Loop was done 1 times.


$ pico p7.4
$ cat p7.4
echo '$#= ' $#
i=0
for parm in $*
do
   echo "$parm"
   i='expr $i + 1'
done
echo "Loop was done $i times."
$ p7.4 'a
> b' "c            d"
$#=   2
a
b
c
d
Loop was done 4 times.


$ pico p7.5
$ cat p7.5
echo '$#= ' $#
i=0
for parm in $@
do
   echo $parm
   i='expr $i + 1'
done
echo "Loop was done $i times."
$ p7.5 'a
> b' "c            d"
$#=   2
a
b
c
d
Loop was done 4 times.


$ pico p7.6
$ cat p7.6
echo '$#= ' $#
i=0
for parm in "$@"
do
   echo $parm
   i='expr $i + 1'
done
```

As shown in the previous diagram, the whitespace characters are preserved when the shell assigns the arguments to the parameter list variable ("$*"). The value of parm is the same as this and when the echo displays "$parm," the shell still cannot get to the whitespace characters. Hence, parm takes up only one value, the loop is done once, and the whitespace characters are seen when "$parm" is displayed.

If we only add the quotes around $parm and not $*, then the shell should be able to get to the whitespace characters when the arguments are assigned to $* and replace them with spaces. Placing the quotes around $parm in the echo command will be doing it too late. By that time, all the whitespace characters would be "eaten up" by the shell anyway. Hence, the output of this program is the same as that of p7.1. Here is the diagram:

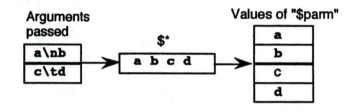

Now we look at a new special variable labeled $@. With $@, we don't get one parameter list as with $*, but we get as many lists as there are arguments, two in our case. Since $@ is not in quotes, the whitespace characters are replaced by single spaces by the shell. When parm is assigned values from $@, there are four values obtained.

Notice that the output isn't any different from that of $*. The output here is the same as that of program p7.1.

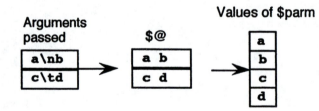

However, when $@ is placed inside double quotes, the whitespace characters are preserved when we assign the arguments to "$@". Now, parm takes upon itself these two values: "a\nb" and "c\td". When echo displays $parm, the shell converts the whitespace characters to single spaces. See the diagram below.

```
echo "Loop was done $i times."
$ p7.6 'a
> b' "c          d"
$#=   2
a b
c d
Loop was done 2 times.

$ pico p7.7
$ cat p7.7
echo '$#= ' $#
i=0
for parm in "$@"
do
   echo "$parm"
   i=`expr $i + 1`
done
echo "Loop was done $i times."
$ p7.7 'a
> b' "c          d"
$#=   2
a
b
c                 d
Loop was done 2 times.

$ ls
file1
$ echo $?
0

$ cat file1
Lovely day!
$ echo $?
0

$ cd file1
- Not a directory
$ echo $?
1

$ pwd
/usr/home/tramteke/unit9
$ echo $?
0

$ pw
sh: pw: not found
$ echo $?
127

$ cat file1 | grep week
$ echo $?
1
```

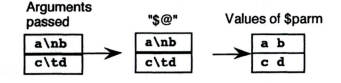

Here is one last example. If $parm is enclosed in quotes, then the whitespace characters should be able to make it to the screen. And they do.

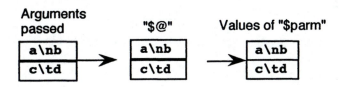

Exit Status

Here we do the ls command. There are no errors.
The special variable labeled $? stores the exit status of the last command which was executed. If it was successful, it stores a 0. Using the echo command we see that the last command, which was ls, was successful. Its value is 0.
Here we do a cat command which is also successful.
Hence, the value of the exit status is 0.

Then we try to change the directory to a file which we cannot do anyway. We get an error.
What is the status code?
It is 1. The non–zero value means it is an error.

The pwd command is successful.

Hence, its exit status is 0.

This is not a valid command so we get an error message.

The error code is not a zero. How does UNIX figure out what value to return for the exit status? It doesn't really matter. Just remember, a status of 0 means the last command was successful and a non–zero value means that it wasn't.
In a pipeline, the last command determines what the exit status is. The grep failed here, so the exit status is non–zero.

Programming in Bourne Shell

```
$ cat file1 | grep day
Lovely day!
$ echo $?
0


$ ls
j.cc m.cc v.cc w.cc
$ cat j.cc
#include <stdio.h>
void main (void)
{ printf("HELLO JUPITER \n");
}
$ gcc j.cc
$ ls
a.out j.cc   m.cc   v.cc   w.cc
$ a.out
HELLO JUPITER
$ gcc m.cc
$ a.out
HELLO MARS
$ w.cc
sh: w.cc: cannot execute
$ gcc w.cc
$ a.out
HELLO WORLD
$ cat m.cc
#include <stdio.h>
void main (void)
{ printf("HELLO MARS \n");
}
$ echo *.cc
j.cc m.cc v.cc w.cc
$ echo *
a.out j.cc m.cc v.cc w.cc
$ echo *.cc > filelist
$ echo *
a.out filelist j.cc m.cc v.cc w.cc
$ cat filelist
j.cc m.cc v.cc w.cc
$ echo `cat filelist`
j.cc m.cc v.cc w.cc
$ cat `cat filelist`
#include <stdio.h>
void main (void)
{ printf("HELLO JUPITER \n");
}
#include <stdio.h>
void main (void)
{ printf("HELLO MARS  \n");
}
#include <stdio.h>
void main (void)
{ printf("HELLO VENUS\n");
}
```

In this pipeline, the grep was successful so its exit status is 0.

Running C Programs

I have already written four simple programs in the C programming language. C programs must have a .cc extension. Here is what j.cc looks like.
Basically, all it does is print "HELLO JUPITER".

To compile the program, we run the gcc compiler. j.cc is an argument provided to gcc.
The compiler creates an executable file from j.cc. The executable file is always called a.out. Notice its presence here.
To execute the executable file, we simply enter a.out.
Here is the output of the j.cc program.
If we provide m.cc as an argument to gcc, the a.out file is overwritten. If we execute this new version of a.out, the program prints "HELLO MARS".
Oops! We have to compile the program first.

Compile the program and create the a.out executable file.
Execute the a.out file.
w.cc displays "HELLO WORLD".
The m.cc file displays "HELLO MARS".

Here are all the C programs.

Here are all the files in my working directory.

We are creating a file called filelist which contains the names of all the C programs.
Now filelist is added to the files in the current directory.
Here is the output of filelist. It contains the names of all the C programs.
We can execute the cat command inside an echo command by using back quotes. The output is the same.
We can also execute the cat command inside another cat command using back quotes. This time, instead of seeing the names of the files, we see the contents of the four files. This is because cat `cat filelist` expands into cat j.cc m.cc v.cc w.cc.

```
#include <stdio.h>
void main (void)
{ printf("HELLO WORLD\n");
}
```

Deeper into Loops

Now that we see that `cat filelist` will provide the names of the C programs stored in filelist, let us use that to create a loop. In this shell program file is a shell variable and its first value is j.cc. In the body of the loop, we send j.cc as an argument to the gcc compiler and we then execute the a.out file which it creates. The output is "HELLO JUPITER." Then the next value of file is the next filename which is provided in the `cat filelist` command. This is m.cc. Hence m.cc is compiled and executed. Similarly, the other two files are compiled and executed as seen in the output of the shell program.

In this shell program we obtain the same result by using *.cc to provide the C program names.

```
$ for file in `cat filelist`
> do
>         gcc $file
>         a.out
> done
HELLO JUPITER
HELLO MARS
HELLO VENUS
HELLO WORLD
$ for file in *.cc
> do
>         gcc $file
>         a.out
> done
HELLO JUPITER
HELLO MARS
HELLO VENUS
HELLO WORLD
$ for file in *
> do
>         gcc $file
>         a.out
> done
Memory fault (core dumped)
ld: filelist:
read_file_symbols(header):
premature EOF
Memory fault (core dumped)
HELLO JUPITER
HELLO MARS
HELLO VENUS
HELLO WORLD
```

If we use * instead of *.cc, we end up trying to compile the other files which are in the directory, such as filelist and a.out. They cannot be compiled because they are not C programs. Hence, we get errors because of compile failures of these programs, but we get proper outputs from the files which were C programs. In fact, we end up running a.out whether or not gcc was successful. It would be nice to run a.out only if gcc is successful.

if Statements Inside of Loops

Let us first create a shell program called p1.

When we write the program, we don't know which files are C programs and which aren't so we set the for loop to assign all files in the current directory to the variable called file.

Then we compile file using gcc.

Then we check the error status.

If the gcc is successful, we show the output.

If the gcc isn't successful, we give the name of the file and a message saying that the file is not executable and we don't execute a.out.

```
$ pico p1
$ cat p1
for file in *
do
   gcc $file
   if [ $? = 0 ]
   then
      echo "The output is: `a.out`"
   else
      echo "$file not executable"
   fi
done
```

```
$ ls -l
total 6
-rw-------     1 ramteke      filelist
-rw-------     1 ramteke      j.cc
-rw-------     1 ramteke      m.cc
-rw-------     1 ramteke      p1
-rw-------     1 ramteke      v.cc
-rw-------     1 ramteke      w.cc
$ p1
ld: elf error: file filelist:
unknown type, unable to process
ld: fatal: File processing errors.
No output written to a.out
filelist is not executable
The output is: HELLO JUPITER
The output is: HELLO MARS
ld: elf error: file p1:
unknown type, unable to process
ld: fatal: File processing errors.
No output written to a.out
p1 is not executable
The output is: HELLO VENUS
The output is: HELLO WORLD
```

Here are the files in our current directory. When we run p1, we will try to compile and execute these files. The ones with the .cc extensions will be compiled and the others will not.

Let us execute p1.
Here we are attempting to compile filelist. Of course, it fails, and gives us system error messages.

Here is the error message generated by our shell program.
We compile and execute j.cc.
Then we compile and execute m.cc.
Here are the error messages provided by gcc when trying to compile p1.

Here is our error message.
We compile and execute v.cc.
Then we compile and execute w.cc.

It would be nice to separate the system error messages from our output. Let us change p1.

```
$ pico p1
$ cat p1
for file in *
do
    gcc $file 2>> errorfile
    if [ $? = 0 ]
    then
        echo "The output is: `a.out`"
    else
        echo "$file is not executable"
    fi
done
$ p1
a.out is not executable
errorfile is not executable
filelist is not executable
The output is: HELLO JUPITER
The output is: HELLO MARS
p1 is not executable
The output is: HELLO VENUS
The output is: HELLO WORLD
$ cat errorfile
ld: elf error: file filelist:
unknown type, unable to process
ld: fatal: File processing errors.
No output written to a.out
(Many other errors)
```

We will only add this to the file. This will place all error messages generated by gcc into a file called errorfile.

Now run p1.
a.out is tried first and this is our error message.
Similarly, errorfile is not executable.
Also, filelist is not executable.
These two files are executable.

However, p1 is not.

Let us display our error file. This is nice because system messages are not mixed in with the messages from our shell program.

Programming in Bourne Shell

```
$ pico p1
$ cat p1
for file in *
do
   gcc $file
   if [ $? = 0 ]
   then
      echo "The output is: `a.out`"
   else
      echo "$file is not executable"
fi
done 2> errorfile

$ p1
a.out is not executable
errorfile is not executable
filelist is not executable
The output is: HELLO JUPITER
The output is: HELLO MARS
p1 is not executable
The output is: HELLO VENUS
The output is: HELLO WORLD
$ cat errorfile
ld: elf error: file filelist:
unknown type, unable to process
ld: fatal: File processing errors.
No output written to a.out
(Many other errors)

$ ls
a.out      filelist   m.cc v.cc
errorfile j.cc       p1   w.cc
$ ls *c
j.cc    m.cc     v.cc     w.cc
$ for i in `ls *.cc`
> do
>         mv $i `basename $i .cc`
> done
$ ls
a.out      filelist   m    v
errorfile j          p1   w



$ ls ?
j  m  v  w
$ for i in `ls ?`
> do
>         mv $i $i.cpp
> done
$ ls
a.out      filelist   m.cpp v.cpp
errorfile j.cpp      p1    w.cpp
```

Here is another way to create an error file.

Add 2> and a filename after done. Then all errors generated in the loop are collectively placed in that file.

Let us do something different now.
I want to transfer the C programs to my PC and run them on a PC compiler. The PC compiler requires a different extension than .cc, so let us first remove the .cc extension from all the C programs.
Here are all the files.

Here are all the .cc files.

The for loop will select only the .cc files and assign each one to the i variable, one filename at a time.
This move command will change the name from one having the .cc extension to a name without it. The basename command will remove the .cc extension from the value of $i.
Here is our listing of the current directory. Notice that all extensions have been removed.

Now let us proceed to add the correct extension for my PC compiler, which is .cpp.
Here are all the files which have only one character for their names.
The for loop will select these filenames.

And the move statement will simply add the .cpp extension.

Here are the C programs with the proper extension. Now I am ready to transfer these files to my PC.

The read and case Statements

We can read data from the keyboard by using the read statement. After we enter the read statement, the shell waits for us to enter characters. Here we are reading two variables, called x and y. After we enter the data on one line, the first word is assigned to the first variable, x in our case, and the rest of the words to the end of the line are assigned to the second variable. If we were to read only one variable, then the entire line would be read into that variable.

```
$ read x y
hhhh jjjjjjj kkkkkkkk lllll
$ echo $x
hhhh
$ echo $y
jjjjjjj kkkkkkkk lllll
```

In this simple program we are setting the for loop to execute four times for each time i is assigned a new value.

Then we display a message explaining to the user what is expected of them.

Then we read the name of the file; the case statement, using the value of file, checks to see if the value is j, m, v, or w. For these values the corresponding C program is compiled and executed. If the user enters some other incorrect value, then the * catches it and displays the "try again" message.

Notice that $file is in quotes. If the user simply pressed the enter key, then the shell would give an error message because the case statement would have nothing to compare against. Just as do and done are required for a for loop, in and esac are required for the case construct. Also, each case is terminated with two semicolons.

```
$ pico p2
$ cat p2
for i in 1 2 3 4
do
    echo "Enter j, m, v or w: "
    read file
    case "$file"
    in
        j )   gcc j.cc
              a.out;;
        m )   gcc m.cc
              a.out;;
        v )   gcc v.cc
              a.out;;
        w )   gcc w.cc
              a.out;;
        * )   echo "try again";;
    esac
done
```

Let us run our shell program.
Here is the prompt message.
We enter a v and the case statement runs the v.cc file and executes it.

Then we run the v.cc program again.

We enter r.cc by mistake and get a "try again" message.

Last, we choose the j option.

```
$ p2
Enter j, m, v or w:
v
HELLO VENUS
Enter j, m, v or w:
v
HELLO VENUS
Enter j, m, v or w:
r.cc
try again
Enter j, m, v or w:
j
HELLO JUPITER
```

EXPERIMENTS

```
$ for i in 1 2 3 4
>do
>   echo $i
>done

$ for file in *
>do
>   echo $file
>done
```

9.1 Do all your labs in the Bourne shell.
Show all the outputs and conclude what you learn from each try.

```
$for file in *
>do
>   cat $file
>done


$for file in *
>do
>   echo Here is $file
>   cat $file
>   echo
>done
```

For the remainder of the labs in this unit, remember from unit5 that you must make the files executable before you can run them. For example,

  $chmod 700 pgm1

You must also set the path to include the current directory or else run the programs as:

  $./pgm1

and so on.

```
$cat > pgm1
# start of the program.
#! /bin/sh
echo The first argument :$1:
echo and the second is  :$2:
echo there were $# arguments.
echo the argument/s were $*
ctrl-d
$
```

9.2 Create the shell program called "pgm1"; then run it at the command prompt several times as shown on the left side of the page. Draw your own conclusions and write them down.

```
$pgm1
```

What is the meaning of each of the following?

  $1

```
$pgm1 mustang
```

  $2

```
$pgm1 mustang sally
```

  $#

```
$pgm1 "mustang sally"
```

  $*

```
$pgm1 mustang sally baby


$pgm1 *
```

```
$cat > pgm2
if [ $1 = ramteke ]
then
   echo welcome  $1
else
   echo bug off $1 !
fi
ctl-d
```

9.3 Create the "pgm2" shell program. (You can use your own name instead of my name.) Then run it twice as shown here. Use arguments so that the condition is false once and true once.

Programming in Bourne Shell

163

```
$./pgm2  romanteke

$./pgm2  ramteke
```

```
$cat > pgm3
if [ $# —ne 1 ]
then
   echo "\n Usage: pgm3 username"
else
   outstuff=`grep "$1" /etc/passwd`
   if [ —z "$outstuff:" ];
   then
     echo "$1 ain't a user"
   else
     echo "$1 is in system"
   fi
fi
```

9.4 Draw your own conclusions here. When you run this shell program, use a user name that you know exists in the system, and then use a name that doesn't exist.

No spaces on either side of the equal sign.
—z means the string has no length.

```
$./pgm3
```

```
$./pgm3  romanteke
```

```
$./pgm3  ramteke
```

```
$read x y
this little
$echo "|$x|$y|"
```

9.5 Now read values into variables as shown here. Write down what you conclude for each experiment.

```
$read x
this little       light of mine
$echo "$x"
```

```
$read x
this little       light of mine
$echo $x
```

```
$read x y
this little light of mine
$echo "|$x|$y|"
```

```
$cat > pgm4
#pgm to lookup users
#! /bin/sh
```

9.6 When you run this program, give a name that is in the system and give a few that are not. Explain the logic in your own words.

```
i=1
while [ "$i" -le 3 ]
do
   echo Give me your user number $i :
   read name
   outstuff=`grep "$name" /etc/passwd`
   if [ -z "$outstuff" ];
   then
      echo "$1 ain't a user"
   else
      echo "$1 is in the system"
   fi
   i=`expr $i + 1`
done
ctl-d
$
```

$pgm4

$cat > datafile
ramturkey
raMTeke
ctl-d

```
$cat > pgm5
#! /bin/sh
while read NAME
do
   USERNAME=`echo $NAME | tr '[A-Z]' '[a-z]'`
   grep -q ^$NAME: /etc/passwd
   if [ "$?" -eq 0 ];
   then
      echo "User $USERNAME is in system"
   else
      echo "User $NAME is not in system"
      echo " "
   fi
done
$
```

$cat datafile | ./pgm5

9.7 Create a file called "datafile" with both user names that have accounts on your system and some that don't. Mix in upper-case and lower-case letters.

HOMEWORK

1. Show the output for each part of the following without running it:
   a.

```
$x=night
$export
$echo "x =   day" > file
$./file
$echo $night
```

Programming in Bourne Shell   **165**

```
                    b.
$var=*
$echo  $var
$echo  "$var"
$echo  '$var'
```

2. Here is a shell program called hw2:

```
if [  $1  =  joe  ]
then
    echo "$1 is ok"
else
    echo "$1 is no—k"
fi
```

Show the output for each run:
a) hw2   b) hw2 jill
c) hw2 "joe "   d) hw2 "joe"
e) hw2 ""   f) hw2 joe

3. Here is a shell program called hw2:

```
if [  "$1"  =  joe  ]
then
    echo "$1 is ok"
else
    echo "$1 is no—k"
fi
```

Show the output for each run:
a) hw2   b) hw2 jill
c) hw2 "joe "   d) hw2 "joe"
e) hw2 ""   f) hw2 joe

4. Here is a shell program called hw2:

```
if [  "$1"  =  "joe"  ]
then
    echo "$1 is ok"
else
    echo "$1 is no—k"
fi
```

Show the output for each run:
a) hw2   b) hw2 jill
c) hw2 "joe "   d) hw2 "joe"
e) hw2 ""   f) hw2 joe

5. Here is another shell program called hw5.

```
shift 3
echo $#
echo $*
echo $2
```

Show its output. It was executed this way:

```
$hw5 eins zwei drei vier funf sechs sieben acht neun zehn
```

6. From page 155 to page 157, shell programs p7.1 through p7.7 were explained. For each of these seven programs, show the output if the arguments passed were as shown here for program p7.1:

```
$ p7.1 'a b' c d "e
>f"
```

Programming in Bourne Shell

LAB ASSIGNMENTS

1. Read one line from the keyboard into a variable called line and display it 3 times.

2. Read in one number and a sentence from the same line entered on the keyboard. Display that line as many times as the number.

3. Create a directory of email addresses. Call the file email. The format of this file will simply be the person's nickname and his/her full email address. For example,

```
joe    jban2435@alankay.nj.devry.edu
```

Write a shell program that will ask the user if they want to add an entry or display the address of a person. The program will receive an 'a' for add, 'd' for display, or 'q' for quit from the user. It will use a case statement. The file is not necessarily sorted. No one can be deleted from the file.

4. Make a list of user names of users, some of which have an account and some of which don't. Then store these names in a file. Every ten minutes your program should check and see which of these users are on the system and which ones aren't. You may need to use the sleep command to wait every ten minutes.

5. Use the file created in assignment 4 above and see if a user is a valid user on the system. If he or she isn't, print an appropriate message. Otherwise, print a message stating whether that user is currently logged on or not.

Appendix A

The vi Editor

EXPERIMENTS

Creating a Simple File

In this unit, we will look at an editor that is widely available in UNIX. This is the vi editor. When you do this lab, press keys carefully and slowly so you can stay in step with the lab. Also, be sure to use the proper case of letter. In order to invoke the editor, simply type the following:

```
%vi myfile1
```

A.1 Here, "myfile1" is a file name. Do you see a new screen?

A.2 Is the name of your file given? If so, where? Is it an existing file or a new one?

There are two modes of operating in vi: one is the *command mode* where commands are given to the editor, and the other is the *text input* mode. Here, text is placed in the buffer, or what you see on the screen. The buffer is part of RAM which has the text as you see it on the screen. Whatever is in the buffer is not necessarily saved as a file on the hard drive.

To get into the command mode, press the [Esc] key. Nothing will seem to happen, but you are now in the command mode.

The first thing you should always do after getting into vi is to have vi display the mode that you are in. Press the colon ":" key and your cursor should go to the bottom of the screen or the command line. Enter the following:

```
:set showmode
```

A.3 What is now different on your screen? Write down what you see:

A.4 What do see after pressing the letter "a"?
Press [Esc] again.

A.5 What do see after pressing the letter "i"?
Press [Esc] again.

A.6 Now enter the following:

```
:set noshowmode
```
and redo Experiments A.4 and A.5. What difference do you notice?

Then set the showmode again.

```
:set showmode
```

A.7 Let us type in some text into our buffer. In order to do that, we must get out of the command mode and go into the text input mode. Enter "i" to insert text. Type the following file with four lines. If you make a mistake, hit [Esc] to go into command mode, type "dd" to delete a line, and type "i" to go into insert mode again. Don't type the dashes.

```
- - - -
I went out
to look
for a friend,
and
```

Now enter the command mode (by pressing [Esc]) and try these two commands in this sequence:

```
:w
:q
```

Are you still in vi?
Can you type out myfile1 on the screen without going into vi?
Can you determine the purpose of each of these two commands?

Moving the Cursor

A.8 Go back to editing myfile1 using vi.

```
%vi myfile1
```

Can you remember how to make vi show the mode? See Experiment A.2. Using the letters "h," "j," "k," and "l" in the command mode, move the cursor around the text. Once you get the hang of it, place the cursor between the words "I" and "went" on your screen. What does each of these commands do? If a command doesn't appear to do anything, then try it from a different place in the file.

```
h

j

k

l

x
```

A.9 Do each of these commands (in the command mode, of course). Do them in the given sequence, going across and then down. While you are doing them, write the purpose of each of them in your own words. If a command doesn't appear to do anything, try it from a different place in the file.

`2j`	`2k`
`<return>`	`G`
`^`	`$`
`3k`	`w`
`^`	`e`

The vi Editor

How do you move the cursor so that it goes to the

	beginning of the. . .	end of the . . .
file.		
line.		
next word.		

Figure A.1 Complete the chart.

1G   3w

b   3e

2b

Now complete the chart shown in Figure A.1.

Adding Text

A.10 You may want to do the above experiment over again using your own version so that you can get comfortable moving the cursor around. Bring the cursor back between the words "I" and "went" on your screen. In the command mode, press "i" and then "zzz". Then press [Esc]. Originally your cursor was on the space. Did the triple "z" get placed before or after the space?

A.11 Now place the cursor on each of the "z"s, one at a time. Each time press "x" in the command mode. What does "x" do?

A.12 To experiment with each of the given letters below, bring the cursor back to where it was, between the "I" and "went" on your screen. Your cursor should be on the space. Then, in the command mode, press each given letter, "zzz", and then [Esc] as shown below. Explain where the triple "z" was placed in each case and how that command behaved. Then erase the "z"s, and restore the file to its original form.

a zzz [Esc]   o zzz [Esc]

O zzz [Esc]   A zzz [Esc]

I zzz [Esc]   R zzz [Esc]

In Figure A.2 the condition of the original screen is shown on the left of each arrow. Label each arrow with one of the above letters and "i" to change the display pointed to by the arrow as shown.

Working with More than One File

A.13 In this experiment, we will to use myfile1 to create myfile2. We want to leave myfile1 unchanged. This operation is very handy when a new document has to be created from an existing large document. This saves a lot of unnecessary typing. Use one of the commands from the last experiment and add one more line to our file as shown below:

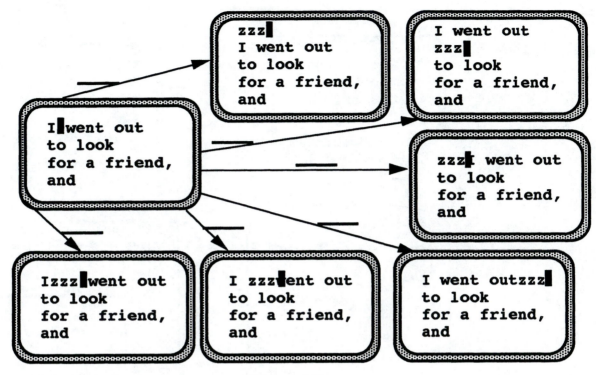

Figure A.2

```
I went out
to look
for a friend,
and
I just couldn't find
```

If we just use the ":w" command, the file will be overwritten. Instead of overwriting the file, let us save this as a different file, giving it a new name. Then we will have two files, the old one and the revised one.

:w myfile2

Now quit vi. If you were to do a write here, you would overwrite myfile1.

:q

In Figure A.3 (Before), what command will save or resave a file called myfile1?
In Figure A.3 (After), one line has been added. What command will save the file as myfile2 without changing myfile1?

A.14 In the UNIX shell, do the command that will produce a listing of files whose names begin with "myfile".

%

Type out the contents of each file. Show the commands and the files.

%

%

A.15 Let us suppose that I forgot that there was already a file in my account that was named myfile2 and that I am about to inadvertently wipe it out by overwriting it with the new file which I am editing.

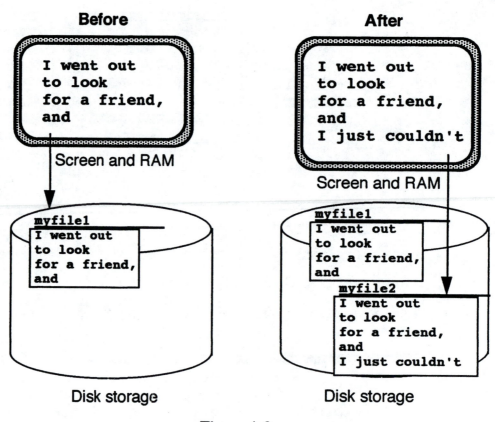

Figure A.3

Let's get back into vi without specifying any filename.

`%vi`

Now type out this file again. I just want to make a point that you will see in a moment. Notice the extra line at the end.

```
I went out
to look
for a friend,
and
I just couldn't find
any.
```

Now try to save it as myfile2.

`:w myfile2`

Can you do it? What error message, if any, do you get?
Now try the same thing with a bang. (A bang in UNIX jargon is an exclamation point.)

`:w! myfile2`

Is this successful? What is the difference between using and not using a bang with the write command?

If you don't use a bang, can you overwrite an existing file?

A.16 Try the following commands and explain their purposes:

```
:set number
:set nonumber
```

A.17 Place the cursor after the comma and press "J" in command mode. Then press "i" and <Enter>. What word do you think "J" stands for? What does it do? Try the same thing after the word "find" in the buffer. The command should behave the same way.

A.18 Place the cursor between the words "a" and "friend." What does the following command do?

```
d$
```

Then try this: What does this do?

```
u
```

What does this do?

```
dd
```

This?

```
u
```

A.19 Now try this sequence of keystrokes anywhere on the screen:

```
[Esc]
```
to get into command mode.
```
R
```
to start typing over or replacing the characters.
```
zzz
[Esc]
```
to get back into command mode.
```
u
```

Do this experiment over again, but this time use the command "o" instead of R. In general, can you tell what the "u" command does?
(The "u" is for undo, not undelete.)

A.20 Leave the triple "z" in the buffer (on the screen). Try this:

```
:q
```

Does the editor allow you to quit without saving the changes first? Try this command:

```
:q!
```

Does a "q" with bang allow you to quit without first saving the changes? Sometimes when I edit a file, I get it so messed up that I would rather start editing the original file than continue editing the current one with all the changes. In such a case, this command is essential to quit vi without first saving the changes to the file.

A.21 Figure A.4 shows what we want to do next. We want to merge one file into another. We will do this by first entering "vi myfile3". "myfile2" already exists in our account. "myfile3" will be created on the screen by entering the four lines as shown below. Then we will retrieve "myfile2" at the beginning of "myfile3" and, finally, when we write the file, it will be saved as "myfile3".

Let's start. Invoke vi with a new file called "myfile3". How is that done?
Now type this content on the screen for "myfile3":

```
So instead, I went out
to be a friend,
and I found
oh so many!
```

Save this file:

```
:w
```

The vi Editor

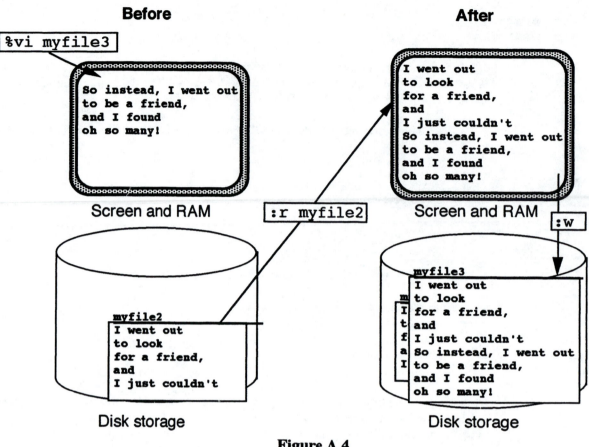

Before

`%vi myfile3`

So instead, I went out
to be a friend,
and I found
oh so many!

Screen and RAM

`:r myfile2`

After

I went out
to look
for a friend,
and
I just couldn't
So instead, I went out
to be a friend,
and I found
oh so many!

Screen and RAM

`:w`

myfile2

I went out
to look
for a friend,
and
I just couldn't

Disk storage

myfile3

I went out
to look
for a friend,
and
I just couldn't
So instead, I went out
to be a friend,
and I found
oh so many!

Disk storage

Figure A.4

How can we merge or combine the two files?

Place the cursor under the capital "S" , type "O" (that's a capital "O"), the <Esc> key, and then try this:

`:r myfile2`

Are all ten lines on the screen? Let us not update myfile2 or myfile3, but instead save this ten–line file as myfile4. How do you do that? See Experiment A.13.

`:`

Miscellaneous Commands

A.22 We want to make sure that there are four files in our working directory.

`:!ls —l myfile*`

With what must you precede a UNIX shell command when you are still in vi?
Do these commands work?

`:!cat myfile3`
`:!date`

Move the cursor to the last line. What command will do that?
Move the cursor to the end of that line. What command will do that?
Try the following:

```
:r  !whoami
:wq
%cat myfile4
```

What did the command **r** **!whoami** do?

A.23 When you display "myfile4," your screen should look like this:

```
I went out
to look
for a friend,
and
I just couldn't find
any.
So instead, I went out
to be a friend,
and I found
oh so many!
```

Now try these keystrokes with the cursor placed on the "I" of the first line:

```
x
3x
xp
i
zzz
[Esc]
U
```

What did each of the following keystrokes do?

```
3x
xp        Transpose.
U
```

A.24 Get your screen looking like it did when you started Experiment A.23. Place the cursor on the "I" of the first line. As you try these commands explain what they do.

```
5dd
u
5j
3w
```

A.25 Get your screen looking like it did when you started Experiment A.23. Place the cursor on the "I" of the first line. As you try these commands explain what they do.
Nothing seems to happen here, but vi is copying something to the buffer.

```
8yy
G
p(lowercase)
p(lowercase)
p(lowercase)
P(uppercase)
```

A.26 Get your screen looking like it did when you started Experiment A.23. Place the cursor on the "I" of the first line. As you try these commands explain what they do.

```
/friend
R
FRIEND
```

The vi Editor

```
n
R
FRIEND
n
.   (This command is small — it is just a period)
?I
```

A.27 Get your screen looking like it did when you started Experiment A.23. Place the cursor on the "I" of the first line. As you try these commands explain what they do.

```
:1,$  s/friend/crab/g
:1,$  s/FRIEND/crab/g
<ctl>d
<ctl>u
H
3dd
5j
P
```

HOMEWORK

Complete the following summary sheet for vi by providing the correct command on the left side of each description. An italicized *n* means a whole number representing a number of lines, characters, etc. Precede the commands that are given on the command line by a colon ":". The "buffer" is the text that is available on the screen. Use the words "string" and "newstring" to denote strings. Use "file" to denote a file name. Use "cmd" to denote a shell command.

File Functions and Options
Write or save the buffer
Write and quit vi
Read the file into buffer
Read the output of a shell
  command into buffer
Execute a shell command
Write to a new file
Overwrite a file
Quit
Quit, no questions asked
Show line numbers
Remove line numbers
Show mode
Remove mode type display

Moving the Cursor
n characters to the right
n characters to the left
n lines up
n lines down
End of line
Beginning of line
Beginning of next line
Go to the last line
Go to the first line of the file
Beginning of *n* words forward
End of *n* words forward
Go back *n* words
Scroll down
Scroll up

Undo the last command
Undo the last command
Undo all changes on current line
Repeat last text change command

Creating Text
Append after the cursor
Insert before the cursor
Replace (type over)
Go to end of line and append
Go to start of line and insert
Open line below
Open line above

Deleting Text
Delete one character
Delete *n* characters
Delete *n* lines
Delete word
Delete to end of line

Copying Text
Yank *n* lines into "clipboard."
Place after current character
Place before current character

Moving Text
(Use delete instead of yank)

Searching and Changing Text
Do a reverse search of a string
Forward search a string
Repeat the last search
Repeat the last text change
Join 2 lines
Transpose 2 characters
Replace all occurrences of
  "string" with "newstring"

Index

Symbols

–z 164, 165
! 11, 19, 20
!! 11, 15, 18, 20
!! | more 23
#! 126, 163, 164
$ 105, 107, 120, 150, 151
$# 147, 154 – 156, 163, 164
$* 147, 154 – 156, 163
"$*" 155
$? 147, 157 – 159, 165
$@ 156
"$@" 147, 157
$1 147, 153, 163 – 166
% 52, 58, 59
& 52. *See also* backgrounding
* 19, 23, 107, 120, 151, 162
.cshrc 114, 115, 118, 126
.forward 130, 134
.login 126
.plan 130, 134
.signature 130, 134, 141
'/^$/d' 78
/bin 26
/dev 26
/etc 26
/etc/passwd 69, 70, 75, 97, 133, 140
/tmp 26
/var 26
< 68, 74
<Tab> character 76
> 11, 16, 17, 21, 22, 67, 68, 73, 74, 105, 161
>> 11, 17, 21, 160
? 19, 24, 161

[152, 166
[!a–b] 24
[0–9] 19, 23
'[A-Z]' 19, 73, 78
'[a-z]' 73, 78
\ 105, 108, 121
'\012' 78
^Z 52, 58, 59, 62
` 105, 108, 120. *See* quote, back
| 82, 87, 88, 89, 90, 91, 96, 105. *See also* piping

A

a.out 50, 158, 159
address book 48
alias 105, 112, 113, 115, 118, 119, 127
appending *See* >>
arguments 152
arp 130, 138, 143
assembler 6
assembly language 2, 6

B

backgrounding 58. *See also* bg
backslash *See* \
basename 161
batch 5
batch processing 1
bg 52, 58, 63
buffering 6

C

C or C++ programs 49, 158. *See also* gcc
cal 12, 14
case 149, 162

cat   12, 16, 17, 18, 21
cd   26, 27, 28, 29
cd -   116
cd ~   28
changing directories   39. *See also* cd
chfn   134, 140
chmod   27, 35, 110, 117, 126, 150
clear   12, 14, 21
comm   82, 84, 95, 99
command interpreter   102
command mode   50
compiler   1, 6
Compose Message   48
correct   117
cp   12, 18, 23, 27, 32
CPU   1, 2, 3, 4, 6, 102
creating a directory   38. *See also* mkdir
csh   102, 111, 115, 116, 117
cut   67, 71, 72, 77, 78, 79
cwd   113, 123, 125

D

date   12, 15, 20
device driver   4
diff   83, 84, 94, 99
directories   26
directory
  login   26
  root   26
double quotes   *See* quotes, double

E

echo   11, 16, 17, 21
EDITOR   104
emacs editor   50, 56, 61, 64, 65
email   141
environment variables   104, 111, 114, 124, 127
exit   12, 16, 73
exit status   157. *See also* $?
export   149, 150, 165
expr   106, 120, 154, 165

F

fg   52, 58, 59, 63
file access   6
file completion   *See* filec
file permissions   42
file structures   26, 44
file system   6
file types   5
filec   104, 112, 122, 123

files   26
  command   117
  handling many   91
  looking for   95
  start-up   114
  working with many   99
  working with similar   93
filters   82, 96
find   27, 32, 33, 34, 83, 85, 86, 92, 95, 99
finger   130, 133, 134, 140
Folder List   48
for   149, 155, 159, 161, 162, 163
foreground   58. *See also* fg
Free Software Foundation   49
ftp   83, 92, 130, 134, 135, 141, 142
  anonymous   141

G

gcc   50, 64, 158, 159
get   135, 142
grep   67, 69, 74, 75, 79
gunzip   83, 93, 98
gzip   83, 92, 98

H

head   67, 69, 71, 75, 77, 79
history   12, 14, 20, 104, 112, 123
HOME   104, 114
HOST   112
hostname   12, 15, 132

I

I/O devices   4
ICMP   144
if   149, 152, 159, 163, 165, 166
ifconfig   130, 137, 139, 143
INBOX   48, 53
inodes   6
insertion mode   50
interfaces   137

J

job control   52, 62, 64, 65
jobs   52, 57 – 59, 63

K

kernel   1, 2, 102
kernel mode   3
keyboard   73
kill   52, 58, 59, 63

L

LAN 1
language
  high–level 1, 6
  machine 1, 6
less 18, 70
logout 12, 14, 16, 21
long listings 42
loops 154, 159
ls 12, 16, 17, 18, 19, 22

M

MAIL 104, 114
mail 48, 141
man 12, 14, 17, 23
memory management 4, 5
mesg 130, 133
mkdir 27, 28, 29, 30
modem 1
more 12, 17, 18, 22, 74, 79
moving 39. *See also* mv
multiprocessing 1, 3
mv 12, 18, 23, 27, 32, 33

N

netstat 131, 137 – 139, 142, 144
network cards 130
NIC 1, 130
noclobber 104, 113, 123
NOS 1, 8
noshowmode 169
number 173
nyplgate.nypl.org 141

O

open systems 7
operating systems 1, 2
  advantages of 2
  components of 3
  examples of 7

P

paging 5
parameter lists 153
partition 1, 5
passwd 12, 13, 20
password file 66
paste 67, 72, 77, 78, 79
PATH 104, 114, 124, 150
path 26, 104, 109, 110, 117, 124 – 126, 137

pathname
  full 26, 39
  relative 26, 39
pattern matching 11, 19, 23, 24
pico 48, 49, 54, 59, 63
PID 58
pine 48, 52, 60, 63, 64
piping 8, 82, 86, 90, 96, 99. *See also* |
portability 7
POSIX 8
printenv 105, 112, 124
process 1, 3
process table 4, 59
prompt 104, 113, 116, 123
ps 12, 15, 16, 52, 57
put 135, 142
pwd 27, 28, 29, 30, 36

Q

quotes 105, 106, 128
  back 105, 107, 108, 121
  backslash *See* \
  double 107, 120, 148, 151, 154
  single 108, 120, 151

R

RAM 5
read 149, 162, 164, 165
redirection *See* >
registers 5
removing directories 41. *See also* rmdir
rm 12, 18, 23, 27, 32
rmdir 34, 35
routing 137, 138, 144

S

script 80
sdiff 83, 84, 94, 99
sed 67, 70, 76, 78, 80, 115
session
  printing of your 9
set 105, 106, 107, 110, 111, 112, 119, 123
setenv 105, 111, 124
sh 12, 16, 69, 75, 102, 150
SHELL 104, 114, 118
shell 3, 4, 11, 12, 102, 103, 114, 115
  Bourne 150
  kinds of 11
shell variables 106, 122, 127, 147
  system-defined 103, 122
  user-defined 104, 119

shift 150, 154
showmode 168
sleep 52, 57, 62
SMTP 141
sort 67, 68, 74, 77, 79, 94
  by field 70, 71, 77, 97
sorting 76
source 105, 115, 118
spawning 1, 4
standard input 66, 73, 79
standard output 11, 66, 73, 79
stop 52, 58, 63
string replacements in emacs 51
stty all 52
substitution
  rules for 147, 151
swapping 5

T

tail 67, 70, 75, 79
talk 131, 133, 140
tape archiving 82. *See also* tar
tar 83, 92, 93, 98
TCP/IP 8
tcsh 12, 102, 103, 116
tee 89, 96
telnet 2, 12, 13, 56, 93, 131, 141
TERM 104, 114, 124
term 104, 124
text blocks 51
text file 6
timesharing 2, 4, 5
touch 12, 18, 120
tr 67, 73, 78, 80
traceroute 131, 137, 145
transpose 78

U

uid 66
umask 27, 36
unalias 104, 113, 119
uniq 83, 85, 94, 99
UNIX
  advantages of 7–8
  connecting to 9
  logging into 11
unset 112, 123
uptime 12, 15, 17, 21
USER 104, 124
user 104, 113
user mode 2

V

vi
  adding text 170
  miscellabeous commands 174
  moving the cursor 169
  working with files 170
vi editor 50, 55, 60, 64, 65
virtual memory 2, 5

W

w 131, 140. *See also* who
WAN 2
wc 67, 69, 74, 79
whereis 83, 96, 99, 109, 117, 124, 137
which 83
while 165
who 12, 13, 20, 133. *See also* w
who am i 12, 15, 20, 22
whoami 15
windows in emacs 51
working in directories 31
write 131, 133, 140
WS–FTP 80